Palgrave Macmillan Studies in Family and Intimate Life

Series Editors: **David Morgan**, University of Manchester, UK; **Lynn Jamieson**, University of Edinburgh, UK; and **Graham Allan**, Keele University, UK

Titles include:

Graham Allan, Graham Crow and Sheila Hawker
STEPFAMILIES

Harriet Becher
FAMILY PRACTICES IN SOUTH ASIAN MUSLIM FAMILIES
Parenting in a Multi-Faith Britain

Elisa Rose Birch, Anh T. Le and Paul W. Miller
HOUSEHOLD DIVISIONS OF LABOUR
Teamwork, Gender and Time

Harry Blatterer
EVERYDAY FRIENDSHIPS
Intimacy as Freedom in a Complex World

Ann Buchanan and Anna Rotkirch
FERTILITY RATES AND POPULATION DECLINE
No Time for Children?

Deborah Chambers
SOCIAL MEDIA AND PERSONAL RELATIONSHIPS
Online Intimacies and Networked Friendship

Robbie Duschinsky and Leon Antonio Rocha (*editors*)
FOUCAULT, THE FAMILY AND POLITICS

Jacqui Gabb
RESEARCHING INTIMACY IN FAMILIES

Dimitra Hartas
PARENTING, FAMILY POLICY AND CHILDREN'S WELL-BEING IN AN
UNEQUAL SOCIETY
A New Culture War for Parents

Stephen Hicks
LESBIAN, GAY AND QUEER PARENTING
Families, Intimacies, Genealogies

Clare Holdsworth
FAMILY AND INTIMATE MOBILITIES

Janet Holland and Rosalind Edwards (*editors*)
UNDERSTANDING FAMILIES OVER TIME
Research and Policy

Mary Holmes
DISTANCE RELATIONSHIPS
Intimacy and Emotions amongst Academics and Their Partners in
Dual-Locations

Rachel Hurdley
HOME, MATERIALITY, MEMORY AND BELONGING
Keeping Culture

Peter Jackson (*editor*)
CHANGING FAMILIES, CHANGING FOOD

Riitta Jallinoja and Eric Widmer (*editors*)
FAMILIES AND KINSHIP IN CONTEMPORARY EUROPE
Rules and Practices of Relatedness

Lynn Jamieson and Roona Simpson
LIVING ALONE
Globalization, Identity and Belonging

Lynn Jamieson, Ruth Lewis and Roona Simpson (*editors*)
RESEARCHING FAMILIES AND RELATIONSHIPS
Reflections on Process

Carmen Lau Clayton
BRITISH CHINESE FAMILIES
Parenting, Relationships and Childhoods

David Morgan
RETHINKING FAMILY PRACTICES

Petra Nordqvist and Carol Smart
RELATIVE STRANGERS
Family Life, Genes and Donor Conception

Eriikka Oinonen
FAMILIES IN CONVERGING EUROPE
A Comparison of Forms, Structures and Ideals

Róisín Ryan-Flood
LESBIAN MOTHERHOOD
Gender, Families and Sexual Citizenship

Sally Sales
ADOPTION, FAMILY AND THE PARADOX OF ORIGINS
A Foucauldian History

Tam Sanger
TRANS PEOPLE'S PARTNERSHIPS
Towards an Ethics of Intimacy

Tam Sanger and Yvette Taylor (*editors*)
MAPPING INTIMACIES
Relations, Exchanges, Affects

Elizabeth B. Silva
TECHNOLOGY, CULTURE, FAMILY
Influences on Home Life

Lisa Smyth
THE DEMANDS OF MOTHERHOOD
Agents, Roles and Recognitions

Vilna Bashi Treitler (*editor*)
RACE IN TRANSNATIONAL AND TRANSRACIAL ADOPTION

Katherine Twamley
LOVE, MARRIAGE AND INTIMACY AMONG GUJARATI INDIANS
A Suitable Match

Palgrave Macmillan Studies in Family and Intimate Life
Series Standing Order ISBN 978-0–230–51748–6 hardback
978-0–230–24924–0 paperback
(*outside North America only*)

You can receive future titles in this series as they are published by placing a standing order. Please contact your bookseller or, in case of difficulty, write to us at the address below with your name and address, the title of the series and the ISBN quoted above.

Customer Services Department, Macmillan Distribution Ltd, Houndmills, Basingstoke, Hampshire RG21 6XS, England

Everyday Friendships

Intimacy as Freedom in a Complex World

Harry Blatterer
Macquarie University, Australia

First published 2015 by
PALGRAVE MACMILLAN

Palgrave Macmillan in the UK is an imprint of Macmillan Publishers Limited, registered in England, company number 785998, of Houndmills, Basingstoke, Hampshire RG21 6XS.

Palgrave Macmillan in the US is a division of St Martin's Press LLC, 175 Fifth Avenue, New York, NY 10010.

Palgrave Macmillan is the global academic imprint of the above companies and has companies and representatives throughout the world.

Palgrave® and Macmillan® are registered trademarks in the United States, the United Kingdom, Europe and other countries.

ISBN 978–0–230–27252–1

This book is printed on paper suitable for recycling and made from fully managed and sustained forest sources. Logging, pulping and manufacturing processes are expected to conform to the environmental regulations of the country of origin.

A catalogue record for this book is available from the British Library.

A catalog record for this book is available from the Library of Congress.

Typeset by MPS Limited, Chennai, India.

For Sveva

In memory of my father, Robert Blatterer
(1927–2014), worker, craftsman, musician, poet.

Contents

List of Tables

Series Editor's Preface

The remit of the *Palgrave Macmillan Studies in Family and Intimate Life* series is to publish major texts, monographs and edited collections focusing broadly on the sociological exploration of intimate relationships and family organization. As editors we think such a series is timely. Expectations, commitments, and practices have changed significantly in intimate relationship and family life in recent decades. This is very apparent in patterns of family formation and dissolution, demonstrated by trends in cohabitation, marriage, and divorce. Changes in household living patterns over the last 20 years have also been marked, with more people living alone, adult children living longer in the parental home, and more 'non-family' households being formed. Furthermore, there have been important shifts in the ways people construct intimate relationships. There are few comfortable certainties about the best ways of being a family man or woman, with once conventional gender roles no longer being widely accepted. The normative connection between sexual relationships and marriage or marriage-like relationships is also less powerful than it once was. Not only is greater sexual experimentation accepted, but it is now accepted at an earlier age. Moreover heterosexuality is no longer the only mode of sexual relationship given legitimacy. In Britain as elsewhere, gay male and lesbian partnerships are now socially and legally endorsed to a degree hardly imaginable in the mid-twentieth century. Increases in lone-parent families, the rapid growth of different types of stepfamily, the de-stigmatization of births outside marriage, and the rise in couples 'living-apart-together' (LATs) all provide further examples of the ways that 'being a couple', 'being a parent', and 'being a family' have diversified in recent years.

The fact that change in family life and intimate relationships has been so pervasive has resulted in renewed research interest from sociologists and other scholars. Increasing amounts of public funding have been directed to family research in recent years, in terms of both individual projects and the creation of family research centers of different hues. This research activity has been accompanied by the publication of some very important and influential books exploring different aspects of shifting family experience, in Britain and elsewhere. The *Palgrave Macmillan Studies in Family and Intimate Life* series hopes to add to this list of influential research-based texts, thereby contributing to existing knowledge and informing current debates. Our main audience consists of academics and advanced students, though we intend that the books in the series will be accessible to a more general readership who wish to understand better the changing nature of contemporary family life and personal relationships.

We see the remit of the series as wide. The concept of 'family and intimate life' will be interpreted in a broad fashion. While the focus of the series will clearly be sociological, we take family and intimacy as being inclusive rather than exclusive. The series will cover a range of topics concerned with family practices and experiences, including, for example, partnership; marriage; parenting; domestic arrangements; kinship; demographic change; intergenerational ties; life course transitions; stepfamilies; gay and lesbian relationships; lone-parent households; and also non-familial intimate relationships such as friendships. We also wish to foster comparative research, as well as research on under-studied populations. The series will include different forms of book. Most will be theoretical or empirical monographs on particular substantive topics, though some may also have a strong methodological focus. In addition, we see edited collections as also falling within the series' remit, as well as translations of significant publications in other languages. Finally we intend that the series has an international appeal, in terms of both topics covered and authorship. Our goal is for the series to provide a forum for family sociologists conducting research in various societies, and not solely in Britain.

Graham Allan, Lynn Jamieson, and David Morgan

Acknowledgments

I'd like to thank Philippa Grand of Palgrave Macmillan for encouraging me to write this book, and the editorial staff for their assistance. Thanks go to my colleagues and friends in the Department of Sociology at Macquarie University for their support and intellectual engagement. I'm particularly grateful to Shaun Wilson for his invaluable insights. I'm grateful also to the graduate students with whom I've spent many hours discussing aspects of the book, especially to Penelope Faulkner and Yin Yin Ye. Thank you to Ingeborg Lux and Vinzenz 'Zenz' Grabner for help with the manuscript. My gratitude goes to Mira Crouch, Jessica Hall, and Jayne Kearney for their interest in, and generous intellectual contribution to, my thinking on the topic. Special thanks go to the three extraordinary people without whom this book would not have been possible: Maria Markus infected me with her interest in, and fine scholarship on, friendship during my undergraduate years; she continues to lead by example – in scholarship as in private life. Pauline Johnson invited me some years ago to teach a course on 'the intimate sphere', which gave important impetus to the research. Her dedication to teaching, research, and sociology as well as her personal integrity, are benchmarks that 'keep me honest'. Sveva Magaraggia opened my eyes to the problem of gender in sociology and everyday life. She took the brunt of my uncertainties; she shared my passion for the discipline – generously and even with delight. For this alone I'm indebted to her.

Introduction

Without friendship life seems incomplete. It is no accident that the history of Western thought is also a history of friendship: Homer, Plato, and Aristotle; Cicero, Augustine, and Aquinas; Montaigne, Hume, Ferguson, and Smith; and later Nietzsche and Emerson, but also C. S. Lewis and many others make up an illustrious pantheon of thinkers who have contemplated the virtues, ambiguities, and pitfalls of friendship. For that reason it seems odd that friendship should be as underrepresented as it is in sociology. Apart from the extraordinary heterogeneity of the phenomenon, Nedelmann mentions two interconnected reasons for the relative paucity of engagement with friendship in the social sciences: the avoidance of topics to do with 'individualistic sentiments' in private life; and a focus on large-scale social structures to the near exclusion of 'interactions that are transient and diffuse' (Nedelmann, 1991, my translation). To say that friendship is underrepresented in sociology is to acknowledge that there *is* work on the topic. This book, after all, draws liberally on existing research, old and new. It is, however, still relatively marginal in the discipline, especially concerning friendship as an intimate relationship between two people. There is a sense that the *dyad* isn't a 'large' enough social relationship to merit serious attention. Sociologists' greater ease with more extensive organizations is reflected in studies of friendship *networks* or *communal* solidarities, rather than the close ties between two individuals, something that is largely left to (social) psychology. This is particularly perplexing, because Georg Simmel, who is often added to sociology's founding triumvirate Marx–Weber–Durkheim, had a great deal to say about the dyad and advocated for its inclusion in the sociological enterprise. As I hope to show, dyadic friendships are not only tremendously important to the lives of real people, but are significant units of analysis because

(a) the discipline seems to be uncertain concerning how to categorize them, and (b) they cannot but refract aspects of the social system and so give clues to the workings of social trends in everyday life. The relative sociological neglect of the dyad is a result of accrued practices over time. An overwhelming research focus on other-than-private, intimate relationships helps congeal an unarticulated norm: sociology is not about these intimate interactions because sociologists aren't really concerned with them – and so the cycle goes.

Taking up the challenge to investigate the friendship dyad from a sociological perspective is to take people's experiences seriously by paying attention to a type of bond that is central to our sociality, a bond that may even have life-changing effects. Friendship can open our eyes to capacities we never knew we had. We might think of what it might be like to move to another country; to leave one's friends behind and be unable to make new ones. Can there really be 'integration' into a new cultural environment without learning new ways of life through the mutual generosity of friendship? Of course friendship doesn't have to precipitate a series of earth-shattering experiences. Whatever its potentials and real-life manifestations, it is a significant social relationship and deserves renewed sociological attention. Rather than subsuming friendship under the sociological key concepts 'community' and 'networks', I approach it as a relationship in its own right, with its own personal and social significances.

While friendship is important to people, we might argue that it is not particularly important to society. In moral and political philosophy the intimate bonds of friendship are often considered in terms of narcissistic self-concern. On that view, friends turn their backs on society. Intimacy equals a withdrawal into an inner sanctum of privacy, a retreat from the *vita activa* of public life. There are echoes of that stance in Hannah Arendt, but also in Adam Smith and Tocqueville (Mallory, 2012). Implicitly at least, that take justifies sociology's marginal interest in the relationship; it is further justified by the assumption that friendship is somehow free-floating, because friends need take few if any cues from society in the construction of their relationship. Thus, I have set the task for myself to fathom the friendship dyad for connections to culture and society. Such connections are not only important in order to test the narcissism thesis, but also to qualify the freedom thesis. As part of that task, the study highlights friendship dyads' embeddedness in the gender order. It shows that friendships are implicated in the gendered constitution of our societies; that they refract existing inequalities, contain them *in nuce*, and help undo some of these, but are also implicated in their maintenance. Explaining friendship's situatedness in the gender order is to explain that the social embeddedness of friendship constrains the extent to which its freedom can be fully lived.

My approach follows the interpretive as well as the critical traditions in sociology. It attempts to situate friendship in a heuristic background of culturally shared meanings. I am interested in concepts, in the meanings these hold in everyday life as well as in the social sciences, in their semantic differences and overlaps, and their power to orient ways of thinking, behaviors, and practices. 'Social relationship', 'dyad', 'institution', 'gender', 'heteronormativity', but also 'intimacy', 'recognition', 'discretion', 'social self', and the much-debated notion of 'modernity' are among the concepts I utilize to thicken the description and analysis in order to make sense of friendship.

A few preliminary words on love and intimacy. Following a long tradition that views friendship as a form of love, I compare what is typical in friendship with what is typical in love. When I mean 'love', I refer to it in its orthodox everyday sense, as erotic attachment between two people, with all the cultural trappings the 'culture of romance' attaches to it (Illouz, 1997). When Ann Swidler (2001) set out to investigate how Americans thought about love, she quickly realized that although people drew on cultural heuristics, when they were asked to reflect on 'love' their beliefs and perceptions were full of uncertainties and contradictions. Swidler was interested in the everyday, practical reinterpretation of love against the background of 'traditions, rituals, symbols, and pieces of popular culture' (2001, p. 4). Rather than the everyday reworking of love, I take the unreflected-upon but shared and constantly reproduced notion of monogamous, romantic coupledom as the heuristic background against which I reflect on friendship. This is no methodological sleight of hand. I'm aware of the immensely varied and complicated experiences of love relationships. To the contrary, as I hope will become clear, that approach recognizes the ambiguities and contradictions that the orienting semantics of love contain, and so sheds light on the social drivers of the great contemporary uncertainties that suffuse love (e.g. Luhmann, 1998a; Swidler, 2001; Evans, 2003; Illouz, 2012).

The concept on which this analysis turns is 'intimacy'. Taking my lead from others, I use it as a normative concept. Maria Markus writes: 'Intimacy ... is emotional, spiritual, intellectual and bodily closeness as *a chosen form of life*. ... on the basis of mutual trust and respect' (2010b, p. 13, original emphasis). Others share this interpretation. Anthony Giddens (1992), for example, sees the modern ideal of intimacy as equivalent to the ideal of democracy: it is nonhierarchical and open to mutual discussion and thus central to the relationship ideal he calls the 'pure relationship'. For Axel Honneth (1996), intimacy connotes noninstrumental relations of affection and care based on social recognition or institutionalized relations of respect. It is a cornerstone of the modern freedom to lead a self-directed life. Taking my lead from such interpretations, intimacy as I understand it has to do with noninstrumentality, justice, trust, respect, affection, and care in practical relations to concrete others. That normative yardstick also means that the standards for friendship are set very high indeed. Taken to 'love' it is immediately evident that intimacy is neither always realized in popular representations, nor are its ingredients – take justice for instance – necessary for relationships to be interpreted as love relationships. Concerning friendship, which is anchored in the practical realization of intimacy, this normative concept serves to separate friendly relations from friendship. It helps distinguish between relationships in a way that makes sense in the social sciences, is adequate to common sense, and so speaks to everyday experiences.

A teacher of mine once said to me, 'we academics tend to reinvent the wheel, albeit at ever-diminishing circumference'. She urged me to remember that much of what we think is original has in fact been thought and written about by others. With that piece of advice in mind, the book draws on Weber, Simmel, Elias, Goffman, and others, although it is a formidable task to do the nuance of their thinking justice. There are German and Italian language publications on friendship that are central texts in other-than-English language sociologies. Francesco Alberoni's *L'amicizia* (2009), Friedrick Tenbruck's (1989) paper on friendship, and Siegfried Kracauer's essays in *Über die Freundschaft* (1990) are examples that are integrated to various degrees of prominence in the book to enable dialogs between different perspectives on and approaches to the topic.

Structure of the book

I elaborate the freedom of friendship and its limits. Friendship is marked by a relational freedom that makes it relatively resistant to reification, especially when compared to erotic love. The case in point I offer is friendship's immunity to therapeutic culture. Offering a sociologically workable way to think about institutions, I compare the institutional trajectories of love and friendship and suggest that friendship lacks important institutional characteristics. Friendship's *institutional deficit* explains both its freedoms and limits: there is freedom of interaction, while normative barriers to their formation persist. In particular, heteronormative assumptions about how the sex categories 'man' and 'woman' are to interact continue to challenge the formation and maintenance of cross-sex, or heterosocial, friendships. Friendship is thus free in principle, but not necessarily in fact. In the context of cross-sex friendships, that freedom needs to be carved out against the background of ingrained cultural assumptions concerning normative forms of sociality. This suggests that the analysis of friendship can provide significant clues concerning the state of gender relations today. So the argument of the book, crudely sketched. It is developed over the following six chapters.

Freedom of association, autonomy, equality, trust, respect, justice; these are the watchwords of liberal democracies. But they also belong to intimacy and denote ingredients of the friendship ideal. Friendship embodies the public norms and ideals we associate with politically, economically, and socially mature societies. As in democracy so in friendship: these characteristics are historically and culturally specific. They developed in the course of modernity via processes of differentiation. Chapter 1 traces important aspects of that process, including the development of a distinct private sphere with its own internal norms, and an emerging appreciation of privacy. Privacy becomes central to the modern freedom to lead an autonomous, self-directed life in the context of modernity. Modernity is more than 'modernization' in the political, economic, and private spheres; it is above all synonymous with existential uncertainties. It is under these conditions that intimacy offers itself as shelter, as the space to be ourselves. Anxiety and excitement mingled in the works of the Scottish Enlightenment philosophers. Especially Adam Smith hailed the new possibilities for friendship, and friendship's advantages to commerce, at a time when feudal relations met their rapid decline and market society began to emerge. His work is often cited as ushering in modern friendship. I disagree. Using intimacy to evaluate Smith's take we can see that his notion of 'sympathy' has little to do with friendship, but has everything to do with an emerging networking ethic. I suggest that the modern ideals of friendship emerge in the Romantics' emotive outpourings. Bridging the Enlightenment and Romanticism, Hegel too contemplated the new ideals of intimacy. The chapter concludes with Axel Honneth's reconstruction of Hegel's approach to intimacy as one cornerstone of modern dynamics of social recognition.

Chapter 2 turns to words, to concepts, in order to sensitize the reader to the conceptual ground on which I base my approach.

Weber's take on social relationships and Simmel's work on the dyad provide some preliminary insights into the specifics of friendship as a form of sociality. But what is friendship? Time and again sociologists have struggled over the question. In everyday life these uncertainties are reflected by some handwringing about the proliferation of online friends and the ostensible weakening of the relationship. 'Can 457 *Facebook* friends really be friends?', goes the tenor of concerns. It turns out that when it comes to the semantics of 'friends' and 'friendship', the different relational qualities these words describe follow long-term linguistic developments. With recourse to work in cultural pragmatics – that branch of linguistics that focuses on culturally specific language use – we can see that the semantics of 'friend' and 'friendship' have taken shape over several centuries. Present uncertainties have some historical pedigree – just as the conflation of the terms has some historical pedigree in the social sciences where despite persistent calls for the differentiation of 'friends' and 'friendship', synonymous usage persists. As a consequence, little is said about friendship itself; it has been turned into a sinkhole concept for all sorts of personal relationships. Especially Siegfried Kracauer and Georg Simmel have made major contributions to a differentiated approach to friendship. Building on their work, I pursue a constructive critique of contemporary conflations of relationship categories and distinguish between them, and hence significantly narrow the view to intimate friendship.

My comparative approach to friendship begins with Chapter 3, where I briefly describe the historical trajectories of love and friendship, and where I undertake a comparative institutional analysis of both types of intimacy.

Distinguishing between institutions' *normative infrastructure* and their *connectivity*, that analysis shows that friendship cannot be assigned a place in the raft of modern institutions; that it is deficient in so far as it lacks connectivity to other social institutions with the exception of heterosexuality. That *institutional deficit* is at the heart of what I call friendship's *relational freedom* – the freedom that friends have to construct the relationship free from cultural prescription. Friendship's connection to heterosexuality explains that freedom's limits, explored in greater depth in Chapters 5 and 6. The analysis begins with a selection of key anthropological research on institutionalized friendship in order to bring to light the particularities of modern friendship as a personal and private relationship. That done, I will go on to explore friendship's relational freedom, suggest a modification to Honneth's approach to friendship, and highlight the empirical consequences of its freedom. Its institutional deficit, I suggest, renders the relationship resistant to the therapeutic ethos whose logic has suffused intimate relationships.

Chapter 4 continues to investigate friendship's freedom from the perspective of the relationship's internal dynamism. How friendship contributes to the making of selves is the question to which I turn here. The approach to the self is self-consciously sociological; it perceives the self as fundamentally social. For Simmel, accelerating social and cultural differentiation had precipitated the differentiation of personalities to such an extent that friends can no longer complement one another in all aspects of their lives. This does not undermine the possibilities for intimacy; to the contrary – friendship gives us a sense of 'home' as we negotiate the vicissitudes of modernity. It also provides us with developmental opportunities. Friends may encourage us to realize our potentials, take on new interests, change course, or see things in ourselves we may otherwise not be aware of. Friendship's relational freedom is *generative*: it enables creativity. And it enables creativity precisely because that freedom is 'limited' by another person. Not because the other curtails our freedom to act, but because here we can be 'ourselves in another', to evoke Hegel. The generative potential of friendship exemplifies that creativity relies on our human sociability. From a structural perspective, that potential is fostered by friendship's position between the private and the public spheres and the possibilities of subversion that result from it. Friendship's may 'subvert' norms of public propriety, as much as they may challenge the norms of private secrecy.

Chapter 5 begins my exploration of gender as limiting friendship's relational freedom and generative potential. More specifically, I explore what I intimated in Chapter 3, namely that friendship's connection to the institution of heterosexuality continues to matter. I argue that gendered assumptions concerning the interactions between men and women continue to pose challenges to the relationship. The taken-for-grantedness of male homosociality both drives and indicates persisting inequalities. Of course, women and men do have fulfilling, generative friendships with one another. Nevertheless, especially among the heterosexual mainstream, gender constrains the formation and maintenance of cross-sex friendships. Heterosocial friends have to overcome cultural barriers that do not apply to same-sex friendships. I begin with a discussion of gender as a social organizing principle before I elaborate friendship's institutional connectivity to heterosexuality. At issue are assumptions about masculinity and femininity and the normative intimate interactions between and among women and men: in 'love' heterosociality is normative while homosociality is nonstandard; in friendship homosociality is normative while heter-osociality is nonstandard. I call this cultural scheme the *love–friendship paradox*, and explain its cultural efficacy by drawing on research on gender stereotyping. What I call the process of *presumptive prioritization* explains how stereotypical judgments order interaction, and discuss the everyday consequences of that cognitive scheme. The discussion provides the basis for the analysis of cross-sex friendships in the fol-lowing chapter.

'Friends with benefits', 'hook ups', recreational sex – these social trends can easily lead to a triumphalist stance on gender relations in the 21st century. 'Who needs feminism when all is fair in lust and sex?', we might ask. There is a significant gap between the fiction of 'equality' and contemporary realities, however. Apart from persisting structural inequalities – easily overlooked in an era where the ideology of indi-vidual choice assigns individual responsibility, especially where there are structural causes – the unspoken, silent tensions between genders in everyday life are no less indicative of the differentiating force of the gender order then gender pay gaps, or the unequal distribution of labor at work and in the home. Chapter 6 discusses the symptoms and con-sequences of the normative assumptions I condense in the love–friend-ship paradox. Here cross-sex friendships move center-stage. Gendered intimacies, that is, the social construction of different types of intimacy for men and women, often inhibit cross-sex friendships, as does the normativity of sexual attraction irrespective of friends' sexual identi-ties. Platonic heterosocial friendships challenge received notions about normative sexual attraction and the gendered attribution of intimacy. But they may just as well reproduce deep-seated cultural norms about gender, and bring into relief the contemporary reduction of intimacy to sexual practices. It is under these conditions that some construct 'erotic friendships' in an attempt to reconcile sex and friendship with-out partaking in the cultural staging of romance. To whatever extent these relationships are successful depends on friends' capacities to improvise relationships against the backdrop of a strongly prescrip-tive love ideology. To the extent that they exist, they speak to human ingenuity and creativity. The reality of heteronormative barriers regard-ing what is ostensibly the 'freest' of all interpersonal relationships tells us something about the gendered distribution of power in, and the gendered constitution of, our societies. The friendship dyad refracts some of the everyday uncertainties and inequalities in personal rela-tionships. And it appears to do so even though this particular analysis cannot engage with the specifics of friendships between women, nor friendships in queer contexts that a more extensive engagement with gender necessitates.

The concluding chapter offers some reflections on the main themes: apart from reiterating the basic premises of the book, I revisit my take on love as well as reflecting on the love–friendship paradox by bringing nonheterosexual (male) friendship into view. I offer some considerations concerning a 'sociology of friendship', and advocate for the retention of a focus on privacy in the 'sociology of personal life'. I conclude with some thoughts on the 'decent society', and contemplate the position of friendship *vis-à-vis* that ideal.

Something that Sarah Matthews wrote nearly three decades ago focused my research from the first day, and it should serve to focus the reader also. Research on friendship, she wrote,

> confronts the sociologist with a critical test to theoretical formulations, not only about friendships but about the social organization of societies more generally. Noninstitutionalized relationships, of which friendship is a prime example, either have been relegated to the field of psychology or forced to fit into the available theoretical framework and described as if they were institutionalized. Reformulating sociological theory so that it can embrace this social relationship would seem to be more fruitful. (Matthews, 1986, p. 159)

But before I begin, a final note on my approach: much that speaks of love and friendship speaks most eloquently and meaningfully in literature, in art. There are no pretensions to such an achievement in this book. Its voice has the brittleness of social science writing, not least because, as always, the last line read was the language of the next line written. But for all its linguistic distance it could not have been written without the few generative and ultimately life-transforming friendships I have had the great privilege to call mine.

1
Modernity, Intimacy, and Friendship

> They who would confine friendship to two persons,
> seem to confound the wise security of friendship with
> the jealousy and folly of love.
>
> Adam Smith

Intimacy is a fundamental human need. But the modalities of its enactment and experience, its possibilities and constraints, depend on context and on place, as well as time. In this chapter I will address intimacy as part of Western developments without which the contemporary meanings attributed to friendship are unthinkable. I have chosen to sketch some key structural and cultural transformations in private life. The autonomy promised by intimate relationships takes on particular significance with the rise of industrial capitalism. But already in the commercial society described by the thinkers of the Scottish Enlightenment these personal bonds are discussed. In the literature on the history of friendship, works by Adam Ferguson and David Hume, but above all by Adam Smith, are almost always held up as the first modern documents lauding the intimacy of friendship. That thesis bears rethinking. Scholars have argued that this commonly reiterated interpretation misses the highly instrumental approach to intimacy taken by the Scots, and especially by Smith. I argue instead that early Romanticism is key to the meaning of intimacy in the modern sense; that the Romantics' often exaggerated outpourings of sentiment prefigure a cultural valorization of intimacy in terms of mutual disclosure, something that gains particular traction with the diffusion of therapy culture in the 20th century.

A century before, however, it is Hegel who conceptualizes intimacy as offering the kind of modern freedoms we take for granted today. Via Honneth's reworking of Hegel's approach we will be able to address the central promise of intimacy – to find freedom in another – as central also to friendship.

The modern experience, public and private

When Siegfried Kracauer (1990, p. 54) writes about friendship as an 'ideal community of free, independent persons', he presupposes a modern society inhabited, made, and constantly remade by modern individuals. But what's modernity and what do we mean by modern individuals? The various prefixes attached to describe its present qualities – post, late, second, reflexive – are testimony to different approaches. But there are some aspects that many perspectives on modernity share and that I will now draw in broad brush strokes.

It is a sociological commonplace that from about the 17th century, in European societies and then in societies that drew on European models of social and political organization, the arenas of human activity multiplied and became more differentiated, in the sense of both a pluralization of ways of life and internal fragmentation. The development of modern subjectivities is intertwined with the displacement of religious authority through science, the challenge to absolutism, and the struggle for a representative politics. Connected to these changes was the formation of a social imaginary that views individuals as closed units of cognition, a view that was systematized by the rationalist philosophers of the Renaissance (Burkitt, 1991; Elias, 2011). In the European imagination the birth of the individual is traced to the Reformation and the Renaissance, when individual identity is said to have replaced collective identity as the center of subjectivity.[1] Its 18th century emergence in the modern sense presupposes structural changes that spell a thorough differentiation and pluralization of social subsystems: economy, politics, science, religion, art, law, and a distinct private realm gradually decoupled from one another and developed their own inner logics and mutual tensions.[2] Science and art, for example, exit their service to religious and feudal authority, become relatively autonomous, and develop their own internal norms. Scientific refutations of religious dogma, but also scientists' attempts to reintegrate science and religion, and the 19th century bohemian creed 'art for art's sake' illustrate the changes.

Especially from the 19th century – earlier or later, even much later, depending on place – European populations were caught up in 'the maelstrom of modern life', well depicted by Marshall Berman:

> the industrialization of production, which transforms scientific knowledge into technology, creates new human environments and destroys old ones, speeds up the whole tempo of life, generates new forms of corporate power and class struggle; immense demographic upheavals, severing millions of people from their ancestral habitats, hurtling them half-way across the world into new lives; rapid and often cataclysmic urban growth; systems of mass communication, dynamic in their development, enveloping and binding together the most diverse people and societies; increasingly powerful national states, bureaucratically structured and operated, constantly striving to expand their powers; mass social movements of people, and peoples, challenging their political and economic rulers, striving to gain some control over their lives; finally, bearing and driving all these people and institutions along, an ever-expanding, drastically fluctuating capitalist world market. (1983, p. 16)

With these structural and cultural changes heterogeneity becomes the normal 'order' of things and an internalized fact of life. But 'differentiation', the sociological keyword describing this heterogeneity, does not merely describe the fragmentation and pluralization of the tangible infrastructure of modernity, but draws into its semantics the intangibles of existential uncertainties. 'The more nuanced become religious ideas and practices, concepts and language, family structures and parenting practices, professions and positions, feelings and principles, concerns and joys, and thus the richer for each individual becomes the cosmos of possibilities', writes Friedrich Tenbruck (1989, p. 235, my translation), 'the greater the risk that everybody falls into hopeless uncertainty and disorganization, because in all social connections the characteristics of the one must inevitably influence the other'.

In Luhmann's language (2010, 4), these processes render life both complex and contingent: complex, because life's possibilities outnumber what can be done and experienced in a life-time, and contingent, because things could always be otherwise. Contemporary processes of globalization, precipitating a disconnection of time and space and a constant 'intrusion of distant events into everyday consciousness', raise complexity and contingency to unprecedented levels (Giddens, 1991a, p. 27) and move the comprehensibility of an already fragmented social environment out of reach. That this is not merely an abstract development, but impacts lived experience is well put by Zygmunt Bauman, who articulates contemporary, ultimately modern, longings:

> The anxiety would be lessened, tensions allayed, the total situation made more comfortable were the stunning profusion of possibilities somewhat reduced; were the world a bit more regular, its occurrences more repetitive, its parts better marked and separated; in other words – were the events of the world more predictable, and the utility or uselessness of things more immediately evident. (1995, p. 145)

That need for clarity, for a simpler life, for greater order, and for more straightforwardly articulable meanings also keeps alive tradition, which seems to offer existential anchorage, provides the illusion of permanence, and becomes all the more important the more acute the uncertainties, the less adequate collective identifications, the less appropriate recipes for living, the less self-evident the cues to a life worth living become. Rather than simply being overcome or constantly replaced by the new, tradition persists and even thrives precisely because it calls on modernity to justify itself against enduring significances. As we shall see, intimate relationships are not exempt from these dynamics. Thus, we moderns are torn between the meaning-giving calls of tradition and life-orienting convention on the one hand, and the call of innovation and self-created freedom on the other.

The processes of differentiation are implicated in new possibilities for social mobility, the formation of political collectivities and new freedoms, but they also presage the specters of atomization, anonymity, and alienation, leitmotifs of early sociology. Time and again, sociologists attend to private life as a refuge from the shadow side of modern life, as that realm of interaction where the warm light of intimacy glows charged with the promise of authentic life. Because 'the ultimate and most sublime values have retreated from public life into the transcendental realm of mystic life or into the brotherliness of direct and personal human relations', wrote Weber, '[i]t is not accidental ... that today only within the smallest and intimate circles, in personal human situations, in pianissimo, that something is pulsating that corresponds to the prophetic pneuma, which in former times swept through the great communities like a firebrand, welding them together' (Weber, 1977, p. 156). The hope with which private life is invested – that in its shelter we can nourish the soul and actualize our real selves, authentically, in harmony with cherished others – does not do justice to its often less than ideal realities. But those realities have done little to undermine the expectations with which private life and intimate connections are imbued.

Privacy, private life, and intimacy

The social history of private life cannot be recounted in a linear fashion. We need to be sensitive to the reality that the social processes and sensibilities that give meaning to privacy, private life, and intimacy 'include, on the one hand, the "deprivatization" and "depersonalization" of certain aspects of life and, on the other hand, the "privatization" and "intimization" of others' (Markus, 2010b, p. 8). In his *On the Process of Civilisation* (2012a [1939]), Norbert Elias has shown how from about the 16th century, first among the medieval nobility and then also the peasantry, all sorts of once-acceptable behaviors were pushed from public view; they were deleted from the social repertoire by an advancing 'shame threshold', 'civilized' in the sense that they came under increasing pressure to conform to emerging standards of etiquette and manners: from blowing noses into fingers to the use of handkerchiefs; from eating with hands to the use of cutlery; from the constant presence and normality of nudity to modesty, embarrassment, and eventually the sexualization of the body. Today, we can observe trends in the opposite direction, a kind of 'decivilization'. Consider the increasing preparedness of people to disclose what once would have been considered private information in public forums, in a range of media, during 'private' cell phone conversations in public spaces (remember the phone booth?), or the cultural imperative of extroversion, assertiveness, and expressive optimism (Ehrenreich, 2009; Blatterer et al., 2010).

The meanings of privacy and publicness in premodern Europe were different from today's variants in fundamental ways because they played out in a context of a hierarchical social organization. The lives of the nobility were wholly lived in the service of public functions, and were subordinate to the reputation of 'the house' (Elias, 2006). It is only with the emergence of a bourgeoisie that, under fast-changing structural conditions, begins to divide work from family life that an inward looking and increasingly autonomous intimacy emerges. From a perspective that emphasizes the links between private life and 'civil society', the lines between the *bourgeois* public and private spheres ran, by the 18th century, between public authority (state, court, police) and the world of private commerce, of literary, political, and cultural discourse (private salons, coffee houses) and the central nub of bourgeois life, the conjugal family with its own internal norms of intimacy. Both civil society and family came to share a private realm where private property ownership and patriarchal authority meant both freedom from public powers and the freedom to cultivate a new bourgeois subjectivity (Habermas, 1991, pp. 27–56). That subjectivity included reflection on the place of the self in a rapidly changing world, and the stabilizing effects that interpersonal relationships may offer.

In the course of that development privacy takes on its specifically modern value: it is anchored in a liberal notion of freedom whose normative core is individual autonomy. At base, writes Rössler, a 'person is autonomous if she can ask herself the question what sort of person she wants to be, how she wants to live and if she can then live in this way' (2005, p. 17). From this it follows that privacy is worth protecting because it permits personal control over our lives, something that has been shown to be fundamental to our sense of wellbeing (Mirowsky & Ross, 2003). This normative conception of privacy goes beyond the traditional spatial distinction between a public and private realm whose gendered conception has been comprehensively critiqued by feminists – a critique that is (for the most part) compatible with the liberal appeal to personal autonomy (Rössler, 2005 pp. 23–27). The connection between intimacy and privacy is not straightforward, however. 'What is intimate is private, but not vice versa',[3] states Rössler, and so points to the multidimensional semantics of privacy.[4] The principal standard by which its substantive reality can be analyzed is *control over access to privacy* concerning our decisions, personal data, and personal spaces, which need to be protected in order to ensure our freedom *qua* personal autonomy. Privacy in the intimate sphere refers, therefore, to an 'agent having control over a realm of intimacy, which contains her decisions about intimate access to herself (including intimate informational access) and her decisions about her own intimate actions' (Innes cited in Rössler, 2005, p. 7). Thus, beyond the differentiation of a public and a private realm, but inseparable from it, is the social value of privacy as guarantor of a kind of freedom that enables us to live autonomous lives. To that end, transformations in the economic structure of societies – the expansion of capitalism not merely as a mode of the production, consumption, and distribution of goods, but as a way of life, as a 'culture' (Sennett, 2006) – was pivotal.

In its nascent state, just before Britain and then continental Europe and the United States enter the industrial age, philosophical attempts were made to bring intimacy and changing economic conditions into accord. A new morality befitting a new economic order was described by Enlightenment philosophers. Especially the contributions of the Scottish Enlightenment are significant, not least because it is here that modern friendship is thematized.

Friendship and commercial society revisited

Whether in the public or the private sphere, social change is acutely perceived in threshold periods. Think about Marx's writing from the center of the Industrial Revolution, Durkheim's concerns with social integration around the time of the Paris Commune, or the great outpouring of European literary, philosophical, and scientific creativity around 1900 (Schorske, 1981; Berman, 1983). The writers of the Scottish Enlightenment too wrote in one of those threshold periods: at the dawn of industrial modernity. What we know today as 'capitalism' began slowly to be extended beyond relations in the market place. Societies were in the process of becoming *market societies*. During that time thinkers such as Adam Smith began to contemplate societal cohesion in a newly emerging society of strangers. But there is another reason why it is worth turning to Smith. Just as much sociological commentary tends to caricature the 'classical' sociologists as thinkers who thought about Western history in terms of linear progress,[5] the taken-for-granted notion has settled among sociologists that Smith is the first thinker to contemplate modern friendship. That social philosophical common sense owes much of its strength to Allan Silver's (1990, 1996) important analyses. At times it has, however, led to a skewed interpretation of friendship's position among the constellation of modern institutions. This has significant consequences for our thinking about friendship. I begin my reinterpretation with some historical context to Smith's work.

According to historian Fernand Braudel, the settled notion that capitalism begins with industrialization is misleading. Already, much earlier, 'capitalism was what it was in relation to a *non-capitalism* of immense proportions' (1985, p. 239, original emphasis). What changed, however, was that from about the late 18th century on (earlier here and later there), in tandem with political changes, urbanization, and industrialization, and on the back of existential doubts raised by the fragmentation of the sense-lending totalities of a religious world picture and religiously ordained feudal authority, a market logic that raised exchange value to the status of central value of all things, including human relationships, came to offer itself as the paradigmatic logic for life *per se*.

Situated between mercantilism and the highly differentiated system of production that was to follow the first Industrial Revolution, the 18th century is a watershed in Western economic history. The French *physiocrats*, with Quesnay and Turgot the central figures, believed in *laissez-faire* economics as a system allowing the relatively unhindered establishment and maintenance of a natural order and social equilibrium, with feudal administration based on 'reason' playing a guiding role (Elias, 2012a, pp. 51–52). Their concerns were confined to relations between agriculture and business and disregarded industry; their aim was to simplify a complex and often arbitrary tax system; their solution was to tax the producers only. While freedom from constraint was clearly advocated by some, fair distribution of wealth was not.

Adam Smith, who had met Quesnay on his French sojourn in the mid-1760s, also advocated for free market interaction, but he saw labor, rather than nature, as the true source of economic value. Like the *physiocrats*, he believed in economic transactions based on self-interest as conducive to social harmony. But his view was more nuanced, his notion of social accord more considered, than that of his intellectual French cousins. He was more circumspect about the market's role as the dominant regulator of human sociability, although he did see in its burgeoning differentiation a leap toward better human relations (Nisbet, 1973, pp. 352–54 Heilbroner, 1999, pp. 42–74). According to Smith, in 18th century Britain – where according to one author, '[o]utside the drawing rooms of London or the pleasant rich estates of the counties, all that one saw was rapacity, cruelty, and degradation mingled with the most irrational and bewildering customs and traditions of some still earlier and already anachronistic day' (Heilbroner, 1999, p. 43) – interactions based on contract best guaranteed social order. And it is under the newly contractual conditions of that 'commercial society' that friendship takes on new meaning.

Scholars have suggested that 18th century thinkers among the growing bourgeoisie praised the virtues of intimate friendship. In two important and highly influential articles, 'Friendship and Trust as Moral Ideals' (1989) and 'Friendship in Commercial Society' (1990), Allan Silver argues that contrary to 'liberal' sociological perspectives, which, according to him, overstate the Romantic revolt against a new industrial, urban instrumentalization of social relationships, it was 'commerce' before the industrial age that set the scene for intimate friendship to emerge as an integrative social force. On that view, friendship did not simply emerge as a reaction to the anonymity of industrial and urbanized societies of strangers. Rather, preindustrial commerce already encouraged the establishment of friendly intimacy. Silver finds his evidence in the writings of the Scottish Enlightenment.

Indeed, in *The Theory of Moral Sentiments* of 1759 (1813), Smith is enthusiastic about the passing of friendship under feudalism, which was based on good will and personal inclination, and so was, for Smith, subject to the fickleness of human emotion. He saw a society based on commercial interaction and contract guided by principles of prudence, justice, and reason as conducive to friendly bonds because it *avoided* the vicissitudes of all-too-personal ties. Importantly, these new relationships were entered into according to agents' free wills. Among the well-to-do, says Smith,

> the necessity or conveniency of mutual accommodation, very frequently produces a friendship not unlike that which takes place among those who are born to live in the same family. Colleagues in office, partners in trade, call one another brothers; and frequently felt towards one another as if they really were so ... The Romans expressed this sort of attachment by the word *necessitudo*, which ... seems to denote that it was imposed by the necessity of the situation.
> (cited in Silver, 1990, p. 1481, original emphasis)

The notion of *necessitudo* in Smith becomes, at least for Silver, a key term denoting the replacement of necessity with a new voluntarism that marks 'a morally superior form of friendship' where 'sympathy', not 'exchange', are the 'universal mechanisms' of personal relationship in this nascent modernity (1990, p. 1482). According to that thesis, an evolving liberal society, rather than giving rise to instrumental interactions, rather than undermining the moral fabric as anti-conservative critiques would have it, fosters amicable, warm relations (at least among wealthy men).

More recent scholarship has tested Silver's thesis, and has shown some of its core assumptions to be problematic (Hill & McCarthy, 1999, 2004). It appears that Silver has misunderstood Smith's notions of *necessitudo* and 'sympathy', and so has misinterpreted the quality of intimacy that Smith was supposed to have treasured. Contrary to common wisdom, Smith was no advocate of a self-regulating market; he recognized the potential infinity of human desire and self-interest and the social disequilibrium that might follow from *laissez-faire* economics. That, however, did not translate into a vision of central government regulating the market. Rather, Smith posited an 'internal spectator', a conscience that as a hypothetical observer monitors our impulses. This is the locus of our 'sympathy' for others, whose main function is to facilitate interaction and whose degree and quality have to be checked and calibrated by the internal spectator. Smith's one-time mention of *necessitudo* is not supposed to highlight the demise of imposed necessity in commercial society, but its redefinition: sympathy, good will, and 'positive identification' with another become necessary ingredients of harmoniously functioning commercial society. 'Clearly, for Smith, the function of sympathy', state Hill and McCarthy,

> is to bring about harmony and not, as we see in Silver's account, merely to generate the positive virtue of beneficence or the classical virtues identified with warm friendship such as candor, humility, or self-sacrifice. In other words, the moral impetus of the impartial spectator is largely negative, guarding propriety and delivering both prudence and justice. Thus, we caution against seeing the function of sympathy in positive terms; it has only limited potential, if any, to generate the capacity for warm friendship. (2004, p. 5)

None of this is to deny the possibilities for warm friendships during that time; it is simply to point out that commercial society did not so much furnish better conditions for intimacy, but rather for civility, for 'cooler' bonds conducive to the harmonious integration of interaction in a differentiating society. This revised interpretation challenges the thesis that Smith speaks about intimate friendship in the modern sense, and is elaborated further on. In so doing it resolves the so-called 'Adam Smith problem', that is, the supposed tension between Smith's emphasis on moral integration in *The Moral Sentiments* and his trust in the 'invisible hand' of the market in *The Wealth of Nations*: Smith marshals 'sympathy' in the service of contractual interaction and thus does not, as is commonly held, stand in opposition to instrumental market rationality. For the thinkers who centrally shaped the culture of nascent capitalism, and who took cues from and critiqued it, as well as contributing to British utilitarianism (Broadie, 2003), friendship fulfilled its role best in the service of commercial prerogatives, as a means to strategic ends.

Moreover, their conception excluded the illiterate masses, and women were taken into account mainly with reference to the greater ease with which a new friendliness could enable more relaxed interaction among bourgeois frequenters of salons and learned societies. The 'essentially democratic spirit' (Pahl, 2000, p. 58) of friendship in commercial society is therefore 'democratic' only in so far is it gives ethical legitimacy to commercial exchange relations among businessmen. Democracy did not need to be extended to the rest of society because betterment for all was believed to quasi-naturally result from market efficiency. Smith, rather than presenting us with a first model of intimate friendship, developed a model of 'commercial friendship', a version of Aristotle's 'friendship of utility',[6] albeit under different social and economic conditions. It had purchase chiefly among a particular stratum of the society of his time, and so principally figures as a forerunner of the 'networking' ethos of latter-day capitalism.

Smith's is a first and enthusiastic attempt to articulate the utility of an ethics of private life in a domain of human action that is, for all intents and purposes, extrinsic to it. It shows that even before we can speak of a fully integrated self-regulating market thinkers turned to the problem of how to capitalize on noncontractual norms of everyday interaction. Whether or not this was due to a genuine belief in social progress is immaterial. What matters is that from then on the norms of market exchange expanded into other areas of life and so began to work as drivers behind the rise of market society. That market society can, however, only then be called 'modern' when a self-regulating market economy, underpinned by a strongly elaborated philosophy of economic liberalism, becomes the organizing center of societies (Polanyi, 2001, pp. 71–80). Concerning the private sphere, the instrumental, goal-oriented logic of the market enters into a symbiosis with conceptions of the personal observable in the kind of exchange logic that enters the vocabulary of intimacy. Over time, that trend threatens to hollow out the shelter of private life because it is fundamentally depersonalizing and dehumanizing: 'The people who meet on the exchange market, says Hannah Arendt,

> Are primarily not persons but producers of products, and what they show there is never themselves ... The impulse that drives the fabricator to the public market place is the desire for products, not for people, and the power that holds this market together and in existence is not the potentiality which springs up between people when they come together in action and speech, but a combined 'power of exchange' (Adam Smith) which each of the participants acquired in isolation. (1958, pp. 209–210)

Thus, friendship in Smith's conception has nothing to do with intimate friendship, and least of all with the friendship dyad in intimate mode, which he in any case considered an inferior form of sociability.[7] Thus he states in his *The Theory of Moral Sentiments* (1813, p. 78), 'They who would confine friendship to two persons, seem to confound the wise security of friendship with the jealousy and folly of love'. It seems, rather, that Smith's conception has everything to do with integrating informal types of sociability and the demands of commercial society. We are, of course, no strangers to such attempts. Some two hundred years later, albeit in the context of a developed market economy, Dale Carnegie sold Smith's vision to a public long primed by a culture of capitalism to regard exchange relations as natural in his bestselling *How to Make Friends and Influence People* (Carnegie, 2009). From there on in, that vision was seamlessly integrated into a late-modern 'networking' logic for all occasions.

As commercial society gains momentum and begins to transform into a market society, private life and intimacy too gain important impulses:

> The moment private sentiment begins to be marshaled in the service of market interaction is also the moment when the bourgeois family begins to retreat behind the fiction of independence from the market, thus crystallizing the intimate sphere partly through the denial of the economic origins ... that provided the bourgeois family with its consciousness of itself. It seemed to be established voluntarily and by free individuals and to be maintained without coercion; it seemed to rest on the lasting community of love on the part of the two spouses; it seemed to permit that noninstrumental development of all faculties that makes the cultivated personality. The three elements of voluntariness, community of love, and cultivation were conjoined in a concept of the humanity that was supposed to inhere in humankind as such and truly to constitute its absoluteness: the emancipation ... of an inner realm, following its own laws, from extrinsic purposes of any sort. (Habermas, 1991, pp. 46–47)

The fiction of self-contained intimacy, of a sphere into which a newly self-aware middle class could retreat, memorably labeled *Haven in a Heartless World* (1995) by Christopher Lasch, begins strongly to orient love and family life, and the more so the more industrialization and urbanization advance. That process of bourgeois sequestration marks both a greater orientation to the other as someone worthy of respect, of 'love', as well as acute cultural anxieties about the felt impersonality of industrial society.

Contrary to Silver, the notion of private life as the site of authenticity is marshaled against the impersonality of a burgeoning industrial system, whatever the enduring inequalities resulting from patriarchal power. With the emergence of industrial, capitalist society that intimacy takes on the kind of meaning to which we contemporary moderns can relate. It develops against a background, that is, that saw not only (uneven) improvements in material conditions but also meant that 'psychologically, Europeans were seriously disturbed' as a result of massive social transformations (Davies, 2010, p. 780–781). The new complexities of modern life translated not only into an optimism about progress, but caused existential uncertainties and anxieties. And so it is under these conditions, and as part of people's attempts to come to grips with the experience of modernity that friendship takes on the contours that mark it as the kind of intimate relationship we understand it to be today. Crucially, then, the thinkers of the Scottish Enlightenment were in no historical position to fully rethink that modernity and the place of intimacy in it, however valid their concerns and prescient their views may have been. That period, I suggest, was yet to come.

Intimacy, recognition, and romanticism

Possibilities for a self-directed life – in principle for some, in fact for others – under modern conditions of complexity and contingency heighten the need for meaning and for a meaningful, 'authentic' realization of the self-chosen life. German philosophers and writers, such as Herder, Fichte, and Schiller, grappled with the demise of a totality of meaning, insightfully interpreted later by Max Weber (see Grumley, 1988). They were strongly influenced by Rousseau's 'rebellion of the heart', as Hannah Arendt (1958, p. 39) has called his pitting of individual authenticity against the leveling trends of a new conformism. Rousseau's thought echoed strongly into the following century and resonated with the early Romantics.

Modern friendship and the Romantic ideal

In his lectures on Romanticism, Isaiah Berlin called it 'the largest recent movement to transform the lives and the thought of the Western world', precipitating 'a great break in European consciousness' (2001 [1965], pp. 1, 8). And in a passage that condenses disparate artistic and philosophical enterprises, he argues that early Romanticism – whether in Victor Hugo or the Schlegels, Goethe or Tieck, Coleridge or Byron, whether in Britain, France, Italy, or Germany – was unified by a particular kind of idealism made up of 'such values as integrity, sincerity, readiness to sacrifice one's life to some inner light, dedication to some ideal for which it is worth sacrificing all that one is, for which it is worth living and dying' (2001, p. 8). That idealism was anti-Enlightenment in all its facets: passion challenged reason, worship of all that is natural opposed mastery over nature, chaos was valued over order, subversion over convention, and religiosity and spirituality over established Church practices (Davies, 2010, p. 783). It was, then, an 'outburst against abstract reason' as well as against a society the Romantics perceived as 'sunk in the mire of commerce and industry, activities that blunted the senses, narrowed the mind, killed the imagination' (Barzun, 2003, pp. 465, 474).[8]

It is this face of Romanticism that has come down to us as a pure type of sorts. This is what Taylor has called the pre- and early Romantic 'expressivism' with its strong links back to Rousseau, but also to Herder who considered 'self-realization' not just in terms of individual difference but concerning the uniqueness of *moral* actors, whether individuals or peoples, the uppermost goal of human progress (Taylor, 1977, pp. 13–27). Both Rousseau and Herder, if with different approaches, railed against the Enlightenment split of human will and objectified nature, which amounted for them to the objectification of *human* nature as such. They shared with all the thinkers and artists of their generation the attempt to solve a 'central problem', namely 'the nature of human subjectivity and its relations to the world' (Taylor, 1977, p. 3). That question became particularly pressing in the aftermath of the French revolution, when a first enthusiasm came up against the horrific realities of the Reign of Terror of 1793–1794. Belief in political progress and the rule of law conflicted with the need for an authentic life irreducible to the strictures of reason. As we will see below, this is the context in which Hegel, both a critic and central figure of Romanticism, formulated his vision of society as an institutional order, articulated the role of intimacy, and in so doing did his share to modernize it.

Intimacy from the late 18th century and into the 19th is marked by rapid structural transformations, the differentiation of a private sphere, the rise of a society of strangers, and an outpouring of philosophical, artistic, and scientific innovation. Toward the end of the 19th century, the psychoanalytical reconceptualization of subjectivity emerges from a 'bourgeois experience' that begins to teeter ever more self-consciously between new-found freedoms and new uncertainties (Gay, 1999). New forms of sociability in new contexts and the beginnings of social mobility clash with the real possibility of anonymity, alienation, and loneliness; individuals are increasingly 'thrown back upon themselves' (Tenbruck, 1989, p. 235, my translation).

Enlightenment philosophers provided the first intimations that transformations in the social order are especially conducive to friendship.

Even earlier we can see the beginnings of a psychologization of friend-ship as part of a nascent 'culture of reflection' that was otherwise given to cool appraisal rather than heartfelt expressivity (Kon, 1979, p. 57, my translation). Montaigne articulated friendship's intimacy and its benefits to self and other (in his case for La Boëtie) 'rather than perceiv-ing friendship primarily in terms of its societally integrative functions the way this was ordinarily the case during the Renaissance' (Kon, 1979, pp. 55–59, my translation). During the Enlightenment the uncertain-ties, but also the excitement, of first-glimpsed possibilities with the challenge to absolute rule and dogma proved fertile for a kind of intimate communication that helped stabilize experience. But by and large, ideals of human intercourse had not yet undergone the shift from public orientation to an ideal of voluntary, mutual, and personal enrichment. This is evident in Smith's attempt to play the cool hand of (contractual) reason in personal relations. Now add the French revolu-tion, the Napoleonic wars, the onset of industrialization and urbaniza-tion, the bureaucratization of state authority and the emergence of a literate bourgeois civil society to the mix, and we can understand that the conditions for a highly personal vision of intimacy met with ever more acute needs for shelter and the recognition of one's unique self. What Rousseau envisaged and Herder advocated found the social and cultural affinities to become a general ideology during Hobsbawm's (2010) 'age of revolution'.

The Romantics, then, counter 'the hardness and impersonality of social relations with the intensive subjectivity of one's own "I"' forged not only in introspection and creativity, but in intimate relationships' (Kon, 1979, p. 62, my translation). For, however uppermost their own sense of self, their own sensibilities, feelings, predilections, and however keen their sense of their own uniqueness, that knowledge is accom-panied by just as intense a feeling of aloneness, both in terms of the creative nourishment of solitude, and the anxiety-provoking specter of loneliness: 'the lonelier the reflecting subject feels, the stronger is his need for an alter ego, for friendly conversation, for a unification of souls' (Kon, 1979, p. 62, my translation). Increased individualization and decreasing chances for deep identification with social statuses and roles facilitate the formation of intimacy, whether in romantic love or friendship; it is now beginning to be conceptualized and enacted pri-marily in subjective terms (Rapsch, 2004, pp. 42–46).

From our 'disenchanted' perspective, much of what goes for the aes-thetic realizations of a bare-all intimacy in friendship during the early Romantic period borders on the ridiculous. Much of it strikes us as narcissistic, or at least as a radical subjectivism exalted by and entangled in an expressivism so strikingly prefigured by Friedrich Schiller, whose work was crucial for the next generation of German Romantics. Take this excerpt from one of his letters to a friend:

> But what is friendship or platonic love other than a sensual confusion of character? Or the view of ourselves in another glass? [...] Oh, a friendship built such as this could have lasted in eternity! ... Believe, believe unashamedly, we were the only ones that resembled us; believe me, our friendship had the most glorious shimmer of heaven, the most beautiful and mighty ground, and foretold us both no less than heaven. (cited in Kon, 1979, p. 79, my translation)

It is sentiments such as these that lead Russian literary critic Vissarion Belinsky to deal with the Romantic ideal in the sharpest fashion. The Romantics are 'not drawn to friendship because they have, in their younger years, a particular need for sympathy', he writes in his 1847 reckoning with his own past,

> but rather because they want to be sure of someone in their vicinity whom they can ceaselessly tell about their own valuable person. To speak in their own highfaluting jargon, the friend is for them a precious vessel for the outpouring of the most intimate and secret feelings, thoughts, hopes, dreams, etc. while in reality the friend is for them merely a toilet bowl into which they can pour the refuse of their own self-love. (cited in Kon, 1979, p. 71, my translation)

Unkind words, perhaps. There is, however, another interpretation that moves the Romantic friendship ideal into a different light. It foreshadows the kind of 'disclosing intimacy', the contemporary ideal of intimacy described by Lynn Jamieson (1998). The constant revelation of 'inner thoughts and feelings to each other', an 'intimacy of the self' prefigures the 'second industrial revolution' with its redefinition of intimacy in a therapeutic mode (Zaretsky, 2004)[9], and so prefigures a general cultural integration of what Eva Illouz (2008) has called the 'therapeutic persuasion'. The diffusion of clinical, psychoanalytic practice as a way of life – ubiquitously represented in the cultural productions of the self-help genre, TV talk shows, celebrity culture, relationship counseling, and online and offline advice columns – is part and parcel of the contemporary self and its various interactions to such an extent that the pioneering work of the Romantic period is easily overlooked.

Intimacy's therapeutic turn (see Chapter 3), owes a fair share to the slow development of modern subjectivity from the end of the Middle Ages via Romantic expressivism.

Hegel, Honneth, and the promise of intimacy

For Adam Smith the overdrawn emotionality of the Romantics would have been just so much folly. The usefulness of such sentiments would have been unclear, their contribution to a pre-capitalist society too intangible. Not so for Hegel. He had a keen sense that modalities of intimacy including friendship have a part to play in our modern freedoms, not despite but precisely because of their irreducibility to contractual norms. What is modern in Hegel is that intimate relationships are not simply about a natural unity, but are spiritual and, most of all, *ethical*; they involve two people determining that they will form a unity through which they propose to reach a higher level of self-assured identity. The institutional form with which Hegel is concerned is marriage, though as we shall see friendship too was significant to his thinking. For Hegel, marriage is supposed to be not just a transaction of convenience, but an undertaking of each partner to seek to refashion and enrich themselves in and through the relationship, with love its ethical core: 'Love, the ethical moment in marriage, is, as love a feeling [*Empfindung*] for actual individuals in the present, not for an abstraction' (1991[1821], p. 219).

Theorization of this process began with Immanuel Kant who sought to establish a contractual model of the family in order to bring to bear on it the general requirements of justice. Later, Hegel criticized the Kantian model on the grounds that affection and care cannot be reduced to juridical presuppositions. What is important here is that toward the end of the 18th century and into the 19th the intimate core of the private sphere becomes increasingly autonomous, and that this also means that inequalities, rather than mostly envisaged in terms of the relations between the family and authority external to it, move to the center of the family, become intrafamilial business. This kind of intimacy – whether fictitious or real – could only enter the heart of private life once the family had come to be perceived as sufficiently independent from political and economic exigencies to facilitate its institutionalization based on justice and affection (Honneth, 2007b).

The tensions between the justice model of the family that codifies rights and obligations and a model of intimacy based on mutual respect, care, and affection remain to this day, and thus call for an increased capacity to articulate and negotiate relationships; they characterize intimacy in the modern sense. But Hegel's conception not only elaborates the irreducibility of intimacy to Kantian justice, but also binds the emotions, the passions, to an institutional order whose very basis is an ethical orientation to an other *qua* person (Honneth, 2007b). What we see here is a first concerted effort at describing the freedoms potentially available to us in a distinct intimate sphere of its own, freedoms that became possible in marriage not least because the perceived virtues of friendship – for a time valued as a higher form of love because of its non-erotic ambit – came slowly to be integrated into the conjugal bond to became its underpinnings.[10]

Modern culture has embraced the idea that individuals can and ought to look at their lives as a project of self-development. Hegel makes the point that this project of self-fashioning is not something that can be meaningfully undertaken in isolation. Rather, I discover who I am and what I can become in my interactions with people and social institutions that I in turn recognize as legitimate. This mutual recognition (*Anerkennung*) lends to individuals self-worth not because they see themselves simply reflected in an alter ego, but because our freedom emerges in the limiting factor of respectful orientation and interaction. In paragraph 7 of his *Elements of the Philosophy of Right* (1991 [1821]) Hegel writes:

> But we already possess this freedom in the form of feeling (*Empfindung*), for example in friendship and love. Here, we are not one-sidedly within ourselves, but willingly limit ourselves with reference to an other, even while knowing ourselves in this limitation as ourselves. In this determinacy, the human being should not feel determined; on the contrary, he attains his self-awareness only by regarding the other as other. (1991 [1821], p. 42)

For Hegel, this is the cultural significance of the intimate relationship: it is a mode of interaction in which one seeks a sympathetic recognition not simply for who one objectively is, for one's 'social standing', but rather for one's efforts to fashion oneself as a self-aware, unique, and autonomous individual in relationship to another, in a dialogical or 'intersubjective' process.[11] The fact of our human *interdependence*, our irreducible sociality, contains the very possibility for our freedom and nowhere more so than in those freely chosen personal relationships where we can 'be ourselves'. That is the modern promise of intimacy, the promise of its freedom; a promise that undermines those versions of freedom that can render it only in terms of the greatest possible *independence* from others. We need to keep in mind here that for Hegel that freedom was best preserved by institutional arrangements embedded in state, market, and family.

Honneth, social recognition, and 'love'

Hegel's formulation has in recent years been taken up by social philosophers who attempt to build conceptual bridges between the Hegelian project of making sense of modern subjectivity, and the sociological project of explaining the mutual constitution of individual and collective actors, and of trying to fathom the social and cultural terms of their flourishing in the contemporary context. For Axel Honneth, recognition is an intersubjective process between actors and their social environments that allows both for the development of autonomous identities and for the possibility of social change. Individuals and collectives drive social change when they demand social recognition for their uniqueness, when they seek to change the very expectations, conformity to which confers recognition. This interplay between the dependence of identity on the recognition of others and individuals' demands for the recognition of their unique characteristics, capacities, and circumstances enables the development of individuals in and *vis-à-vis* the community, of social groups in and *vis-à-vis* their social environments, and of societies as a whole. In Honneth's approach, this model for the formation and assertion of identity is the mirror that is held up against the realities of conformity and injustice.

The premise at the heart of theories of recognition is to conceptualize social dynamics of misrecognition, or disrespect, in order to reach a better understanding of how forms of social injustice can be mitigated through the transformation of 'institutionalized patterns of cultural values' (Fraser, 2000, p. 114). To that end, Honneth (1996) outlines three historically differentiated spheres of recognition: 'love', 'law', and 'solidarity'. Together they constitute the cornerstone of Honneth's interpretation of 'bourgeois-capitalist society as an institutionalized recognition order'; it is, moreover, an attempt 'to show that the distinctively human dependence on intersubjective recognition is always shaped by the particular manner in which the mutual granting of recognition is institutionalized within a society' (Fraser & Honneth, 2003, p. 138).

With 'love', as the Hegelian catch-all term for intimacy, Honneth refers to an affective type of recognition that is vital to people's trust in their physical integrity and the value of their physical and emotional needs.[12] We gain this type of 'self-confidence' through socialization and the mother–child bond where it is reaffirmed by the experience of affection and care. Social-historical processes like the emergence of childhood as a discrete stage of life, and the development of the perception of children as beings with unique rights to protection and care, love is institutionalized. Another example is the gradual freeing of relationships between women and men from economic and social imperatives, and their anchoring in feelings of mutual affection in marriage 'as the institutional expression of a special kind of intersubjectivity, whose peculiarity consists in the fact that husband and wife love one another as needy beings' (Fraser & Honneth, 2003, p. 139). For Honneth, recognition through mutual affection and care shored up by institutional 'guarantees' is no less than a prerequisite for individuals' self-confidence in their bodily integrity.

From this perspective we arrive at intimacy as a private and personal, noninstrumental relationship of care, support, and affection in the context of trust and respect. Indeed,

> it is true of both familial relationships and friendships that they can continue to exist only as long as the subjects involved show moral consideration and care out of affection; indeed, caring actions of this kind lose their moral value as soon as they are performed not for reasons of love but because of the rational acceptance of duty. (Honneth, 2007b, p. 158)

The juridification of intimate relationships is an example where intimacy is obliterated. In cases of divorce, especially in custody battles and claims to property entitlement, the other – once loved for their unique, non-substitutable qualities – is treated as a mere legal subject. A juridification of self and other ensues. Monitoring for possible legal transgressions by what is now one's nemesis goes hand in hand with an acute self-monitoring and the presentation of a morally impeccable self to elicit empathy from magistrates and judges (see Honneth, 2011, p. 157–172). Friendship is 'protected' from such processes, not because it is integrated into the repertoire of institutional arrangements, but because it is subject to an 'institutional deficit' which is central to its freedom. This is a modification to Honneth's thesis that I will elaborate in Chapter 3.

Conclusion

The modern vision of intimacy crystallized in processes of differentiation that changed people's relationships to themselves and to others in fundamental ways. The capacity to recognize one another for each other's unique endowments, capacities, and individual authenticity presupposes a shift in social organization: from a strongly hierarchized type, in which 'honor' is distributed according to rank and station, to social arrangements that allow for social mobility and give individuals the chance to turn the fate of 'contingency into destiny' (Heller & Fehér, 1988, p. 27), to live autonomous lives. The freedom we find to express ourselves in our intimate relationships, and so the very meaning of intimacy depends on the cultural and social infrastructure in which it finds nourishment – on ideas and practices that change over time, are valued today, or are without power to stir the social imagination tomorrow. Adam Smith saw in friendship the possibility to grease the wheels of commerce; the early Romantics saw in it yet another way to express their subjective sensibilities and to counter the coldness of contract and instrumental reason that threatened to corrode the ties that bind. For Hegel, intimacy promises the kind of freedom that best expresses our humanity: the freedom to work, create, become, or simply 'be' within limits that are not imposed but generated freely in interaction with others. That promise may very well explain the very attractiveness of intimate relationships; and arguably it is most readily realized in friendship. But what is friendship? How can we think about it? To describe the relationship type, what it offers to us as well as its challenges, we need to come to terms also with what it is not, to distinguish it from other kinds of relationships whose meanings are, if contested, also shared. That is the task of the next chapter, where, the benchmark of modern intimacy is applied to the concept of friendship and to those relationships with which it is sometimes conflated.

2
Friends, Friendship, and Sociology

What in everyday life are mostly unarticulated, intuitive distinctions must be taken seriously in sociological research. The discipline is about 'defamiliarizing the familiar' (Bauman & May, 2001), about reflecting on everyday interactions, social processes, trends, and their meanings with the intention to feed clarifying reinterpretations back into social life. In that context it is well to remember what Alfred Schutz (1973) had to say about the relationship between common sense thinking and social science knowledge. In everyday life we use abstractions, constructs, and concepts that help us cut through the complexities of daily living; they help us select meanings relevant to given situations. What differentiates common sense and the social sciences is, according to Schutz, that 'the constructs used by the social scientist ... are *constructs of the second degree*, namely constructs of the constructs made by the actors on the social scene whose behavior the scientist observes and tries to explain' (Schutz, 1973, p. 6, my emphasis). Social scientists not only describe common words in their own terms, but also seek to understand the patterns of behaviors, practices, and attitudes they denote. Moreover, as Anthony Giddens (1984, p. 284) has made clear, the concepts that may result from social science research may become re-appropriated by people in the context of their everyday lives by way of the 'double hermeneutic', the interpretive feedback loop between research and everyday understandings.

This has nothing to do with telling people how to think. Contemporary sociology is suspect of 'normativity', and that with some reason. There is today a great sensitivity to approaches that pretend they can offer blueprints for living, or to make judgments from up above about ways of life here below. Thankfully that is no longer what sociologists are about. But a more empathic and inclusive stance, with its now extraordinary sensitivity to agency – something that is likely to be not only a matter of advanced method but also a defensive stance versus the ever-looming charge of social determinism – has at times also meant that the semantics of concepts have become so diffuse that it is often difficult to use them in any meaningful way. Whatever it is that people do or say is given credence to such an extent that unreflected upon actions are taken as if they are ready-made concepts that are no longer in need of interpretation. As we will see, usage of the term 'friend' is a good example.

Conceptual clarity is no less important in studies that are 'essayistic' or theoretical than in 'applied' research. Concepts need to refer clearly to concrete social relationships. 'Theory is of value in empirical science only', wrote Herbert Blumer nearly sixty year ago,

> to the extent to which it connects fruitfully with the empirical world. Concepts are the means, and the only means of establishing such connection. ... If the concept is clear as to what it refers, then sure identification of the empirical instances may be made. ... Thus, with clear concepts theoretical statements can be brought into close and self-correcting relations with the empirical world. Contrariwise, vague concepts deter the identification of appropriate empirical instance, and obscure the detection of what is relevant in the empirical instances that are chosen. Thus, they *block connection* between theory and its empirical world and prevent their effective interplay. (1954, pp. 4–5, my emphasis)

Blumer breaks with a positivist tradition that seeks to narrow the complexities of social life by subsuming interactions under quasi-natural laws, and by narrowing the range of meanings attributed to 'definitive concepts'. Blumer advocates instead for what he calls 'sensitizing concepts' – concepts that rather than 'provid[ing] prescriptions of what to see ... merely suggest directions along which to look' and 'rest on a general sense of what is relevant' (1954, p. 7). Taking my lead from Blumer, I seek to construct a conception of friendship that has interpretive purchase because it is understandable from a lay perspective and hopes to clarify some of the more entrenched notions regarding the relationship type.

I begin by approaching the subject matter from a general level and then narrow that approach to friendship itself. The first step in that process is to think, with Max Weber, about friendship as a *social relationship.* Not only does this basic concept move friendship squarely into the purview of sociology, it prepares the way for a central argument of the book, namely that friendship, although a social relationship, cannot be considered a full-fledged institution. This is important because I show in Chapter 3 that friendship's 'institutional deficit' lies at the core of the kinds of freedom friends can enjoy. Further, the fact that friendship 'exists only as a *relationship*' (Markus, 2010b, p. 16, original emphasis) but as rule is not thematized as a relationship by friends, has very real consequences. Second, because I'm concerned with one-on-one friendships rather than networks, I go on to highlight some of the basic sociological characteristics of the *dyad* by engaging with Georg Simmel's writing on the topic. Third, I turn to the words 'friends' and 'friendship' in order to show how social change has precipitated considerable overlaps in everyday usage of the terms, but also in order to point out what I think is a persisting methodological problem in sociological analyses of friendship: the conflation of friendship and friendly relations.

Sensitizing concepts: social relationships, dyads, friendship

Weber on social relationships

Max Weber has written extensively about the methods of the social sciences. In *Economy and Society* (1978) he elaborates key sociological concepts, among them the term 'social relationship', which is for him no less than the basic focus of the discipline. Here is the leading statement:

> The term 'social relationship' will be used to denote the behavior of a plurality of actors insofar as, in its meaningful content, the action of each takes account of that of the others and is oriented in these terms. The social relationship thus consists entirely and exclusively in the existence of a probability that there will be a meaningful course of social action – irrespective, for the time being, of the basis for this probability. (Weber, 1978, pp. 26–27)

The key ingredients in a social relationship are thus more than one actor – whether it is a group, organization, or person – and a mutual orientation, a taking account of one another that makes it likely that there will be a meaningful interaction. Weber then goes on to clarify the statement: what matters is a mutual orientation, but not whether that orientation is hostile or friendly, and it need not be reciprocal concerning the actors' motivation. Think about diplomatic dissimulation between states, bluff in business transactions, or unrequited love. 'A relationship is objectively symmetrical only', says Weber, when 'according to the typical expectations of the parties, the meaning for one party is the same as for the other'. But because we are dealing here with 'typical expectations' on the level of culture, such symmetries can only ever be approximate. 'A social relationship in which the attitudes are completely and fully corresponding is in reality a limiting case' (Weber, 1978, p. 27), something that in love and friendship in any case can never be proven, but is more or less assumed. Again, the actual attitudes and motivations that actors bring to an interaction are not the relationship's sole defining characteristics. The basic criterion here is mutually oriented and meaningful action. Thus, according to Weber, 'the absence of reciprocity will, for terminological purposes, be held to exclude the existence of a social relationship only if it actually results in the absence of a mutual orientation of the action of the parties' (1978, pp. 27–28).

'Meaningful' here refers to commonly agreed upon norms, whether formalized in law or simply taken-for-granted shared cultural understandings about 'how things are done around here' and about expectations concerning interactions between certain types of actors. Hence, an interaction is probable to the extent that it makes sense to the actors concerned in an appropriate context. The context could be family, business, or politics; the actors husband and wife, merchant and customer, government department and university, etc. For Weber it is the mode of interaction that denotes what we understand by a given entity such as 'the state', and by extension 'the family', 'the economy', or 'friendship'. He asks us to 'avoid the "reification" of those concepts', as if they were self-sufficient, self-organizing, and autonomous units independent of human action. Rather, these concepts are products of human interaction, can only be properly understood as such, and so 'cease to exist in a sociologically relevant sense whenever there is no longer a probability that certain kinds of meaningfully oriented social action will take place' (Weber, 1978, p. 27). Weber understood that in the social sciences, unlike in the 'dogmatic disciplines ... such as jurisprudence, logic, ethics, and esthetics, which seek to ascertain the "true" and "valid"', concepts are never semantically fixed (1978, p. 4). It is in that spirit that Herbert Blumer (1954) warned against treating concepts in the social sciences as 'definitive', and urged us to treat them as 'sensitizing', as guiding research but not as constructs that unduly narrow down conceptualization of interactive possibilities. After all, it is social scientists who interpret actions and categorize them, while actors 'construct' them more or less unawares. They change the meaningful content of relationship types 'on the ground'. We, the observers, are in a sense always playing catch-up.

For Weber, the cultural meaning of a concept – 'typical' or 'average' expectations or 'sense' which is contingent on time and place – is crucial, and is identified as an interaction, or set of interactions, that can be observed and categorized as typical for a certain kind of relationship:

> Thus that a 'friendship' or a 'state' exists or has existed means this and only this: that we, the observers, judge that there is or has been a probability that on the basis of certain kinds of known subjective attitude of certain individuals there will result in the average sense a certain type of specific action. (1978, p. 28)

Should the content of the relationship change – from solidarity to conflict, for example – we may give it a different name, or insist that the 'what' remains the same and that only the 'how' has changed, but it still remains a social relationship. What typically remain constant in a social relationship are its internal norms, its 'maxims' as Weber calls them. And these are more likely to be 'rational', formalized, contractual, articulated, and formulated the less intimate the relationship: 'There is far less possibility of a rational formulation of subjective meaning in the case of a relation of erotic attraction or of personal loyalty or any other affectual type than, for example, in the case of a business contract' (Weber, 1978, p. 28). These aspects of the social relationship take on particular significance and shading in the dyad.

Georg Simmel on the dyad

In two articles published in *The American Journal of Sociology* (1902a,b), Simmel gives a fascinating account of how the qualities of interactions change with the number of interactants. Testimony to the fundamental importance of these considerations, Simmel elaborated them as part of his methodological treatise *Soziologie: Untersuchungen über die Formen der Vergesellschaftung* (1908a) and in the same year published an excerpt in a Berlin newspaper that spells out the sociological significance that dyads held for him:

> If sociology is to be true to the fact that the single human being does not exist alone, but is determined by the coexistence of others, then its gaze can not be limited to the great collective entities that are

circumscribed by politics and economy, the law and church, family and culture in general. Rather, it must turn to those finer, more ephemeral relationships ... that unfold between person and person, to those often abandoned and then recovered threads on which, after all, the inner vitality and solidity of our existence depend. (Simmel, 1908b, my translation)

For Simmel it is clear that dyadic interpersonal relationships are *the* elementary social form and as such ought to be fundamental to a discipline that deals with social relationships. He then goes on to sketch in greater detail what in such relationships is of sociological significance, something that he already attended to in his earlier American publications.

In 'The Number of Members as Determining the Sociological Form of the Group' (1902a,b), his first publications on the peculiarities of dyads expanded later in his *Soziologie* (1908a), Simmel juxtaposes the dyad with the triad and first notes the dyad's irreducibility: if one actor exits it ceases to exist. Thus, all dyadic relationships are by definition temporary, with death or relationship break-ups the most obvious examples. Less drastically, children leaving the nest, migration, and – in today's flexible labor markets which require unprecedented mobility – the increasing asynchronicity of life trajectories exert pressures on dyadic relationships (Beck & Beck-Gernsheim, 1995, 1996; Blatterer, 2009).

Although from the perspective of audiences dyads constitute distinct social entities, from an insider perspective this is usually not the case. Rather, the relationship is perceived in terms of one's immediate relations to the other. According to Simmel there is hence no development of a group identity the way this is already possible among three actors, and secondly, there is no place to hide – both in the sense of anonymity and responsibility. For instance, in the case of such reified constructs as 'the economy' or 'the State', individuals often need reminding that they are part of these entities' very constitution, because the great numbers that comprise them also appear to afford anonymity, which feels like independence – until financial crisis or political upheaval brings home the sociological reality of *inter*dependence. The larger the number of participants, the greater the leeway for dissimulation, for the diffusion of accountability, 'the *shifting* of duties and responsibilities' (Simmel, 1902a, p. 43, original emphasis). In a relationship of two, one is not confronted with an abstract entity, but with the factual reality of the other, with all the visibility and accountability this entails. The structural fact of number therefore determines to a significant degree the quality of interaction.

Concerning lack of identification beyond immediate interaction there are, for Simmel, important exceptions, 'the most decisive of which' is marriage (1902a, p. 40). Irrespective of the spouses' character qualities, the bond is imbued with 'the feeling that marriage is something super-personal, something in itself worthy and sacred, which stands over and above the unsanctity of each of its elements' and goes beyond the 'mere I and thou' (Simmel, 1902a, p. 41). There are two reasons for this in Simmel's mind: intimacy and tradition. Intimacy is, for him, 'a miracle' in so far as it goes beyond that which is rationally comprehensible and explicable and enables the reconciliation of otherwise irreconcilable individualities. This intimacy is, in turn, 'promoted by the superindi-viduality of the marriage', by the fact that the *institution* has preceded the couple and will outlive it:

> This projection of traditional elements into the matrimonial relation-ship, *which puts it in significant contrast with the individual freedom that is possible, for instance, in molding the friendly relationship* ... favors the feeling of an objective constitution and superpersonal unity in mar-riage; although each of the two partners has only the single other in juxtaposition with himself, yet he feels himself at least partially so situated as one feels only when in correlation with a collectivity – i.e., as the mere bearer of a superindividual structure, which in its essence and its norms is independent of himself, although, to be sure, he is an organic member of it. (Simmel, 1902a, p. 42, my emphasis)

There are, of course, other dyadic relationships between non-intimates that are more than the sum of the interactions between two indi-viduals that too are subject to a 'superpersonal unity'. For example, transactions between business associates abide by the rational rules of contract and are therefore subject to external norms that usually preexist the exchange; they are 'institutionalized' interactions. Simmel recognizes this and sees as the main difference between intimate and non-intimate dyadic relationships their diverging objectives:

> The reciprocal relationship of the business associates has its purpose outside of itself; whereas in the case of marriage it is within itself. In the former instance the relationship is the means for the gaining of certain objective results; in the latter everything objective appears really only as a means for the subjective relationship. (1902a, p. 43)

While the business person may, literally, close the door on the interaction *qua* transaction at the end of the working day, for spouses the institution 'marriage' remains an ever-present reality and 'psychologically increase[s] in contrast with immediate subjectivity' (Simmel, 1902a, p. 43). But whatever the normative force of the institution, the person cannot hide behind abstract maxims, norms, and promises. 'Until death do us part' can hardly protect us from the possibility of deception and acts of disrespect. Again Simmel holds that the number of interactants alone mitigates the shirking of responsibility. In a memorable passage he says:

> Economic combinations make demands of such shameless egoism, colleagues in office wink at such crying malfeasances, corporations of political or of scientific nature exercise such monstrous suppressions of individual rights, as would be impossible in the case of an individual if he were responsible for them as a person, or at least they would put him to shame. As a member of a corporation, however, he does all this with untroubled conscience, because in that case he is anonymous and feels himself covered and, as it were, concealed by the totality. (1902a, p. 44)

By contrast, in a relationship of two it is much more immediately obvious who did or said what. And it is from that particular situation that the dyad draws its strengths and encounters challenges:

> Precisely the fact that each knows he can depend only upon the other, and upon nobody else, gives to such a combination – for example, marriage, friendship, and even more external combinations up to political adjustment of two groups – a special consecration; each element in them is, in respect to its sociological destiny and everything dependent upon this, much more frequently made to confront the alternative of all or nothing than in other associations. (Simmel, 1902a, p. 45)

In the second part of the article, Simmel foreshadows his perspective on friendship, further elaborated in his 'The Sociology of Secrecy and of Secret Societies' (1906). In 'Number of Members II', he attends to friendship more directly in order to differentiate it from marriage, and in so doing he touches upon two concepts that exercise his imagination throughout his life: 'individuality' and 'differentiation'. Simmel uses these terms in specific ways. With *individuality* he refers to the degree of relative personal independence from social determinants – what in the literature is commonly meant by the term 'individuation' – but he also uses the term in the everyday sense of 'personal qualities'. These qualities diminish in importance to the degree that group membership expands (see also, Simmel, 1908a, pp. 86–88). On the upper end of that scale, the smooth operation of the modern bureaucracy is premised on the very negation of individuality; function trumps personality. With *differentiation* he not only refers to the gradual development of separate domains of social activity – economy, politics, family, etc. – but also to a parallel development of the personality that renders it more complex, less bound to single ascribed roles and called upon to act and think in plural and diverse contexts. And so, for Simmel, friendship in contrast to marriage presupposes a capacity to enter social relationships that lack the institutional scaffolding that holds up and solidifies marriage *vis-à-vis* the individual; it presupposes a personality that is 'differentiated' and so 'individual' enough to relate directly from person to person without the guiding and constraining influences that institutions provide: '[F]riendship', he writes, 'is a relationship entirely founded upon the individuality of the elements, perhaps even more than marriage, which, through its traditional forms, its social fixities, its real interests, includes much that is super-individual and independent of the peculiarity of the personalities' (1902b, p. 159).

Simmel illustrates this point with reference to the 'very general opinion' of the day that women are less capable of friendship. Indeed, from Aristotle to Montesquieu and beyond, women were either ignored in discussions of friendship, or were deemed unable to establish and maintain them. Their structural position – in the home rather than in public – was cited as both cause and symptom of that alleged incapacity, while the realities of gendered power that underpinned that position remained ignored. Simmel recognized that the structural position of women has had negative consequences for their potential to individuate, and so to enter into the one intimate relationship that requires a maximum of 'individuality': friendship. Connecting individuality, differentiation, and social position to distinguish marriage from friendship he maintains that,

> [t]he fundamental difference upon which marriage rests is, in itself, not individual, but it pertains to the species; friendship, however, rests upon a purely personal differentiation, and hence it is intelligible that in general real and permanent friendships are rare at

the inferior levels of personal development, and that, on the other hand, the modern highly differentiated woman manifests notably enhanced capacity and inclination for friendships, alike with men and with women. The entirely individual differentiation has, in this case, attained decisiveness over that which pertains to the species, and we thus see the correlation formed between the sharpest individualization and a relation that at this grade is absolutely limited to duality. (1902b, p. 159)

Simmel refers to marriage as a social category (*Gattung*), but to friendship as too open, too beholden to the relational dynamics between two distinct personalities to achieve anything like the institutional status of marriage. But – importantly – it is still a *social relationship* because it emerges as a product of meaningful interaction. Add to that the fact that it is articulable, describable, and a potential subject for communication, and so holds shared cultural meaning on the level of everyday life, and friendship emerges both as more than the emergent property of dyadic interaction, and less than an institution. That in-between status means that how an individual friendship is 'done', how friends interact, trumps social prescription; it is the core of what I will elaborate in Chapter 3 as friendship's 'institutional deficit' – a structural peculiarity that affords friendship its characteristic freedom.

It is debatable whether or not Simmel's conception of 'real' friendship overly relies on masculine constructions of a valuable public and devalued private domain. After all, there appears to be an implicit assumption that it is only with differentiation – with the rise of the 'modern' woman – that friendships between women become possible, while friendships between men were already prevalent in antiquity. This is in line with Simmel's conviction that friendships the way we think of them today are possible only due to the development of distinct arenas of human interaction and the increasingly individualized individuals that construct and inhabit them. Contemporary friendships are quintessentially modern; differentiated society furnishes the social conditions necessary for more or less autonomous individuals to enter into more or less unmediated relations of intimacy. On that count male friendships in European antiquity could not have been analogous with modern friendships. Possibilities for friendships in our sense, then, arise for both men and women with modernity, although these possibilities remain strongly circumscribed by gendered norms, as we will see in Chapters 5 and 6.

Friends and friendship

In his *Philosophical Investigations* (2010 [1953]), Wittgenstein warned us from laying too much store by words, these inadequate constructs that we have made to mirror experience. Garfinkel (1967) too has reminded us not to overemphasize the power of concepts in sociological explanation, because people on the ground by and large make little use of them and tend to rely on habit and routinized actions. We need, then, to keep the imperfections of words and concepts in mind. But we also need to acknowledge that words, labels, names do work – work of explanation as much as obfuscation, of inclusion as well as exclusion, and that not despite but often because of their inadequacies in respect to experience.

The social media age has prompted a new public reflexivity about friendship. The ease with which we can accumulate great numbers of *Facebook* friends has not only spawned the verb construction 'to friend' and neologisms such as 'defriending', 'unfriending', and 'friend farming', but has sparked curiosity and sometimes consternation about what friendship is, who our real friends are, and who our are. It has raised questions as to whether this age of ubiquitous but loose connections is not also an age that no longer prizes friendship the way we may have done before the advent of social media. At least among the affluent denizens of the Global North[1] a gap seems to have opened up between our technological capacities to connect with others and the social conventions that orient the 'what' and 'how', especially of these mediated relationships. Connectivity, so it seems, has outpaced our capacity to create rules and then build a consensus around how to maintain these relationships, even what to call them and what meaning to attribute to them. 'There are *Facebook* friends', says *Guardian* writer Oliver Burkeman (2012),

> with whom you want to share everything, those you've grown apart from, and those you've barely heard of. (You can assign them to different lists, but then you've introduced a whole new layer of decisions: who belongs where? What qualifies someone to be switched from one list to another? And so on.) There are Twitter followers with whom your acquaintance is strictly professional, those you know from school, but didn't necessarily like, and those who are your dad. Not long ago, I realised with a feeling of dismay that I'd started to think of some of these contacts – not most of them, but some – as clutter.

Already busy lives, far from finding the relief that the gurus of techno-logical innovation preach and promise, are not only made busier by increasing work hours, or by the constant offloading of public respon-sibilities onto the shoulders of today's 'individualized individuals' (Bauman, 2001), but by a need to connect for its own sake. The prolif-eration of connections goes hand in hand with a new unmanageability of social relationships, a kind of connectivity overload. Quantity and quality clash. The greater the number of connections, the less certain we become about the qualities of the single relationships, and the more reflexive – thoughtful, introspective, circumspect – we need to be about them. We are still novices at trying to negotiate trends whereby people willingly disclose visual or textual information about themselves to a whole gamut of others, from the very close to the barely known; to many, that is, with whom we don't actually have 'personal relation-ships' as once understood (Markus, 2010a).

Before we might be tempted to put all this simply down to individual choice, preferences, and proclivities, let's not forget that this connectiv-ity for connectivity's sake has quickly become a normal imperative of sorts, over and beyond the fact that it is simply easier to keep in touch with others or to stylize our identities by following consumer trends. The collective need for connectivity comes to light especially when the mere thought of non-participation conjures fears of social ostracism, of falling outside the informational loop of events, of becoming invisible. In consequence, participation, connectivity, and visibility are increas-ingly pursued at the expense of privacy (Blatterer, 2010).

The public equation of participation in the social media game with morality adds its fair share of motivational impetus, and that not only because those who are little concerned with privacy can be seen as peo-ple who have nothing to hide (Solove, 2007), but because individual non-participation may be read as a sign indicating a predisposition to a whole range of antisocial behaviors. Suspicion falls on those who don't do as others do. At the same time as the need for connection heightens anxieties about being left out or being considered socially inept, com-mentators warn about yet another phenomenon, namely a kind of isolation that is, paradoxically, shared by the connected many, by the millions that are 'alone together' (Turkle, 2011). It remains to be seen how these changes, obvious to those of us who have witnessed their emergence, will be negotiated by the 'digital generations' who are and will be born into an already altered infrastructure of sociality.

It is in this context, then, namely under the conditions of a social media society, a society in which connectivity proliferates while the principles of interaction lack ethical consensus, that the terms 'friends' and 'friendship' have become especially ambiguous. 'We have so many online friends', states one German advertisement, for example, 'that we need a new word for the real ones'. And yet, these terminological uncertainties are not new. Discussion in the social science community on what friendship is and who friends are has some historical pedigree. A selection of statements on the problem – one linguistic, the others sociological – provides some context to contemporary uncertainties.

Language and social change

Like many trends that have been made to sport the shiny veneer of newness, the semantic ambiguities around 'friends' may have become more topical, but at the same time they can be traced back in history. Viewed over the *longue dureé* of our shared sociality contemporary consternations lose some of their novelty. Anna Wierzbicka, a linguist whose corpus of work constitutes a formidable challenge to the highly reductionist cognitive explanation of language (e.g. Pinker, 2010), has pursued important work on the meaning and usage of everyday words across cultures. As part of that work Wierzbicka has turned to semantic changes in *friend* and *friendship* in several languages including English.

Wierzbicka begins her chapter in *Understanding Cultures Through Their Key Words* (1997) by reminding us that, contrary to some Anglophone social scientists, friendship and the characteristics attributed to it cannot be generalized across cultures. Those who do are guilty of ethnocentrism, and often more specifically still, of anglocentrism. Despite common recourse to the cultural pedigree invoked by references to European antiquity, neither *friend* nor *friendship* can be assumed to describe personal relationships intrinsic to human nature everywhere and at all times. A good illustration of cultural variability is Hendrick Smith's commentary on the Russian meaning of *friend*:

> Their [the Russians'] social circles are usually narrower than those of Westerners, especially Americans, who put such great stock in popularity, but relations between Russians are usually more intense, more demanding, more enduring and often more rewarding. ... They want someone to whom they can pour out their hearts, share their miseries, tell about family problems or difficulties with a lover or mistress, to ease the pain of life or to indulge in endless philosophical windmill tilting. As a journalist I sometimes found it ticklish

because Russians want a total commitment from a friend. (cited in Wierzbicka, 1997, p. 55)

That is not to say, of course, that relationships and their various modes of interactions cannot be interrogated with the use of English words. Wierzbicka's aim is, above all, to remind us that the lack of precise equivalence across languages speaks to cultural variability, which unless taken into account as 'important and revealing' will have the result 'that the habitual Anglo perspective on human relations will be mistaken for the human norm' (1997, p. 32). This is an important observation. It reminds us not only of cultures beyond our own, but also of the fact of modern societies' thoroughgoing pluralization.[2]

Wierzbicka's analysis of centuries-long semantic changes of the words *friend* and *friendship* in English is instructive on at least two grounds: first, linguistic semantic changes are inseparable from changes in the web of human interdependencies and so contain clues to the social developments of personal relationships. Second, an understanding of these changes provides a good platform from which to begin the subsequent analysis of how some sociologists have thought about and used these concepts.

Over the centuries the word *friend* has been subject to processes that Wierzbicka (1997, p. 36) describes as devaluation, broadening of scope, and a shift from exclusivity to inclusivity. They indicate a semantic cooling – from traditional connotations of intimacy to relative affective distance – and connected to it a progressive multiplication of those others who are labeled friends. Again, the example of *Facebook* friends is apposite here. 'Broadly, the meaning of the word friends has "weakened"', says Wierzbicka, 'so that to achieve anything like the same "force" it is now necessary to use the expression *close friend*.' As a consequence,

> Something of the old value of the word *friend* has survived in the derived noun *friendship*: whereas in the older usage, *friends* were related to one another by *friendship*, in the current usage one can have many more *friends* than *friendships*, and only 'close friends' can now be said to be linked by 'friendship'. (Wierzbicka, 1997, p. 36, original emphasis)

The related processes of affective weakening and greater inclusivity of *friend* are the semantic concomitants of changing expectations on the level of the relationship. For instance, if in the time of William Shakespeare and Christopher Marlowe a friend was expected to do things *for* us, this gradually developed into the expectation that they do things *with* us. Moreover, the semantic cooling and greater inclusivity of *friend* can be seen in the demise of the expression 'my friend' in favor of 'a friend of mine', unless special emphasis is required as in the phrase, 'I can't do it to him, he is *my friend.*' The pronoun 'my' thus connotes greater intimacy and/or familial ties than the construction 'of mine'. Think about the semantic differences between 'my sister' and 'a sister of mine', for example. According to Wierzbicka, this indicates the integration of friends into a homogeneous collective in modern English, implying 'that the relation in question is not personal and exclusive but rather ranges over a whole class of people, defined by a single nonpersonal characteristic' (1997, p. 45).

Going by all indices of this linguistic analysis, it seems safe to entertain that intimacy emerges as the defining characteristic distinguishing friends from friendship. Remember, while George Eliot was well understood when she wrote, 'So, if I live or die to serve my friend,/'Tis for my love – 'tis for my friend alone', today we are expected to *like* rather than love our friends (1997, p. 51). In this social media age of ours we can confidently add that *knowing of* each other, or simply appearing on someone's *Facebook* page is good enough to be identified a friend. What hasn't changed, however, is that *friendship* connotes the kind of intimacy that friends in the broad sense can do without. And yet, what may be puzzling for social researchers who are supposed to reflect critically on commonsense assumptions is frequently outpaced by everyday practices. Witness, for example, the need for *Facebook* to establish the category 'close friends' in 2011 – a corporate nod to users' intuitive understanding and need for the differentiation of levels of intimacy in personal relationships. In sum, Wierzbicka's analysis provides us with strong evidence that owing to centuries of English language development *friendship* retains its name and the concept its power as denoting an *intimate* relationship.

Having discussed some fundamental developments in English usage of *friend* and *friendship*, this is a good place to investigate the enmeshment of lay and scientific usage of these words and the relationships they promise to describe. Awareness of the inextricability of lay and scientific modes of thinking as a central characteristic of the social sciences, and perhaps most self-consciously of sociology, brings to light questions that need addressing: what is the relationship between everyday understandings and sociological takes on friendship? What does that relationship explain and what does it obscure? And why are these questions important in the first place?

Differentiating friendship from friendly relations

Siegfried Kracauer is best known for his work on film and aesthetic and literary theory, for his close friendship with fellow Frankfurt School members Theodor Adorno, Leo Löwenthal, and Walter Benjamin, and is sometimes remembered as the author of a pioneering sociological study of white collar workers, *The Salaried Masses* (1998 [1930]). But Kracauer also wrote two essays on friendship: his 1917 *Über die Freundschaft* and in 1921, *Gedanken über die Freundschaft*. Originally published as separate articles, Suhrkamp released them together in book form in 1971. Despite a glowing review at that time by Johann Siering, who believed that 'nothing of comparable magnitude and elegance had been written on friendship in the German language since the eighteenth century', Kracauer's reflections have been largely ignored – and that not only by sociologists of friendship, but also by Kracauer specialists and biographers (Richter, 1997, pp. 233–234).[3] It turns out that his thought on friendship is a rich seam to mine, although we have to keep in mind the particular historical and cultural context in which he wrote, and the philosophical legacy from which he drew.

'There are words that walk through the centuries by word of mouth, without their conceptual content ever appearing clearly and sharply defined before the inner eye', begins Kracauer in *Über die Freundschaft* and takes us straight to the gap between experience and language:

> The experience of generations, inexhaustible life, numerous events are hidden in them, and one marvels only that these word-vessels, which are made to carry such fullness, always retain their old validity, endure and let themselves be filled with ever new content. Our whole life is pervaded by them, we think with them and take them for unities despite the indeterminate variety [of meaning] that quivers in them. What are these words that grasp the wealth of our inner world other than weak, helpless, meager names for an overflowing substance? Love, loyalty, courage, cowardice, hate, compassion, pride: thousandfold occurrence compresses itself in their shell. (1990, p. 9, my translation)

Including *friendship* among the words that are destined to remain unclear, Kracauer continues: 'It, too, a term to which new experience has time and again attached itself; untamable fullness in the paltry form of a word!' (1990, p. 11, my translation). These comments on the inability of language to articulate and communicate emotions and affect, and so to directly represent our inner worlds, follow in the footsteps of European language philosophy since Fritz Mauthner (1849–1923) and Ludwig Wittgenstein (1889–1951). But that does not imply that the word *friendship* is meaningless. Whatever the difficulties concerning the translation of emotions into cognition, communicable signs, and language, the word holds meaning because we *collectively* attribute meaning to it as a type of relationship.

Kracauer's reflections on friendship and friendly relationships are far-reaching and nuanced. They take into account age and gender, the special bond between mentor and students, distinguish 'ideal' from 'middle' friendship, turn to love, to time, and trouble. But at base, friendship for Kracauer is 'a dispositional and ideal community of *free, independent* persons based on the mutual development of typical possibilities'. And he goes on to state: 'To flourish together without losing oneself in the other, to devote oneself in order to posses oneself in expanded form, to fuse into a unity and yet exist separately for oneself: this is the secret of the bond' (Kracauer, 1990, p. 54, original emphasis, my translation).

That 'ideal', in Kracauer's terms, does not imply 'unreal' or 'statistically insignificant' in the way that the term is sometimes treated in sociology, is plain in his friendship with Adorno, as evident in their four-decade-long correspondence (Adorno & Kracauer, 2008). The troughs and peaks of their relationship show also that 'ideal' in this sense does not mean the same as 'without tension or conflict'. It speaks, rather, to a basic orientation of mutuality grounded in respect and affection. Only on that basis can intimate friends accommodate differences of opinion, attitude, and lifestyle, and withstand and learn from each other's criticisms as well as encouragement and support, a theme we will revisit in Chapter 4.

Read through the lenses of contemporary social science and everyday discourse on friendship, Kracauer's writing raises difficulties of interpretation. His practical attitude to friendship as intimacy lacks today's self-consciousness and so permits effusive declarations of affection. Take, for example, this excerpt from a letter to Adorno in April 1923: 'I felt, in both these days, again such torturing love for you, so that it seems to me as if I could not even exist on my own. This existence appears so flat, so detached from you, I don't know how this shall go on' (Adorno & Kracauer, 2008, p. 9, my translation). At the time, this type of bourgeois masculinity could still rather unproblematically incorporate effusive affection, perhaps because 'the public homosexual' was yet to fully emerge, and so homophobia had yet to attain its full force in the work of the normalization of heterosexuality (Zaretsky, 2004, p. 42).

But the patina of another time and place coats Kracauer's writing also because he shows masterfully that only informed reflection, interpretation, and poetic nuance, rather than outcome oriented enumeration, measurement, and description, are the stuff of meaningful insight into personal relationships, into the intimate to and fro that makes them. Importantly, there is a methodological lesson in Kracauer's approach that goes beyond the situatedness of his essay in its time and context. He shows that friendship needs to be interpreted against the backdrop of other types of personal relationship so that its generalizable specificities – specificities that are meaningful, recognizable, and legible by us as participants in the culture – emerge with some clarity. His is not a work of definition but of circumscription; it does not simply draw lines in the sand between types of relationships but invites us to reflect on the degree of negotiability of boundaries in everyday life. That does not mean that how people 'do' friendship is therefore unimportant. Quite to the contrary: friendship practices or processes are central to the relationship's meaning; after all they are the stuff of friendship. But I would argue that those kinds of practices that articulate with, challenge, extend or transgress the limits of culturally constituted boundaries are of particular sociological significance. Kracauer's is an important impulse in that direction when he differentiates friendship from other personal relationships. Most likely influenced by his one-time mentor Georg Simmel, Kracauer goes on to delimit the boundaries of friendship against the boundaries of acquaintanceship, comradeship, and collegial relationships – boundaries that are drawn by typical patterns of interaction that find orientation in the shared, though changeable, cultural understandings of each type.

Comradeship

For Kracauer, *comradeship* is a 'goal connection' (*Zielverbindung*) because the personal ties forged under its banner are wholly enabled and determined by objectives external to the relationship. We could think here about the defeat of the enemy among soldiers, the attainment of political power and victory of a 'cause' among party affiliates or social activists, or the restoration of 'normalcy' in relief operations during natural disasters, etc. That is not to say that affective connections are impossible in these relationships; they clearly are and in fact are central to the public esteem accorded to comradeship, as commemorative celebrations of wartime 'mateship', *esprit de corps*, and sacrifice attest. However, the kind of affection at issue for Kracauer – what we understand by 'camaraderie' – is a secondary outcome rather than the premise on which the relationship is based. Comradeship, rather than an end in itself, is for Kracauer primarily a means to a given end: a purposive, instrumental relationship so pointedly expressed by the German *Zweckgemeinschaft*. Without its general societal or communal purpose the relationship type would not exist: 'Comrades are equals before the goal, but nothing besides it' (1990, p. 14, my translation). Time plays an important role here. The mutual orientation to a specific goal over time effects an equalization of personalities; it does not lead to an increasing closeness of unique individualities. And so if cooperativeness, indefatigability, the will to sacrifice, courage, and endurance in the overcoming of obstacles strengthen the relationship and facilitate the achievement of the common objective, mutual 'involvement of the whole personality' would in fact lead to an 'overburdening' of the relationship (1990, p. 15).

Collegial relationships

The degree to which nonintimate external logics impinge on or characterize the relationship is clearly central to Kracauer's differentiating approach. *Collegial relationships* are no exception. Here too the common focus on objective tasks is the prime context of and motivation for the ties. But colleagues are not comrades. If comradeship distinguishes itself by subordination to general goals that effectively render individuals interchangeable, collegial relationships – at least in those professions that call for specialist knowledge and skills – are entered into by people who are aware of their individual professional capacities and a high degree of interdependence. The collective focus on problem solving may give rise to relations that 'can easily transform into friendships'. But they can only become friendships on the basis of 'deep human sympathy' (Kracauer, 1990, p. 16, my translation). As long as professional concerns remain the sole points of reference friendship is impossible. There is, then, a separating line between the private and intimate that runs through collegial relationships:

> Where the world of my dreams, my memories, my yearning, my love begins, there also ends the relationship between me and my colleague. A subtle feeling holds close watch so that no mixing of both realms eventuates. Every transgression of the separating line will, consciously or unconsciously, be repudiated. (1990, pp. 18–19)

Kracauer hastens to reiterate that this does not exclude the potential emergence of friendship, but only under the conditions stated above. Thus, the relationship is either a friendship *or* a collegial relationship, but can never be both, although this does not preclude development in one or the other direction (see also, Carrier, 1999).

Acquaintanceships

Acquaintanceship is next on list of personal relationships that are similar to but decisively different from friendship. The relationship type merits a more detailed treatment, because it is relatively frequently discussed by sociologists. For Kracauer, acquaintanceship is very different from comradeship and collegial bonds, which 'somehow always presuppose the involuntary being together of those who act the same' (1990, p. 19, my translation). Acquaintanceship does not originate in common goals or occupational tasks. Like all personal relationships it too fulfills 'the need to communicate one's self', to 'entrust to another human being a piece of their multifarious soul'. What marks acquaintanceship, however, is the lack of a 'continuous thread' that stretches from soul to soul even if otherwise the relationship has 'developed in a high degree'. This implies, for Kracauer, that once the unspoken 'decision' has been made that the relationship shall develop no further, 'an invisible dividing wall' is erected between acquaintances. As in the other types of relationships, 'a feeling of shame, which is finer than the finest scales, here too makes noticeable the least transgression' (1990, p. 20).

In other words, the relationship turns on *discretion*. Where intimacy lacks, public convention takes its place. Because in these relationships we are not able to feel at home the way we do in friendship, can't 'let our hair down', public conventions guide interaction and so reduce the risk of awkwardness. Also, unlike in friendship, acquaintanceship centers on moments of togetherness, 'its essence is the present' and therefore does not lead to the 'mutual development' of selves: 'However close the acquaintance might be situated: as long as he is only an acquaintance, he does not participate in the construction of our self, does not give continuous nourishment to the imagination, and his image does not live in us as invisible companion on our paths' (Kracauer, 1990, pp. 21, 22, my translation).

Again, Kracauer's differentiation is about the structural root of the designation, about the meaning and so the cultural legibility of the relationship's 'form' whose boundaries are policed in interaction, and whose limits are set because interactants calibrate affective content according to unspoken but shared understandings. Rather than that boundary-setting being aided by external aims, acquaintanceships turn on various social similarities that are without purposive charge – common interests, similar experiences, views, social status, and so on. Once these commonalities are established the relationship is set, solidifies, becomes rigid. As a consequence, '[a]ll further interaction oscillates around the established center of gravity'. It is possible that people who otherwise could establish a friendship remain acquaintances because their relationship crystalizes around commonalities they cannot get beyond. The potential intimates, 'in truth live past one another in an ossified relationship' and remain 'more deeply separated by the falsework of their acquaintanceship than by the most terrible dispute' (Kracauer, 1990, p. 23, my translation). Doubtless, Simmel's legacy comes through in Kracauer's approach.

In 1906 the *American Journal of Sociology* published Simmel's 'The Sociology of Secrecy and of Secret Societies'. The article contains what was to become one of the definitive statements on friendship in sociology, one to which I will return again later. For now, I want to pay attention to Simmel's take on acquaintanceship as a distinguishing 'limit case' to friendship. Like for Kracauer, what constitutes an acquaintanceship as a specific mode of personal interaction is, according to Simmel, a tacit understanding that only some information about oneself is to be offered, and only some information about the other is required for the relationship to work. In fact, '[t]hat persons are "acquainted" with each other signifies in this sense by no means that they know each other reciprocally; that is, that they have insight into that which is peculiarly personal in the individuality'. There is, then, in these relationships a good measure of impersonality and instrumentality, which are anathema to friendship but designatory in acquaintanceships. Simmel gets to the point: 'Knowledge of the *that*, not of the *what*, of the personality distinguishes the "acquaintanceship"'. And drawing the affective boundaries ever more thickly, he stresses that '[i]n the very assertion that one is acquainted with a given person ... one indicates very distinctly the absence of really intimate relationships' (Simmel, 1906, p. 452, my translation).

Simmel draws our attention to the need for discretion in the negotiation of the relationship, something that as we have seen is echoed by Kracauer. Indeed, acquaintanceship 'is the peculiar seat of 'discretion', the central marker of the relationship (Simmel, 1906, p. 452). It is in interaction rather than by articulated norms that the limits between this type of relationship and others are drawn, and that presupposes a tacit understanding about the typical repertoire of behaviors, the typical range of appropriate disclosures and topics of discussion. Whatever is normative is unarticulated but more or less shared. Appropriate behaviors, attitudes, and practices are shored up and reproduced, as well as challenged by *indiscretion* in everyday interaction. Again, in the absence of intimacy the need for a mutual balance of discretion – of what to disclose and what to keep to yourself – is acute; it protects from awkwardness, *faux pas*, shame, and embarrassment. The face-to-face interactions of acquaintances, and the rules that apply to them, are topics to which Erving Goffman had some insights to contribute.

In *Behavior in Public Places* (1963a) Erving Goffman dedicated a chapter to acquaintanceship. He did so not to distinguish types of social relationships like Kracauer, and Simmel, but to explain performative specificities that are elaborated in face-to-face interactions between acquaintances. As always, Goffman is a master of 'thick description' of what at first glance may appear to be trivial interactions. Beginning with a pithy statement on the 'preconditions' of acquaintanceship, Goffman moves from the general to the personal plane, and as so often makes us feel what he explains, offers us visceral insights of what Simmel may have meant by the need to calibrate discretion according to relationship type. The 'preconditions are satisfied', according to Goffman, 'when each of two individuals can personally identify the other by knowledge that distinguishes this other from everyone else, and when each acknowledges to the other that this state of mutual information exists' (1963a, p. 112). Goffman, years before social recognition became a distinct research program in social philosophy, goes on to explain the centrality of mutual recognition to sociality, specifically concerning one-on-one relations in the 'interaction order'.

By distinguishing between, and then explaining the interdependence of, cognitive and social recognition, Goffman is able to show the emotional weight of uncertainty concerning how to behave in encounters with acquaintances. *Cognitive recognition* refers to the process whereby individuals 'place' one another and recognize one another in relation to previous situations or future plans, or by our ability to recognize others as belonging to a social category. Think about 'line ups' in criminal investigations, meeting and then recognizing a blind date by virtue of personal information about them, or (as in another one of Goffman's examples) about pickpockets noticing plainclothes police. 'Cognitive recognition, then, is the process through which we socially or personally identify the other' (Goffman, 1963a, p. 113). *Social recognition*, on the other hand, refers to a process of mutual acknowledgement that on the micro level could be something like the acceptance of a greeting, the return of a smile, or 'the according of a special role within an engagement, as when a chairman acknowledges and fulfills an individual's desire to be given the floor' (Goffman, 1963, p. 113). There is no social recognition without cognitive recognition, and often these processes occur at the same time. The ethical basis for social recognition in acquaintanceships is obligation. More precisely, it is 'the obligation ... to be readily accessible', which according to Goffman can be read off in various types of strategies, that minimize the probability of a 'cut', of slighting the other (1963, pp. 114–16).

The embodied sense of discomfort of situations in which a mutual freezing out threatens brings home the delicate balance that needs to be struck in practice in order to ensure maintenance of the relationship. Goffman illustrates this by way of example from Marcel Aymé's novel *The Secret Stream*, and it is worth recounting. Rigault glimpses Maître Marguet some way off, walking towards him and on the opposite side of the street. Rigault had always felt some unease about encountering the lawyer Marguet, because the latter would only sometimes return Rigault's greetings, who, in turn, has no way of telling whether this might be 'accidental' or 'capricious'. That sense of uncertainty caused Rigault to spend considerable energy reflecting on the right course of action as the encounter unfolded:

> Deciding that the raising of his hat would probably go unnoticed, Rigault resolved to begin this gesture only at the last moment, which left him the possibility of completing it or abolishing it by pretending to scratch his ear. But then a reasonless, almost religious apprehension caused him to hurry his movements. They were still four paces removed from the orthodox, level position when his hand went to his head. Maître Marguet, on the opposite pavement, looked up and replied with an ample gesture; and Rigault, instantly relaxed, felt a wave of well-being pass through him. It was more than gratified vanity; it was the sweetness of a response, the fulfillment of a social instinct. (cited in Goffman, 1963a, p. 119)[4]

Taking intimacy – however imprecise its definitions – as a sensitizing concept to what is going on in Goffman's example can tell us something more about the difference between friendship and acquaintanceship. Friendship's intimacy allows us to be open to and tolerant of a much greater range of transgressions. Conversely, the lack of intimacy in acquaintanceship translates into a mutual second-guessing of the definition of the situation. Because here mutual recognition turns on inference or imputation rather than fairly firm knowledge of mutual attitudes, public convention plays a much stronger role in acquaintanceship than in friendship. In fact, as we will see later, friendship offers us opportunities to subvert public convention whose place is taken by trusting intimacy. The absence of intimacy in acquaintanceship makes the relationship inherently unstable because social norms are context-dependent, and to be effective rely on very similar interpretations of the situation. Rigault's anxiety originates in uncertainty over the degree of mutuality of such interpretation. And so, while 'acquaintanceship is an aspect of all social relationships' (Goffman, 1963, p. 114), as a relationship of its own it easily devolves into estrangement or at least becomes potentially highly awkward, since, once having 'recognized' one another, acquaintances can never again be perfect strangers.

Simmel thought of acquaintanceships as peculiarly bourgeois, as belonging chiefly to 'the higher cultural strata' (1906, p. 452). But even to this day 'acquaintances' (*Bekannte*) is still more readily used in German than in Anglo-American environments, where usage of the word faded quickly during the 20th century and came to be replaced by 'friends'. In his network studies, charting the diffusion of information, Stanley Milgram could still take for granted that people would differentiate unproblematically between 'friends' and 'acquaintances'. For example, in one of his 'small world' studies, whose findings entered the popular imagination as the 'six degrees of separation' phenomenon, Milgram and his colleague Charles Korte asked a set of 'white' participants to send booklets to their 'Negro' 'acquaintances', and another set to their 'friends' in a study that, by the way, helped Mark Granovetter to significantly substantiate his thesis that counter to prevailing wisdom 'weak ties' are more conducive to the transmission of information than 'strong ties'; that ''weak ties, often denounced as generative of alienation, can be indispensable to individuals' opportunities and to their integration into communities, while strong ties breed local cohesion and lead to overall fragmentation' (Granovetter, 1973, p. 1378). Central to this thesis, which since its proposal has been substantiated many times over, is subjects' clarity concerning the relational differences between friends and acquaintances. As Granovetter tells it, 'Often when I asked respondents whether a friend had told them about their current job, they said, "Not a friend, an acquaintance"' (1973, pp. 1372ff.). It is interesting, therefore, that around the same time sociologist Suzanne Kurth noted the increasing usage of 'friend' for what she calls 'friendly relations', and so by 1970 could confidently state, '[s]ociety lacks terminological distinction. We call "friends" people with whom we do little more than exchange "good mornings", members of our high school or college sets, some of our colleagues, and various and sundry others', while, at the same time, to call someone 'a mere acquaintance would generally be considered impolite' (1970, p. 169).

By the early 1980s, Claude Fischer (1982, p. 19), could, on the basis of research, argue that 'friend' is 'to some extent a residual label' applied unsystematically to most nonkin relations with whom people socialize, to people of similar age, and to those they have known for a long time. Fischer's study suggests that when we ask Americans to tell us about their friends, they tend to tell us about almost all of their associates, though they tended, at that time, to exclude neighbors and colleagues. The term '"friend" clearly does not, for example, distinguish an "intimate confidant and counselor" for most Americans', and hence Fischer was emphatic 'that researchers should be wary about using this vague term' and called for distinction (Fischer, 1982, pp. 305–306). Kurth too discerned an increasing conflation of what she considered the strong affective ties of friendship and friendly relations in the social sciences, and according to her that was partly because friendly relations could lead to friendship, are sometimes part and parcel of their development, and because intimate friendships are relatively rare. Despite the difficulties, and admitting that the prevalence of a relationship type (however measured) ought not to determine whether or not we take it seriously in research, Kurth concurred with Fischer and strongly suggested a differentiated approach: 'If we are to find out more about various categories of relationships ... we must distinguish similar but distinctive types' (Kurth, 1970 p, 169).

More recently, David Morgan (2009) has taken to an analysis of acquaintanceship in the contemporary context. Situated somewhere between strangers and intimates, Morgan thinks Simmel's definition of acquaintanceships too narrow because, as we have seen, Simmel does not admit intimacy to enter the relationship. According to Morgan, intimacy is present in interactions between ostensible nonintimates – neighbors, doctors, and patients – and thus cannot be simply used as a delimiting factor in relationship types. Reality is far too complex. At the same time, taking my lead from Simmel, Kracauer, Goffman, and others, I would argue that if we perceive the neighbor's 'Good morning, how are the kids?', or the doctor's touch – conventions of civility, fulfillments of professional tasks – as acts of intimacy, then intimacy is in fact everywhere, and the concept is close to useless. That is, the concept of intimacy needs to retain content for it to be used as a distinguishing characteristic between friendship and friendly relations such as acquaintanceships. Morgan is right in not writing off these individual attributions of intimacy; they are, however, individual business only. And so to make these perceptions part of a categorical description of a relationship type is problematic because it lacks evaluative purchase. It lacks evaluative purchase especially from a perspective that conceives of intimacy as a trust relationship based on affection, care, and respect. The type of intimacy we meet in Morgan's book neither has to be based on trust (I can visit a doctor who 'will do' for the time being because the one I really trust isn't available), nor does it have to be based on respect (I inquire about my neighbor's health as a matter of common courtesy). Dissimulation will do just fine. Put differently, intimacy is only then useful as a concept in research if it retains its normative force.

Semantic conflation and contemporary complexities

There are others who have approached friendship in a nuanced and differentiated way. Friedrich Tenbruck (1989) and Francesco Alberoni (2009) are two exponents of the approach that spring to mind. Yet overall, contemporary sociologists who turn to friendship tend to do precisely what early sociologists like Simmel and Kracauer, and later Kurth and Fischer, have shown to be counterproductive: they conflate the weak ties of friendly relations with the strong ties of friendship. That conflation in turn gives rise to contradictory positions that are rarely made explicit but can be rendered in shorthand: one perceives an increasing ubiquity of friendship (here it functions as a catchall category made to accommodate an assortment of personal relationships); the other diagnoses a thinning out of affective ties and conjures the end of friendship (e.g. Anderson, 2001). Neither side communicates much with the other, although both diminish friendship's analytic purchase. Used interchangeably, the analytic power of *friendship* is diminished to such a degree that it can easily be made not only to take on the semantic loads of 'colleagues', 'acquaintances', and 'neighbors', but, as we shall see, also of 'family'.

Family as friends, friends as family

The central premise of Liz Spencer and Ray Pahl's *Rethinking Friendship* (2006) is to show that despite social theories of long standing that diagnose greater atomization, individualization, and a decline of the social, people's enmeshment in informal social relationships – with friends, family, neighbors, colleagues or associates of all kinds – attests to the fact that 'personal communities' continue to provide the 'social glue' that holds together contemporary societies. These communities include 'friend-like' relationships across the familial and nonfamilial terrains of the social landscape. What is of particular interest in the present context is the authors' usage of the central concept, which they endeavor to rethink. Spencer and Pahl are well aware of the semantic complexities of 'friend' in English:

> Even from everyday observation, it is clear that the word 'friend' encompasses a dizzying array of relationships. For example, those who work at building extensive networks, filling their address books or databases with useful contacts, may refer to these contacts as friends. Primary school children excitedly tell their family they have made a new friend when someone offers them a sweet or invites them to join in a game. World leaders describe each other as friends when they form alliances, even though they have little informal contact outside their roles and spend little time in each other's company. People use the term 'friend' to refer to those with whom they simply have a pleasant association, for example, through neighbourhood, work, joint interests or common activities. People also describe as friends those with whom they have shared a lifelong relationship and to whom they feel closer than a brother or sister. Even our attempts to qualify the term 'friend' lack precision: good friends may be soulmates or simply acquaintances. (2006, p. 58)

Recognition of the semantic expansion of 'friends' is not accompanied by further conceptual clarification. Instead, Spencer and Pahl treat friends and friendship synonymously and so friendship is made to function as an umbrella term denoting various personal relationships. That conflation underpins the conclusion that there is a great 'diversity of friendship', such as 'associates', 'useful contacts', 'favour friends', 'fun friends', and of course also 'soulmates', 'best friends', and 'true friends'. Whatever the variety and great variability in mutual orientation, friendship is the concept that unites them. In these terms friendship is internally differentiated to such a degree that there seems no need to differentiate it from other relationships, such as 'just good neighbours', and workmates with whom the relationship does not extend to respondents' private lives (Spencer & Pahl, 2006, p. 76).

The problem here is that the researchers take their respondents' word for gospel and so do not further interrogate the conceptual overlaps they express, do not investigate the material for latent meanings. As a result we get a curious mix of personal relationships that are on the one hand greatly differentiated in categorical nuance (the diverse friendships listed above are further assigned to 'basic', 'intense', and 'focal' 'friendship repertoires'), while overlaps and contradictions remain unexplored. For instance, while the respondents distinguish acquaintances from friends (read 'friendship'), associates of whom they know next to nothing beyond shared interests in a hobby *do* count as friends. In fact, relationships may even be shot through with disrespect, as is evident in 'the phenomenon of the *heart-sink* friend', described by one subject as those who 'when they phone you think, "Oh no, it's ..."' (Spencer & Pahl, 2006, p. 71). Far from showing solidarity, there is a plethora of relationships subsumed under friendship that may completely lack any notable affective content even remotely close to mutual interest, let alone care or support.

Again, this is a problem of method. The sense emerges here that agency is stressed to such an extent that second-order interpretation – the elucidation of meanings beyond the listing and categorizing of diverse practices – is largely neglected, especially pertaining to the social understanding of friendship. The meaning of friendship is not allowed to emerge from the responses; it is *a priori* chosen to mean 'personal communities' and is attributed to respondents' networks of personal relationships. As a consequence, we learn little about shifts in language use, whether or not the term is now actually used to connote all kinds of personal associations and what that may let us infer about social change in intimate life. What we are confronted with instead is a tautological approach to concept building: friendship is made to cope with the range of informal relationships, and having been pressed into service is then used as evidence of its diversity. The term 'personal communities' would, so it appears, have sufficed very well indeed. On balance, what Spencer and Pahl have done – and done successfully – is to collect and label a variety of stories about people's personal relationships and so have elucidated extant 'hidden solidarities'. What they haven't done is 'rethink' friendship.

Spencer and Pahl also attend to the affective overlaps between friendship and family and propose that just as family relationships can be 'friend-like', so friendships can be 'family-like', which is not to say that actors mistake one category for the other. The blurring of the boundaries between family and friends takes on particular complexity as well as significance in nonheterosexual contexts, where 'family', with its historically loaded heteronormative imprint, has been resignified with the metaphor 'families of choice' (Weeks et al., 2001). That resignification goes beyond the description of affective ties; it is a political move in so far as it seeks to do justice to the lived plurality of nonheterosexual forms of intimacy. But it is also a contested politics. State recognition may be fought for by those who see in it the goal of activism and rejected by others who fear that recognition may erase differences that distinguish nonheterosexual cultures from the mainstream (Düttmann, 2000). The explicit disavowal of the 'family' label is one example here (Rofes, 1997), the queer critique of claims for same-sex marriage another (Conrad, 2010).

Weeks, Heaphy, and Donovan, authors of *Same Sex Intimacies* (2001), paid close attention to how their respondents – 96 self-identified gay, lesbian, and bisexual men and women – described their friendships. Like in earlier research that has described intimate life among nonheterosexual people (e.g. Weston, 1997), here too 'family' emerged as a common denominator (a) because of the word's culturally ensconced connotation of intimacy that 'underlines the poverty of [the English] language in describing alternative forms of intimate life', and (b) because for many respondents their sexuality created tensions and rifts between them and their families of origin. Unlike conservative idealizations of the family as 'an image of mutuality, interdependence and resilience' (Weeks et al., 2001, p. 22), representing 'a haven in a heartless world', 'family' becomes meaningful in these contexts because the respondents' real experiences confirm what in society at large is a promise but by no means a universal truth: they are relationships of care, affection, and support, of 'intimacy' in other words. So, while at first glance the appropriation of the family label may seem to be yet another apotheosis of the family ideal, it is in fact chosen because these self-created relationships actually *realize* potentials of intimacy that are difficult to attain or even unavailable to them in orthodox families.

However, to what extent the appropriation of the family label is or has been successful in decentering the monolithic image of the heterosexual nuclear family in the public imagination – so the hope of Weeks et al. – remains an open question. To be sure, decades of gay activism, local victories in claims for same-sex marriage here and there, greater visibility of same-sex parenting, but also heterosexual family reconfigurations on a massive scale, seem to have broadened the repertoire of what are deemed acceptable, tolerable, or even validated forms of intimacy. But it has done little to change the image of the family as envisaged in the mainstream imagination and as institutionalized in law and policy regimes. Let's reflect on assorted trends: perennial social and political commentary on the need for male role models for children based on the widely held assumption that children need both a mother and father; overwhelming cultural representations of the normative family even if accompanied by representations of 'alternative' forms; handwringing over divorce rates as if 'until death do us part' commitments alone guarantee relationship 'normalcy' and childhood bliss; large-scale aspirations toward conventional coupledom – these are just some of the realities that make explicit that the forces of detraditionalization have not yet captured the normative heart of intimacy the way we are sometimes led to believe or may hope (Gross, 2005).

I would argue they haven't done so because no matter how confidently we might appropriate labels, institutions and organizations are resistant social formations indeed. Of course, collective agency can overturn traditions (just as it may reinstate old ones) and over time this may well happen; but just as an individual appropriation of 'marriage' without formal authorization would be meaningless from the standpoint of the public, appropriations of 'family' to include other-than-heteronormative 'cultures of intimacy and care' (Roseneil & Budgeon, 2004) are up against deeply entrenched heterosexual structural and cultural arrangements. That is – emphatically – *not* to deny advances that have been made, that new forms of intimacy do exist, that the monolithic image of the heteronormative family is problematized by the greater visibility of alternative intimacies. All this clearly pertains. But to speak of 'a battle over meaning' (Weeks et al., 2001, p. 17) concerning 'the family' may not only have been premature a decade ago. We need only take account of diverse experiences of class and cultural background that cut across experiences of and attitudes about gender in our own 'advanced' societies to realize that the challenge to – let alone a subversion of – mainstream norms appears still some way off. For now, the old and new sit side by side and rarely see eye to eye.

None of this devalues the meaning of 'family' in 'families of choice': it functions as a synonym for friendship in the lived experiences of non-heterosexuals in ways that it cannot operate in heterosexual contexts, like, for instance, in Spencer and Pahl's (2006) respondents' descriptions of family-like and friend-like relationships. Families of choice are *intimate friendships* that validate and support whole 'ways of life' in the context of trust and respect – ways of life that gain their political and identificatory purchase as 'families of choice' from the fact that they are both lived in and in opposition to a heteronormative 'gender order'

(Connell, 2009) (see also Chapter 6). It is under these conditions that these relationships flourish and take on their centrality in nonhetero-sexual lives as friendships, and that not simply as the odd, allegedly rare dyad, but as *networks*. It is in this context that Weeks et al. elaborate 'the friendship ethic' as practically underpinning the nonheterosexual social formations at the center of their research. Both the uncertainties and complexities of modern life in general, and the outsider position of nonheterosexuals in particular, give unique meaning and value to friendships; they 'flourish when overarching identities are fragmented in periods of rapid social change, or at turning points in people's lives, or when lives are lived at odds with social norms' (Weeks et al., 2001, p. 51). And raising the issue of what has since been commented on as friendships' 'flexibility' (Allan, 2008), they go on to suggest that they are,

> portable, they can be sustained at a distance, yet they can allow individuals who are uprooted or marginalised to feel constantly confirmed in who and what they are through changing social expe-riences. They offer the possibility of developing new patterns of intimacy and commitment. All theses features give a special mean-ing and intensity to friendship in the lives of those who live on the fringes of sexual conformity. (2001, p. 51)

Same Sex Intimacies shows very cogently that the depth of friendship ties and their prevalence and function depend on the context in which they are lived. In the case of nonheterosexual lives lived in both mainstream society and culture and nonmainstream friendship communities, peo-ple inflect words such as 'family' and 'friendship', work their semantics, and so politicize them, whether consciously or not. And so Eisenstadt and Roniger (1984, p. 17) were surely right to point out that in modern societies, 'the crux of the paradoxical and ambivalent relations between friendship and kinship lies in their sharing many characteristics while, symbolically and organizationally, friendship appears distinct from kin-ship and even potentially opposed to it'.

For some time now, and not unlike 'culture', friendship has been running the risk of being turned into a 'sandtrap or sinkhole' concept (Gans, 2012, p. 2), ready to be filled with whatever meaning suits a given piece of research. Perhaps it is a fear of 'determinism' that fol-lowed the heyday of Marxist sociology and of functionalism, or an antipathy to 'structure' since the heyday of post-structuralism, that has opened a side door to the kind of 'methodological individualism'

(Lukes, 1968) that attributes ultimate truth to what people say and then stops short of questions concerning societal meaning. Whatever the reasons, an emphasis on how people 'do' intimacy, 'do' friendship, love, and family and what they say about it has on the one hand given rise to a premature triumphalism concerning the subversion of taken-for-granted marginalizing categories and, concerning friendship, has periodically caused consternation in the social sciences. For instance, Peter Willmott, in his pioneering British study of informal support networks, asks: 'How can the relevance of friends ... be sensibly examined if there is no agreement about who they are?' (1987, p. 2). Others alert us that '[i]n order to have an adequate theory of friendship, we must have a definition of friendship' (Derlega and Winstead in Wierzbicka, 1997, p. 33). In response to the issue Allan's assertion that 'the notion of friendship needs to be extended so as to include workmates, acquaintances and others who may not always be specified as friends' (1989, p. 10), has, it seems, become programmatic for much of the sociology of friendship. Taking an undifferentiated approach and so conflating weak and strong personal ties is to conflate affectionate relationships with those that are more instrumentally orientated, or with relationships, such as acquaintanceships, in which affection is optional because they are *'not* strictly mutual' (Martin, 2011, p. 41, original emphasis). As a consequence, these words are in danger of being emptied of meaning to such an extent that research on the varieties of social interactions they are supposed to signify teeters on the edge of meaninglessness in relation to everyday experience.

Conclusion

Distinguishing friendship from friendly relations is essentially an 'unblocking' exercise; it aims at differentiating in order to reflect upon common sense understandings and so to reconnect theory and everyday experience – not in order to reduce real complexities, but to do justice to them in a sociologically workable way. That endeavor does require a normative stance of sorts – not one that prescribes how friendships ought to be 'done', but one that is anchored in the social-historical development of intimacy in Western modernity as a relational dynamic enabling the realization of self-chosen lives. According to this perspective, trust, respect, and justice are friendship's necessary conditions; care, support, and affection the ingredients that give it substance. That perspective fundamentally limits friendship to noninstrumental relationships. Here immediate objections could be raised.

We could reasonably argue, for instance, that all relationships, even the closest among them, are underpinned by some kind of instrumentality, because we enter into them for a variety of reasons, to fulfill a range of needs. Take erotic love as an example. It may fulfill the need to be cared for, the need for company, the need for sex, the need for financial security, and the need to 'settle down' in societies where stable love relationships are still part and parcel of the cultural repertoire that makes mature adulthood societally 'legible' (Blatterer, 2009). Likewise, 'friendships' may be entered into for a range of motivations, such as to hang out and have fun, to share common interests, or to further career prospects. Against such qualifications, I suggest that first of all it is part of our humanity to act according to a range of motivations; that altruism can result from self-interest, for instance, without making the action itself necessarily less valuable (Misztal, 1996, p. 182). But if the fulfillment of such needs is my main purpose for initiating the relationship; if therefore the relationship is driven by a narcissistic self-concern that mutuality cannot limit; and if hence the other is no more than a means through which I pursue such purposes, we cannot speak about 'intimacy' in the way it is intended here. That is not to say, however, that therefore friendship is – or ought to be – devoid of any kind of instrumentalism. In real life, it is about the kind, level, and appropriateness of instrumental actions: 'Friends', says Graham Allan, 'can quite legitimately make use of one another in instrumental ways without threatening the relationship, provided that it is clear that they are being used because they are friends and not friends because they are useful' (cited in Misztal, 1996, p. 182). It is that clarity of mutual understanding that intimacy provides.

This preliminary outline of the ethical underpinnings of intimacy will be further elaborated or referred back to in succeeding chapters. But for now it should suffice to give substance to the concept of friendship as thought about here. To reiterate, it is intended as a sensitizing conception of friendship that is open enough to be 'filled' with self-created ways of interacting – with a multiplicity of ways of doing friendship – but sufficiently limited to distinguish friendly relations from the intimate bonds of friendship, but to also heed Carol Smart's call 'that the notions of kinship and friendship should not be collapsed into a formless sludge' (2007, p. 33). The openness of the concept *friendship* finds its limits, then, when intimacy as mutual orientation is absent.

As we saw in the previous chapter, intimacy in these terms – wedded to trust, respect, justice, care, and affection – gains cultural value and practical efficacy in a long historical development and receives its significance with the increasing centrality of individual authenticity, with modern conceptions of freedom to which intimacy became increasingly important. The way that freedom is played out in practical relationships has, as others have suggested, to do with the way and the degree to which they are institutionalized. That is the central argument of the following chapter, which traces the institutional trajectory of friendship in distinction to love in Western modernity, and in so doing elaborates the freedom friends can call their own.

3
Love, Friendship, and Freedom

At least since Emile Durkheim published *The Rules of Sociological Method* (1966) [1895], institutions have been a core focus of the discipline. There is a difference between lay and sociological understandings of institutions. In everyday discourse, they are considered like organizations such as educational institutions, state institutions, asylums, and so on. When we speak about someone being 'institutionalized', we mean that they have become subject to institutional duties of care. Another meaning is the one we attach to the institution of marriage, for example, and it comes closer, and in fact builds an important part of, the sociological conception; it refers to the legal formalization of an intimate relationship that is conferred public recognition by way of religious or civic ritual, and the legal attribution of shared rights and obligations. But sociological perspectives on institutions go further; they incorporate, but also elaborate, everyday discourse.

Like most concepts in the social sciences, the sociological meaning of 'institutions' is contested. This is not the place to go into the nuances of the debate. My conceptualization of institutions builds upon some fairly uncontroversial perspectives. The aim is to use an approach that is workable in the analysis of the peculiar position of friendship in contemporary societies. That position, I suggest, is the condition for the *relational freedom* that friends have to create the relationship according to their own vision; it's the room to move, if you will, without which friendship could not be the 'freest' of all interpersonal relationships. I then sketch a brief, schematic history of the development of love and friendship in Western modernity in order to provide a contrastive frame of reference for my argument that friendship's institutional deficit is the condition for its relational freedom. Some anthropological literature on institutionalized friendship highlights the exceptional status of friendship as a private and personal relationship. Finally, I illustrate the freedom of friendship by interpreting its position *vis-à-vis* contemporary therapy culture.

Love, friendship, and the problem of institution

In his far-ranging analysis of institutions, Hartmut Esser (2000) proposes a working definition. They are 'certain *socially* defined *rules* with societal *validity* that are anchored in actors' *expectations* and from which an "unconditional" binding character of action is deduced' (Esser, 2000, p. 6, original emphases, my translation). For Esser, institutions are bundles of norms that are considered legitimate in a given society or milieu. These norms are legitimate because they are socially meaningful; they orient people's expectations and aspirations in ways that make sense in the context of modern life and so open up a horizon of possibilities in which they can act. But they also restrain actions that go against a prevailing and often unspoken normative 'consensus', against 'the way things ought to be'. We can thus, with Swidler, think of institutions as a kind of 'cultural structuring ... that might be thought of as operating from the outside in, organizing dispersed cultural materials' that are reworked by individuals. '[A]s persons orient themselves to institutional demands and institutional dilemmas, they continually reproduce structured cultural understandings, even when those structured pieces do not add up to an internally coherent whole' (Swidler, 2001, p. 159). These conceptions are value-free, disinterested in whether a given set of norms impacts positively or negatively on individuals, different social groups, or whole societies, whether or not they are 'ethical'; it applies, therefore, to relations of both relatively equal as well as unequal power. What matters is their legitimacy. The more one-sided the distribution of power, the more the holders of power have to marshal ideological effort at sustaining the legitimacy of their position.[1]

If we conceive of institutions basically and minimally as bundles of norms that enable and constrain (rather than simply determine) and so orient our ways of thinking and acting, we also need to distinguish between different kinds. *Formal* norms are those norms that are formalized in law and spell out mutual rights and obligations. *Informal* norms are regulative ideas concerning social action that are part and parcel of a given culture's repertoire of commonsense knowledge. Rituals can underpin the formal or informal constitution of norms.

In marriage, for example, formalization and ritualization go hand in hand.

In *Folkways* (1906), the early American sociologist William Graham Sumner (1840–1910) referred to informal norms as 'mores'. Drawing on German phenomenology, he argued that mores are taken for granted and only become recognizable when we become conscious of them: 'Conscious reflection is the worst enemy of the mores ... because their expedience often depends on the assumption that they will have general acceptance and currency, uninterfered with by reflection' (Hartman cited in Sumner, 1906, p. 66). What brings these norms into consciousness, makes them subject to reflection and so articulable, is their transgression. Norms do their work of orienting and guiding interactions because their transgression, in one way or another, results in negative sanctions – from no more than wagging fingers, snubs, and raised eyebrows, to verbal and physical abuse where transgressions of informal norms are concerned, to various legal sanctions from fines to incarceration when laws are broken.

Interested in informal norms, ethnomethodologists, such as the pioneer of the approach, Harold Garfinkel, were concerned to show how social order is established in small scale or micro interactions. They used 'breaching experiments' to make visible the invisible and unarticulated norms of common sense that guide everyday, routine interactions and make them meaningful to us in the first place (Garfinkel, 1967). Getting students to act like lodgers in their own homes, for example, not only served to show up that interactions that seem natural are in fact a result of adherence to norms that change with context and are constantly negotiated, but also that any type of action that breaches situational expectations is immediately classified as 'deviant' and is subjected to moral judgment and sanction.

Now, when Simmel reminds us that 'in all that we do, we have a norm, a standard, an ideally preconceived totality before us, which we try to transpose into reality through our actions' (1978, p. 458), we might judge his view too determinative. But he also alerts us to the fact of 'superindividual' *ideational* constituents of social actions. Institutional norms are not just 'instituted' by formal-legal means; its matrix is drawn in prevailing ideas and beliefs, in what Emile Durkheim (1966 [1895]) called 'social representations' that are constantly distributed, circulated, reiterated, and challenged in popular culture. For instance, ideas about love and romance, about marriage, about 'the family' (including non-traditional forms) are given form not only in tangibles such as legal norms, but also as ideas in novels, songs, TV sitcoms, movies, newspaper columns, magazine articles, blogs, online discussion forums, dating websites, and so forth; and they are also rallying points for various secular and religious interests.

Bundles of norms that constitute institutions are open to social change: 'an ideal, an ethical standard which has become established is a mortal creation', notes Shils (1981, p. 25). Institutions may be directly challenged by those who advance claims for the recognition of their particular ways of life, or because social changes in related domains have helped reconfigure people's attitudes and practices. For instance, the challenge to the gendered order of the male-bread-winner/female homemaker 'nuclear' family model from the 1970s was the result of dedicated women advancing claims for recognition; that challenge would have been unthinkable without them. But it was also advanced by the introduction of birth control allowing women a say over their reproductive futures, and by the transition from industrial to the postindustrial labor markets, from manufacturing to service industries. All of these changes are linked, of course, and the connections show that institutional change never has simply one cause. Neither are all institutions equally open to change. Some are slower in changing than others, and they may congeal rather than change through generational transmission before yielding to contestation (Luckmann and Berger, 1966). We should keep in mind, for instance, that while the nuclear family today appears like a hangover from the mid-20th century, gendered inequalities in domestic labor persist despite structural changes in family composition (Gerson, 2010).

Not all intimate relationships are institutionalized in the sense discussed; and this has consequences for the typical ways they are enabled and constrained, and for the efficacy of enabling and constraining norms. That efficacy, I argue, depends on institutions' makeup, what I call their *normative infrastructure*, and their availability for societal integration, what I call their *institutional connectivity*. Put differently and broadly, the degree and depth to which norms are socially and culturally shored up, and the degree to which they are connectable to 'external' institutional complexes and other domains of life, correlates with the degree to which they are able to elicit or compel, enable, and constrain personal attitudes, practices, and behaviors. The institutional trajectories of love and friendship – how intimacy has been differentially institutionalized over time – illustrate that thesis. Before analyzing the institutional infrastructure and connectivity of love and friendship, I turn to some historical reflections.

Love and friendship: selective history of a relationship

As discussed in Chapter 1, processes of social differentiation entail (among other things) the development of privacy and personal relationships in the modern sense. Along with other changes, such as the spatial reorganization of living arrangements, literacy, and changing relationships to the body (including changing regimes of hygiene), impersonal and highly mediated relationships increasingly come to characterize modern forms of interactions (Calhoun, 1992). These are also the prerequisites for the development of intimate life as we know it. In *Love as Passion* (1998a), Luhmann traces the morphology of the semantics of intimacy in French, English, and German literature from the Middle Ages to the Romantic era. In his conception and language, impersonal and personal types of communication become differentiated; they develop into distinct communication systems with their own semantics, their own 'codes'. Here Luhmann draws on the Weberian tradition but also nods in Simmel's direction. Just as the economy, science, and art develop around profit and money, truth and method, and aesthetic conceptions, so the emergence of modern subjectivity emphasizes the cultivation and portrayal of one's individuality. Over the centuries, love and friendship develop as different codes for the communication of authentic individuality. In that process, they are institutionalized in different ways and to different degrees.

In premodern Europe, sexuality was integrated into the religious world-picture as necessary for the reproduction of God's worldly order. Marriage was the religiously sanctioned institution in and through which sexual reproduction ensured the reproduction, transfer, and widening of economic and political power. The politics of the Habsburg Empire are a case in point. The guiding motto, *Bella gerant alii, tu felix Austria nube!* (May others fight wars, you, lucky Austria, marry!) speaks to the utility of marriage, which for much of European history not only held true for the forging of imperial alliances. Erotic passion was not supposed to sully marriage. Desire of any form was to be reserved for God, all else being a 'sinful deflection of religious love' (Singer, 1984, p. 25). Evidence of the non-European origins of much of what we may consider indigenous to European culture shows that secular love entered our imaginary around the 12th century from the Middle East via *provençal* troubadours, and from there slowly began to gain general purchase. By the Middle Ages it became something to be pursued, albeit in highly sublimated form: love – sexual or otherwise – acquired a certain idealized nobility and dignity (Singer, 1984; Zeldin, 1994; Luhmann, 1998a; Paz, 2011).

According to Luhmann, a decisive shift occurred when, from about the 1650s, aristocratic women increasingly attained agency in the courting process, and so shed the idealized aura of the previous centuries. Not that they stood any better chances of being valued for their own sakes, as persons in the modern sense. Rather, they were expected to become experts at playing the highly conventionalized roles of temptress, *coquette*, or unattainable love object, to become complicit in the game of seduction. But we do see here the beginnings of love as a *relationship*, even if only in so far as love becomes premised on a constant second-guessing of the degree to which the other is subject to it. Gradually, love begins to crystallize as a third entity between lover and beloved (Luhmann, 1998a, pp. 41–75).

That process, however, is only encoded in the semantics of love with the emergence of what Luhmann calls 'passionate love' in the 17th and 18th centuries, a process that is both symptomatic of and contingent on the emerging belief that existence is about living one's very own, self-fashioned life, true to oneself and uninfluenced by others in order not to 'miss what being human is for *me*' (Taylor, 1992, p. 29, original emphasis). Passion, once seen only in terms of passive suffering, now becomes an imperative, 'a sort of social institution and ... an expected precondition of the formation of social systems', that is, of the kind of social relationships carried out in the name of love (Luhmann, 1998a, p. 60). Love is now invested with, and can eventually be no longer imagined without, the paradoxes of feeling that mark it: falling in love is to be passive, to be subject to overwhelming desires, but fall in love we *must*; it is an imperative miracle, to be experienced simultaneously by lover and the beloved, who is conquered but then submits unconditionally. Whether it is conquest and self-renunciation, blindness and extraordinary vision, illness and healing, or desire and suffering, love promises to reconcile the irreconcilable, to be the one and best vehicle to communicate the incommunicable. Love as a semantic code raises the probability of mutual understanding (1998a, pp. 48–75).

But this passionate, erotic love was not integrated into marriage for some time yet. Absent much knowledge about the personal lives of the lower orders, it appears as the sole province of the aristocratic elites. Its place was outside marriage, which was still a predominantly economic and political institution. Erotic love was an *illicit* love that left the sanctity of that institution untarnished. Seneca's injunction, invoked by St Jerome, 'Men should appear before their wives not as lovers but as husbands', still held sway (Ariès & Béjin, 1985, p. 134). Passionate love still proved too dangerous for the social order to meet the criteria for full social integration. But as individual self-consciousness emerges, as autonomy begins to vie for pre-eminence in the priorities of life, sexuality becomes thought of in other than religious, moral, and political terms: 'The barriers erected to the consummation of sexual relations not only for, but precisely in, marriage were dismantled and replaced by a revaluation of the concept of (physical) nature' (Luhmann, 1998a, p. 113).

That process underwent a two-centuries-long rationalization in the semantics of love, which evolved differently in different cultural contexts. The problem concerning the integration of sexuality and marriage particular to the English context was that for women chastity was a prerequisite for marriage, not least because this enabled proof of paternity and so patrilineal succession. French conceptions of marriage were more or less prepared for that integration, because Eros and love were only ever imperfectly separated in the first place. There, sensibilities were primed to take sexuality into the conjugal bond once emerging subjectivity challenged traditional injunctions. Generally, the exclusion of unpredictable sexual attraction also served social control; it prevented a social mobility driven by status-transcending intimacy that would have threatened the social order – a threat that Austen, some time later, articulates in *Pride and Prejudice*.

But some time earlier, love and friendship competed for supremacy 'as the formulae for the codification of intimacy' (Luhmann, 1998a, p. 116). As far as cross-sex friendship was possible, the ideals of friendship offered themselves as more adequate to the new demands for intimacy because it was unburdened by the emotional pressures of passionate love's paradoxes. Its non-sexual description rendered it non-threatening to social convention, and so friendship became *the* legitimate social relationship in which individualities could flourish without threatening subversion. The utility of friendship, in other words, lay in the fact 'that, in contrast to the semantics of love, it does not claim a radical turning away from society' (Schmidt, 2000, p. 82, my translation). Friendship delivered subjectivity to personal relationships and so is crucial to the development of modern intimacy. But around the same time sexuality is revalued as *sensuality*, is integrated into the range of communicative modes of individuality and individual self-consciousness.[2] Self-expression and sexual life become inseparable. But because friendship figured as the *legitimate* social form for the communication of a type of individuality to which sexuality now becomes increasingly important, it is friendship that delivers an erstwhile illegitimate sexuality into the center of intimacy. Friendship, in other words, enables intimacy between men and women; over time sexual practice becomes normative as the heart of love and gradually evolves as the prime signifier of intimacy. I return to some of the contemporary consequences in Chapter 5. For now we should note that at least in Luhmann's version of events it is in friendship that intimate communication was learned and carried out; but to the extent that sexuality becomes central to individuality, friendship is set aside. Its asexual description renders it insufficient for a gradually modernizing love ideology that soon ceases the day.

Friendship continues to play a central part in the story of love. Its intimacy shores up sexual love and so paves the way for the integration of love in the modern love marriage, of which it eventually becomes the key ingredient. Friendship as the foundation for romantic love helps to shatter the age-old connections linking honor, status, power, and marriage. In the 18th century it becomes an ideal for the love marriage because love's passion is seen as temporally limited and so needs friendship to sustain it. But while love enters marriage via friendship's intimacy, friendship is soon devalued *vis-à-vis* marriage. Schleiermacher's assertion, 'love aims to make one out of two, friendship two out of each' (cited in Schmidt, 2000, p. 87, my translation), gives expression to this apotheosis of love at a time when unity was raised above mere individuality (today, that attitude would be judged as self-compromising co-dependency). Buttressed by an emerging understanding of the individual as a unity of mind and body (as opposed to the Platonic separation of body and soul) the body also asserts its claims for intimacy. Sex, which once rendered love illegitimate, had become its crucible. Sexuality becomes the key distinction between love and friendship. Ever more imperative in love, and inconceivable in friendship, gender lines are more deeply etched into the normative fabric of intimacy: intimate friendship between men and women becomes subject to suspicion, becomes all but impossible, or at the very least causes ambiguities, conflicts, and uncertainties that continue to echo into the present (see Chapter 6). As intimate history's table turns, friendship, once the legitimate form of intimacy, comes to be seen as potentially subversive of the 'natural order' of things (Suttles, 1970; Rawlins, 1992; Vernon, 2006).

With the spread of Romantic fervor, individuals looked for a transcendence of the everyday. Intimacy, as we have seen, began to be conceived as a refuge from societal realities. In the 19th century love and art were seen to 'offer protection and a foothold *vis-à-vis* the dominant markers of modern society – *vis-à-vis* the economic pressures of work and exploitation, state regulation and ... technology. The threatened "I" saves itself in love, regenerates itself in the family, and finds its expressive possibilities in art', says Luhmann (1998b, p. 988, my translation). But, for one, the state of transcendence and the Romantics' exalted sensibility was associated with anti-democratic, elitist sensibilities that could not survive the new egalitarian impulses of the modern world. Secondly, love is culturally encoded as self-referential and irrational. Its existence can only ever be inferred, can never be proven; only love can solve love's puzzles. This causes considerable emotional burdens and so makes romantic love not only the quintessential subject of the novel, and then of psychoanalysis; but it is also a situation that cries out for simplification and standardization. As the 19th century unfolds, love is brought down to earth, is embedded in formulaic cultural scripts that gain mass appeal with the growth of the cultural industries of the 20th century – at a time, that is, when 'love crossed over from books to screens and records', and 'America's media kissed Europe's tired lips' (Theleweit cited in Burkart, 1998, p. 25ff.).

Love as institution

In the course of its social development erotic love became strongly institutionalized. Marriage made love tangible as quasi-proof of love's existence because it was contractually formalized to the extent that eventually, and after considerable struggle, a perceived lack of love became a sufficient cause for divorce. Love, as the foundation of the modern family, is also the driving force that displaces the patriarchal family ideal, including authoritarian parenting.[3] The displacement of public (economic and religious) functions by (secular) love as the main justifier for family formation has also raised the family to an ideal that it can by no means always live up to: loving shelter from the dangers of the outside world. Its interactional realities are riven with ambivalences (Connidis & McMullin, 2002).

Love's *connectivity* to other institutional complexes – to 'external' norms – is particularly great. Consider its connection to the law and religion in the case of marriage, and romance's connection to the market via its cultural commodification. There is love's connection to the institution of heterosexuality, which is shored up by heteronormative assumptions and practices and until very recently was legitimated by marriage as an exclusively heterosexual institution (Wittig, 1992; Jackson & Scott, 2010). Love's institutional connectivity alleviates, but doesn't solve, existential uncertainties that are part and parcel of its modernity, because it is ideologically and structurally anchored in a bedrock of informal notions and formal prescriptions.

As we have seen, the history of love is premised on a heightened sense of individuality, and a need to communicate it. What Luhmann calls 'interpersonal' or 'interhuman interpenetration' describes the new, but equally fragile, basis for love: 'the (selective) inner experience of the partner, and not just his actions, becomes relevant for the actions of the other person'. But these inner experiences can only ever be circumscribed, can never be fully known and remain incommunicable in essential ways: 'Interhuman interpenetration exceeds the possibilities of communication. This refers not only to the boundaries of linguistic possibilities and not only to the meaning of bodily contact. Instead, *intimacy includes what is incommunicable and therefore includes the experience of incommunicability'* (1995, p. 228, my emphasis).

Because the inner experience of the other can only ever be interpreted but never empirically proven, there is a need for certainty that would become unbearable were it not for a social mechanism that reduces uncertainty. For Luhmann that social mechanism is trust (see also Luhmann, 1994). As the fundamental basis of intimate relationships, trust keeps doubts, second-guessing, and insecurities at a minimum. But at the same time, the uncertainties are firmly entrenched in the structural and cultural makeup of love: its normative version is monogamous and heterosexual, with jealousy both love's 'proof' and potential undoing. Intimacy is 'psychologized' some time before the emergence of psychology. But these are brittle foundations indeed and cannot guarantee the continuance of love as institutionalized in the love marriage. The basis for trust asks to be verified, certainty to be given a chance. On that count, capitalism appears to deliver.

The culture of romance, with its roots in 19th century Romanticism, is integrated into the capitalist mode of production and consumption. The norms of the market, which in earlier history attached to the reproduction of social stratification in arranged marriages, now attach to love for love's sake. That love – as stable or unstable as a relationship based on intimate needs may be – becomes legible in material form; a highly commodified culture of romance promises to make the ephemeral tangible and concrete. A thoroughly gendered 'romantic utopia' (Illouz, 1997) furnishes scripts that are given material form in an array of consumer goods whose purchases may just help distinguish true love from lesser kinds and so raises the probability of interpersonal interpenetration. But this cannot be realized. Paradoxes remain unresolved;

the world of love remains self-referential. Only love can spur love. Only love can save love. It is its own cause and effect, its own symptom and remedy. Popular culture gives voice to these complexities in myriad ways. Take, for example, the Beatles', 'All you need is love', or Stevie Wonder's 'Love's in need of love today'. But that giving voice to love's conundrums remains just that: an expression of the pains, joys, and wonders that are embedded in love's essential irrationality. In so doing, popular culture offers diagnoses that don't call for cures – the cures already reside in love – but are proof of a true love that brooks no rationality no matter what pain and suffering it may cause. That endeavor is left to another quarter.

Love and therapy culture

Once confined to the clinic, by mid-20th century a therapeutic ethos had begun to provide new modes of thinking concerning all relationships. 'Expert systems' emerged that specialize in the alleviation of love's pathologies. Marriage and relationship counseling and a growing market of self-help advice, but also a massive literature on childrearing, not only offer solutions to relational problems but generate them. New vocabularies facilitate the diagnosis of ever new problems – for which experts offer ever new solutions. Romance, therapy, and capitalism – mutually supportive, mutually reinforcing, and constitutive, intertwined, and inextricable – imbue the human need for intimacy with dreams of greater freedom and raise expectations of more authentic experience (Bauman, 1991; Furedi, 2004; Illouz, 2008).

It is at the nexus between capitalism, romance, and therapy culture that, according to Anthony Giddens' *The Transformation of Intimacy* (1992), a new conception of love emerges: 'confluent love'. Replacing romantic love, the kind of love that is meant to last forever, confluent love is 'contingent', open to changes including its sudden end. A mutual 'opening oneself out to the other' is essential (Giddens, 1992, p. 61). While in the romantic love ideal the 'rational', 'strong' man provides a shoulder for the 'emotional' woman to cry on, confluent love 'only develops to the degree to which intimacy does, to the degree to which each partner is prepared to reveal concerns and needs to the other and to be vulnerable to that other'. Sexual satisfaction in romantic love is supposed to flow naturally from the erotic power it rouses. Confluent love, on the other hand, includes the 'cultivation of sexual skills, the capability of giving and experiencing sexual satisfaction, on the part of both sexes' with recourse to expert advice, for example. But also, it does not presuppose monogamy: 'Sexual exclusiveness here has a role in the relationship to the degree to which the partners mutually deem it desirable or essential' (Giddens, 1992, pp. 62–63). Confluent love is not tied to heterosexuality in the way that romantic love was. The understanding of the possibilities of a person's varied sexuality is a given here.

This late modern type of love is, for Giddens, a precondition of what he proposes to be the 'pure relationship'. Lovers entwined in such relations raise communication – and above all the communication of emotions, of feeling states – to prime importance for the continuance of a kind of love that is all about fulfillment. Themes of this shift emerge in the literature of the postwar era. Take, for instance, Janice, wife of protagonist Harry 'Rabbit' Angstrom in John Updike's *Rabbit* series of novels. Janice's transformation illustrates the historical shift from romantic attachments based on patriarchal arrangements to the kind of intimacy that requires autonomy, self-reflexivity, and the capacity to articulate desires as well as emotional pain. Having separated from him, and having met a lover whose recognition of her as a person in her own right sparks a once-unknown self-confidence, Janice calls her husband and, assisted by a new-found psychological vocabulary, asserts:

> Harry, I'm sorry for whatever pain this is causing you, truly sorry, but it's very important at this point in our lives we don't let guilt feelings motivate us. I'm trying to look honestly into myself, to see who I am, and where I should be going. I want us both, Harry, to come to a decision we can live with. It's the year nineteen sixty-nine and there's no reason for two mature people to smother each other to death simply out of inertia. I'm searching for a valid identity and I suggest you do the same. (Updike, 1995, pp. 355–356)

Today – and this is a liberalizing development that brings new challenges – fulfillment has less and less to do with conforming to traditional marriage ideals, and more and more with mutually fostered emotional, psychological, and spiritual growth. What Updike's Janice voices post-breakup is a quintessential ideal of contemporary love: that once that type of growth seems irredeemable, so is the relationship. It presupposes the capacity to externalize emotions; to 'look honestly into myself', as Janice says, and to turn feelings into objects that can be made subject to (self) analysis. This type of capacity for self-objectification – that it is a solipsistic illusion is not to say it cannot be effective – is today highly prized as 'emotional intelligence'. This kind of psychologization of love means that marriage, while remaining strongly circumscribed and even prescribed by cultural norms, goes hand in hand with the fact that marriage is ever more subject to individual justification rather than public demand. Questions such as 'Why should we get married?' or 'Why did we?' have only recently become meaningful.

To what extent Giddens' pure relationship is a (middle-class) ideal rather than a generalizable reality is debatable (for a critique see Jamieson, 1998, 1999). As Ann Swidler has shown, the 'therapeutic ethic' may not be drawn on by everyone among her white, middle-class, Californian subjects. Nevertheless, for those who are inclined to value work on the self, 'therapeutic effort ... can deepen their relationships, making them last not because they stabilize their selves, but because they achieve a deeper communication that allows them continuously to adapt to one another'. As a consequence, they believe the relationship to be in trouble when 'they no longer engage the authentic selves of their participants' (Swidler, 2001, p. 143).

Based on mutuality, contemporary intimacy in Giddens' invocation holds out 'the promise of democracy', something that in friendship, as a symmetrical relationship, is actualized (1992, p. 188). When it comes to 'the pure relationship' in the context of erotic love that promise still awaits realization, because gender relations, including the division of household labor and the preeminence of heteronormative assumptions cannot simply be undone by expressing one's emotional and psychological needs. It is here precisely that Giddens' suggestion that all intimate relationships – parent–child, love as well as friendship – can be subsumed under the pure relationship model rings too optimistic. Even if we were to assume that friendship comes closer to the democratic ideal, as long as gender relations remain asymmetrical the notion that all that needs to be done is infuse love with (democratic) friendship, or make friendship the foundation of the love relationship and thus save the day remains suspect. Rather, what the realities show is that sexual relations, because of how they intersect with socially and culturally structured gender relations, remain highly problematic on the everyday level of intimate interactions (see Chapters 5 and 6).

But let's now return to the institutional question. The shift from public obligation to individually negotiated choice can be, and has been, thought of as the deinstitutionalization of love (Beck & Beck-Gernsheim, 1995; Bauman, 2003). But this is only a limited development depending on whether formal or informal norms are considered, and so the normative infrastructure of love is neither uniformly deinstitutionalized nor does this occur in a linear fashion. In a thought-provoking paper

Neil Gross (2005) proposes the differentiation between 'regulative' and 'meaning-constitutive' traditions in his challenge of the detraditionalization thesis which, as the sum total of various contemporary perspectives, has congealed around a radical demise of traditional blueprints for intimate life. 'Regulative traditions' are made up of formal and informal norms whose transgression results in individuals' and groups' exclusion from 'moral communities'. For example, on the level of formal norms there is a continuing struggle over the recognition of gay marriage, which is only slowly being decided in favor of same-sex unions, one jurisdiction at a time. Simultaneously, *de facto* relationships – cohabiting arrangements between unmarried lovers – are either in the process of being recognized as equal to marriage before the law, or already are (e.g. Australia), irrespective of partners' sexual orientations and genders. We are witnessing here the formalization of informal arrangements. Pertaining to gay marriage in particular, this is not merely about a valorization of the institution of marriage – something that is increasingly criticized by gay writers and activists – but also a bid for the choice to say 'no' to an institution that has for so long been closed to same-sex partners. That bid can thus also be conceived as a struggle for the freedom to choose whether or not the relationship ought to be publicly sanctioned. So while marriage may be experiencing a crisis of legitimacy concerning its binding nature and the necessity for its public recognition, unconventional forms of love are beginning to be formally institutionalized. Add to that the long historical demise of marriage as the vehicle for the reproduction of familial status and privilege, a forty year history of no-fault divorce, and the rise of the pure relationship ideal in a therapeutic mode, and there seems to be little left aside from personal arrangements and individual decision making to keep the institution alive.

Yet on the informal level of cultural norms marriage still finds a lot of support. While across the OECD there has been a four-decade-long fall in the crude marriage rate (disregarding other formal cohabitation contracts and informal partnerships), attachment to marriage as a normative institution remains strong (Gross, 2005; OECD, 2012). It also remains one of the 'classic markers of adulthood', marking the transition to full personhood in contemporary societies because it lends practical evidence to the notion of adult 'maturity' (Blatterer, 2009). Against Giddens (1992), but also Zygmunt Bauman (2003), I suggest this to be all the more the case the more 'until further notice' love relationships become, the more they become mired in the brittle ground that is the uncertainty of emotional need fulfillment. Under those conditions tradition promises certainty in the shape of marriage as formalized trust. As well, the culture of romance – with its Valentine's Cards and anniversaries, honeymoon vacations and candle-lit dinners, but also expert counseling and everyday therapeutics – continues to strongly outline love's terrain, sets its boundaries, provides benchmarks with which to test its truths and lies, celebrates its beauties, and suggests exits from its pains. Erotic love is shot through with prescriptions: monogamy, and so exclusivity, is normative. While this does not prevent people from asserting their own desires and alternative practices – think about polyamory as one example (Klesse, 2014) – romantic love would be impossible were it not for the injunction of exclusivity. Love, in other words, is subject to a strong structural and cultural program. While undergoing considerable changes, its lived experiences rely heavily on its normative infrastructure, which for all its uneven institutionalization, is supported by high institutional connectivity. This is only to a limited yet significant extent the case for friendship.

Friendship's institutional deficit as relational freedom

When compared to love, and taking into account a sociologically workable approach to institutions, friendship takes up a peculiar position: it has, in the course of its modernization, retained some broadly institutional features, but has largely been reconfigured to the extent that we cannot subsume it among the range of modern institutions. That reconfiguration is not merely an abstract process, but has significant consequences for everyday experiences of intimacy, because without that transformation friendship would not have attained the level of interactional freedom it has the capacity to deliver to us today.

Anthropology and institutionalized friendship

In sociology the family is the focal point of private life, and sometimes friendship is subsumed under its heading (e.g. 'families of choice'). Similarly, in anthropology 'kinship' – the web of familial relations beyond the parent–child nucleus – was for much of the discipline's history core to the analysis of non-Western societies. Kinship was thought to provide the structural scaffold ensuring the endurance of social arrangements in those societies where centralized political control is absent. By extension, friendship was treated as marginal, with some empirical and conceptual work scattered through the decades. Only fairly recently, albeit sporadically, has its position in the institutional makeup of non-European (as well as within different European) societies become subject to anthropological research (e.g. Cohen, 1961; Brain, 1976; Parekh, 1994; Gurdin, 1996). Some of that literature is important to this discussion because it shows, for one, that the commonsense assumption that friendship is a freely chosen relationship does not hold true everywhere and for all time. Secondly, it shows that important aspects of Western thinking about friendship cannot be universalized. And thirdly, we get here also a glimpse of how trust works in interpersonal relationships, because social practices of trust shape the mutual articulation of the categories family, kinship, and friendship. What follows is not a comprehensive critical engagement with the anthropological literature. I'm simply drawing on some classic statements to make my point.

Firmly embedded in anthropological kinships studies, Gulliver's *Neighbours and Networks* (1971) describes social relationships among Ndendeuli men of Tanzania. The relationship between kinship and friendship he observes is instructive: nonkin personal friends were rare; about half of the men had a single friend and only very few had more than two. Friends 'were rather unimportant to social life' (Gulliver, 1971, p. 302). The main reason for friends' marginality is their perceived untrustworthiness: 'whereas a kinsman could be trusted and had to accede to requests for assistance *because* he was a kinsman, an unrelated man was unlikely to be so considered, could not be trusted, and had no need to entertain obligations nor the right to make demands' (Gulliver, 1971, p. 302, original emphasis). Ndendeuli men were more likely to develop affectionate friendships with men that were part of the kinship network. In one of the rare cases where long-lasting friendships did develop, others in fact assumed the men were relatives. Kinship here was the quintessential site of interpersonal trust, its benchmark and fulcrum.

Robert Brain's *Lovers and Friends* (1976) provides contrasting examples. For one, Brain dismantles any Western pretensions to the universality of friendship's voluntarism. But this time the weight of negative sanctions falls on kinship. For the Ghanaian Bangwa, '[f]riendship is valued far above kinship; between kin there are niggling doubts and witchcraft fears. Friendship lasts till death; kinship is brittle and involves inequalities of age and wealth and status. Friendship alone can cancel these out' (Brain, 1976, p. 35). Here, trust relations are the exact opposite of those in Ndendeuli society. And not only is friendship highly valued, it is thoroughly institutionalized in ritual fashion: girls and boys are assigned lifelong, same-sex 'best friends'. Although the rituals vary, these 'ritual friendships' are common in the literature on

Melanesia, Polynesia, and Africa. Edward Evans-Pritchard's (1963) description of practices among the north-central African Azande, and Yehudi Cohen's (1963) survey of 65 societies across the globe, contain passages describing 'blood bonds' among men. These bonds, whether found in non-Western or premodern European societies are usually described as 'blood brotherhoods'. Brain objects to that description because it conflates kinship and friendship:

> The term 'brotherhood' is ... a misnomer of long standing, based on the misconceptions of early observers of ... [blood] rites. The assumption was that there was no kinship without community of blood and that there were no obligations in primitive societies except those of kinship, so that anyone wanting an alliance of friendship had to adopt the notion of artificial kinship. ... A brother is a brother, while blood brothers are really friends. (1976, pp. 85–86)

There are exceptions to the rule that kinship and friendship constitute different, and differently valued, forms of socially integrative trust. The most striking example may be that of the Swat Pukhtun of Northern Pakistan. According to Lindholm's *Generosity and Jealousy* (1982), this is a society with an unusually high degree of competition, rivalry, and generalized *distrust* amongst its members; there is '*no* paradigm in the lives of the Pukhtun for a relationship of mutual trust, respect, and generosity', (1982, p. 160, original emphasis). Not only is there constant competition over land, but relations of distrust go so far that in the case of enemy threat leadership is entrusted to an outsider. No Pukhtun would accept direction from another Pukhtun. Temporary solidarity dissipates as soon as the threat is over. What holds society together is not trust, but a code of honor based on the belief of Pukhtun superiority. Friendship – imagined possible only between men in this patrilineal and patriarchal society – is idealized to such a degree that realization is all but impossible: 'The friend cannot be more powerful than ego, for this would imply servitude. Nor can he be less powerful, for then he is a servant. Nor can he be an equal, for then he would be a rival' (Lindholm, 1982, pp. 244–245). Pukhtun friendship ideals diminish any universalizing potential that either so-called 'status homophily' (like attracts like) or heterophily (opposites attract) may hold as a necessary conditions of friendship (Lazarsfeld & Merton, 1964; Allan & Adams, 2007). In Swat, difference as well as identity – that is, not just likeness by sameness – are equally to be present should friendship stand a chance. Friends are to merge into one in a process of

mutual possession. That cannot occur in the given social context, however: 'The foreigner is', therefore, 'much sought after as a friend, since
he fits, more than any Pakistani, the necessary qualifications of strange-
ness, equality without rivalry, and an absence of conflicting interests'
(Lindholm, 1982, pp. 244–245). The passionate desire for an ideal
friendship, declared in poetry and songs, is fueled by the practical scarcity of opportunities to realize it. But it is not impossible. Lindholm's
own friendship with Muhammad Zaman Khan, his host and assistant,
is one example. Seeking an answer to the dilemma that friendship exists
among the Pukhtun when it has 'no roots in the structure', Lindholm
advocates for an anthropology that takes the cultural structuring of
emotions more seriously, passes through psychoanalytic terrain, and
finally ends on a high note of pathos: 'Friendship ... in Swat can then
best be understood as the expression, in a world of hostility and fear, of
the necessary counterweight to the Pukhtun man's inevitable sense of
isolation: love' (1982, p. 273) – a theme, we should note, that time and
again recurs in the modern literature on intimacy.

In one way or another all these accounts show that while the boundaries between kinship and friendship are not as easily drawn as may have
been suggested in much of the earlier research, friendship and kinship
articulate on the level of social meaning and practice: either is more or
less socially relevant against the background of the other. That articulation is made meaningful in relations of trust and distrust. Among
Ndendeuli men, although socially anchored relations of trust do not
determine friendship choices, a societal bias toward kin nevertheless
affects their practical likelihood. Like in Ndendeuli society, the articulation between kinship and friendship among the Bangwa is constitutive
of both, even though trust relations work the opposite way, that is, they
are biased in favor of friendship. These arranged, 'ritual friendships' not
only afford friends companionship and affection, but a much needed
'outlet from the claustrophobic restrictions of kinship ties' (Brain, 1976,
p. 37), a role that, as we shall see in Chapter 4, friendship continues to
play today in highly differentiated societies. For the Kwame, friendship
determines the organization of kinship networks. Once friendships are
established, the incest taboo comes into force. Friends are not to have
sexual relations with females of either kinship group (Cohen, 1961).
Seen from this anthropological vantage point, kinship and friendship
are 'repositories of trust', to use Eisenstadt and Roniger's (1984) terminology. Trust is distributed differently according to prevailing societal arrangements. And because trust is an irreducible category (we
can't trust just a little; we either do or don't), kinship and friendship

are each other's *limiting cases*. That is not to say that the boundaries are clear. The vexed questions of the distinction between family and friendship, and between erotic love and friendship, show that theoretical boundary-drawing may serve analytic purposes, while in real life tensions remains.

There are important similarities as well as differences between these societies and ours. As we have seen, the development of intimacy in European history – and this holds true to this day – shows a constant articulation between love and friendship. To the anthropologists visited here friendships are personal relationships, to be sure. But they are *institutionalized and public* and not private relationships. It is only with processes of modernization and differentiation that friendship becomes *personal and private* (Markus, 2010b). In everyday interaction, the personalization and intimization of friendship translates into a particular kind of freedom that lies at the heart of the relationship's very semantic ambiguities and practical tensions.

Friendship's relational freedom

The relational freedom of friendship refers to more than freedom of choice, the in-principle choice concerning when and how to initiate, change, and terminate them (Wolf, 1966; Jerrome, 1992); it refers also to the freedom to construct and maintain the relationship in its own image, relatively independent of cultural prescription, in the context of '*symmetrical, generalized reciprocity*' (Markus, 2010b, p. 17, original emphasis). Several statements help clarify the notion of relational freedom. According to Silver, for example,

> [n]ormatively, friendship is grounded in the unique and irreplaceable qualities of partners, defined and valued independently of their place in public systems of kinship, power, utility, and esteem, and of any publicly defined status. The privacy of friendship is not only cultural but formal. No body of law and administrative regulation brings sovereign authority to bear on friendships; correspondingly, friendship is unprotected by law – for example, friends do not enjoy immunity from testifying about each other in court, unlike physicians about their patients, clergy about congregants, and spouses about each other. (1996, p. 46)

Further on, Silver tells us that, 'an ideal arena for that individualized conception of personal agency central to modern notions of personal freedom', friendship 'is ungoverned by the structural definitions that bear on family and kinship, and, unlike erotic relations, may ignore gender' (1996, p. 47). Others concur. Rawlins, for example, states that 'friendship has no clear normative status within publicly constituted hierarchies of role relationships. ... Friendship cannot be imposed on people; it is an ongoing human association voluntarily developed and privately negotiated ... Appropriate behavior is determined within the friendship and is upheld principally by each individual's affection for and/or loyalty and commitment to the other' (1992, p. 9). Similarly, Budgeon asserts that, '[u]nlike family or kin, friendship is not constituted by socially defined purposes or functions. Therefore, it allows for the recognition of individually defined needs which evolve within the terms of the relationship itself' (2006, paragraph 5.4). Seeing friendship as 'a kind of relationship [that is] ... based on spontaneous and unconstrained sentiment or affection', Carrier reminds us that 'if the relationships is constrained we confront something very different from what we call "friendship", something like bureaucratic relationships, kinship relationship, or patron-client relationships' (1999, p. 21). Vernon, too, puts it well and helps us understand the comparative institutional complexities and tensions of the relationship:

> Unlike institutions of belonging such as marriage which is supported and shaped by social norms ... friendship has no predetermined instructions for assembly or project of growth. People have to create their friendships mostly out of who they are, their interests and needs, without any universally applicable framework. On the one hand, this is a potential weakness, because a friendship may 'go nowhere' or 'run out of steam'. On the other, it is a potential strength because there is also a freedom in this that is crucial to friendship's appeal: it is part of the reason for the diversity within the family of relationships called friendship. (2006, p. 5)

Vernon not only describes the comparative freedom of friendship, but sees that freedom as reflected in the ambiguities concerning the very term.

The *relational freedom* of friendship is not total. For, now Allan's attention to friendship's social moorings as part of his important work of contextualization suffices:

> In principle, at least, each party to an actual or potential friendship is as free as the other to influence its path, and consequently

the choices each can make are limited by the choices made by the other – each of which is, of course, patterned to some degree by their different immediate social environments. (1989, p. 47)

That is, friendship is not disembedded from structural and cultural exigencies. For one, as a personal and private relationship it is linked to centuries-long processes of differentiation (Paine, 1974; Tenbruck, 1989; Luhmann, 1998a; Schmidt, 2000; Markus, 2010b); and as sociologists have shown, class and status, as well as age, cultural background, and race constrain friendships' reputed voluntarism and so matter in their initiation (Lazarsfeld & Merton, 1964; Allan, 1989; Adams & Allan, 1998). As I will argue in Chapters 5 and 6, gender poses the most enduring challenges of friendship formation. But especially, though not exclusively, in its most acceptable (homosocial) form, friendship allows for the self-generation of modes of interaction to a degree that is not given in other interpersonal relationships. For some that relational freedom is *linked* to the institutionalization of intimacy. That point is worth revisiting.

Rethinking Honneth's approach

In Chapter 1, I briefly outlined Honneth's take on intimacy and recognition, and his argument that, following Hegel, our free will and hence our subjective freedom depends on the degree to which it is enabled by social institutions. To varying degrees, and always subject to contestation, that freedom is at minimum *promised* by modern institutions such as states, markets, and intimate relationships, including friendship. The freedom that marks the latter, and that Honneth attempts to flesh out, lies in 'the mutually enabled perfecting of one's own self' (2011, p. 234, my translation). Specifically on friendship, he claims that freedom lies, furthermore, in the will to 'be oneself in another' and so to be able to 'entrust one's will in all its indefiniteness and tentativeness to the other person freely and without fear' (2011, p. 249, my translation). Individual freedom is thus guaranteed by social, that is, intersubjectively constituted, freedom; the other 'is not a limitation, but a prerequisite of individual freedom', which in turn presupposes 'a complimentary obligation to [friendship] roles' (Honneth, 2011, p. 250, my translation). Because Honneth has set himself the task of showing that modern institutions are central to our freedom and so to justice, he must show friendship to be an institution, even though it is the personal relationship that 'possesses the least degree of institutional anchorage' (2011, p. 237, my translation).

What for Honneth makes friendship an institution, then, are its culturally shared norms:

> The action norms of friendships are socially institutionalized in so far as there exists commonly shared knowledge about those practices that together describe what constitutes their normatively relevant realization; as soon as deviations from these intuitively understood rules occur, this is generally experienced as crisis. Massive injuries of relevant norms are perceived as dissolutions of friendships. (2011, p. 239, my translation)

There is no arguing with Honneth's assertion that the transgression of cultural understandings of friendship can be detrimental to the relationship. At the same time, friendship is rarely tension free. It can and does harbor hurts, disappointments, ambiguities, and tensions, these 'dark sides' social research documents (Smart et al., 2012). But because they are established as trust relationships they can – and frequently are – repaired on the same grounds. Moreover these 'action norms' are at once less than regulative norms and more than prerequisites: friendship actually *is* trust relationally manifested; it instantiates and gives particular meaning to intimacy and thus personifies the modern ideals of equality, freedom, and personal justice. While what goes for love can, and often does, continue whether trusting or not, just or unjust, friendship cannot. Unlike in love, where jealousy is culturally coded as a sign of attachment, jealousy in friendship, although possible, does not injures the relationship. And so the cultural artifacts that describe friendship – from biblical David and Jonathan, to Hesse's *Narziss und Goldmund*, to *Tom Sawyer and Huckleberry Finn*, from *Thelma and Louise* to *Friends*, to *Sex and the City*, etc. – can only ever *describe* a range of attitudes and conduct, interactions, ways of communication and a range of interactional possibilities, but they cannot *prescribe* them; they are meaning-constitutive frames of reference rather than binding rules.

Even cultural forms that are most directly concerned with orienting practices and attitudes are full of contradictions, and in any case are subject to cultural variability. Take the myriad maxims captured in proverbs in the course of friendship's history in different places: 'You cannot buy a friend', according to a Russian saying, while a traditional American proverb holds that 'The purse-strings are the most common ties of friendship'. For the French, 'Friends agree best at a distance', while for the Greeks 'Friends living far away are not friends'. Aristides bemoans the fact that 'When a man fares badly, his friends keep away', which for Mark Twain is just as well. He approvingly quotes 'an old time toast': 'When you ascend the hill of prosperity may you not meet a friend'. If Ovid had been a contemporary, on the other hand, he would have advised Twain to be more judicious in his use of 'friend'. For him 'the vulgar herd estimate friendship by its advantages' (Strauss, 1994). The maxims may be legion, but they are contradictory and relativizing, culturally and historically specific rather than universal, and if considered part of friendship's institutional infrastructure hopelessly inadequate for the orientation of meaning.

As discussed in Chapter 1, Honneth follows in Hegel's footsteps when he sees modern institutions – intimate relationships, markets, states – as central to our relational freedom, that is, a kind of freedom that goes beyond the libertarian model of unfettered individual freedom of action, and is instead embedded in collective decision-making and the negotiation of the contents and boundaries of autonomy. On this view, the intimate sphere is where 'individual needs and attributes ... take on social form and are intersubjectivity realized' (Honneth, 2011, p. 233, my translation). And they take on 'social form' as institutions as part of modernizing, differentiating processes.

While erotic love relationships and parent–child bonds retain institutional characteristics pivotal to modern freedom, the situation is somewhat different with regard to friendship. The freedoms that inhere in friendship rest on its *incomplete* integration into the raft of modern institutions. Honneth leans too heavily on the Scottish Enlightenment version of friendship as interpreted by Silver. For him, Smith 'for the first time delineates with systematic ambition the vision that apart from familial relationships there is a second figure of social relationships [friendship] in which subjects can be connected solely on the grounds of reciprocal affection and attraction' (2011, pp. 241–242, my translation). This, I suggest, has consequences for Honneth's theory because he doesn't perceive the instrumentalizing drift evident in Smith, that is, Smith's historically situated inability to conceptualize intimacy in the modern sense. Modifying Honneth's thesis, then, I suggest that friendship's freedom is possible *not despite, but precisely because*, it 'possesses the least degree of institutional anchorage' (Honneth, 2011, p. 237). Thus, what from one perspective could be perceived as a weakness in fact turns out to be a real strength, is in fact friendship's central characteristic from which all its interactional possibilities and potentials flow. To what extent that exceptional status of friendship has a bearing on Honneth's conception of the institutional guarantee of our social freedoms does not need to be discussed in the present context.

Some time ago, Robert Paine (1974) elaborated the normative constitution of friendship and its exceptional place in the institutional order. This is arguably also a better place than Enlightenment visions to contemplate the complexities of modern friendship:

> One invariably talks of friendship as being an *institution*. Inasmuch as friendship is recognized as a social relationship, it is an institution in the limited and rather loose sense of bestowal of recognition; and this is commonly the extent of its institutionalization in our culture where it amounts to a kind of *institutionalized non-institution*. (Paine, 1974, p. 128, original emphases)

With 'institutionalized non-institution' Paine chose a term that speaks to the very ambiguities that make friendship unique in the repertoire of personal relationships. That designation is worth teasing apart. I do so not by using Paine's own distinction, but, for the sake of continuity, by distinguishing between the normative *infrastructure* and the *connectivity* of institutions with specific reference to friendship. To reiterate, institutional connectivity refers to the degree of integration of one institution with one or more other structural social arrangements, and their ideological reproduction in the cultural domain. Put differently and broadly, the degree and depth to which norms are socially and culturally shored up, and the degree to which they are connectable to exogenous institutional and organizational arrangements and cultural representations correlates with the degree to which they are able to orient personal attitudes, practices, and behaviors. The most obvious case of love's institutional connectivity is its legal codification as marriage and the normative force of heterosexuality. Contemporary erotic love, in whatever form, cannot escape – indeed needs for its own self-reproduction, and for it to be 'readable' in the culture – the connection to the nexus capitalism–romance–therapy, which in turn benefits from love's inexplicability, ambiguities, and potential hurts (Luhmann, 1998a; Illouz, 2012).

The same applies to friendship only to a limited – although, as we shall see, decisive – degree. The lack of formalization is self-evident. There are no written contracts that spell out the rights and obligations of friends; neither can sue the other for a breach of terms, nor can friends claim state support or seek help in 'friendship counseling'. Contrary to love, the formal institutionalization of friendship would undermine the very likelihood of its formation, let alone strengthen it, because in modern societies it is a personal relationship that is always already premised on choice, freedom, and interpersonal justice. At the same time, on the informal level friendship connects strongly to the institution of heterosexuality, which continues to order shared cultural assumptions concerning homosociality and heterosociality, rendering cross-sex friendships non-standard. This is just one indication that friendship remains strongly connected to the gender system. This is not so much an indication of the institutional qualities of friendship, but rather indicates the normative force of heterosexuality, and its persistence as an institution. I will elaborate that train of thought in Chapters 5 and 6.

For now I just want to reiterate that compared to other interpersonal relationships friendship is *relatively deficient* in institutional connectivity, and that this deficit is central to its freedom. That is not to say that friendship is free of cultural presuppositions or lacks typification. Were this to be the case it simply wouldn't make sense to us, would remain unrecognizable as a social form. These are the taken-for-granted assumptions about friendship, such as the necessity of trust and loyalty, equality, symmetric reciprocity, and justice, that make friendship meaningful to us and yet do not suffice for its institutionalization. The 'what' and 'how' of that trust and loyalty, the ways equality and reciprocity are enacted, practiced, and 'done', are very weakly delimited in the culture and do not attain the prescriptive force they attain concerning love. Thus it is in friendship's ambiguous position, nestled between a common sense about its character and the weak prescriptive and orientating regimes, that its relational freedom is situated. The strength of that freedom rests, among other things, on friendship's potential to shelter intimacy from exogenous logics.

Relational freedom as resistance: friendship and therapy culture

Whatever its modalities, the aim of therapy is to alleviate psychological and emotional suffering of varying degrees, by way of either professional guidance or self-help. Over the last several decades, therapy culture has attracted its fair share of critics. With some deviation they have mainly taken issue with psychology's individualizing approaches, which are said to reproduce *social* pathologies in the attempt to alleviate *individual* suffering and so nourish rather than change the 'social causes of psychological distress' (Mirowsky & Ross, 2003). Lasch's (1979) 'culture of narcissism' and Bellah et al.'s (2007) convergence of utilitarian and expressive individualism in the North American context and Furedi's (2004) 'victim culture' are well-known examples.

Much of Eva Illouz's work is a sustained attempt at a critical contextualization of the therapeutic turn. In *Consuming the Romantic Utopia* (1997) Illouz shows that erotic love, with commodified romance at its center, is literally unimaginable outside a consumerist frame of reference. Late modern therapy culture, promising guidance and clarity in matters of love for the exchange of money, plays a crucial role here; the trend has been successful in raising 'emotional communication' to imperative status: ideal love is 'an eminently *talkative* love' (Illouz, 1997, p. 234, original emphasis). This form of intimate communicative rationality is more than a prerequisite for the successful negotiation of intimacy (Holmes, 2011); it converges with economic rationality in so far as communicative capacities are seen as personal assets tradable in the dating market (Illouz, 2007). Illouz (2008) has specifically addressed the rise of what she calls 'the therapeutic persuasion'. Again, she emphasizes the emergence of an 'emotional style' that has become central to how interpersonal relations in all spheres of life are imagined, approached, and negotiated. At its core is the notion that people ought 'to transform their emotions into objects, to be watched from the outside, so to speak, by the subject and object of the emotion', who while doing so is supposed to 'keep feelings at bay' (Illouz, 2008, p. 133).

What for Illouz spells a form of reification with the dehumanizing potential that this may entail, for Giddens is a blessing. For him, autonomy and equality level love's playing field, including the terms of its closure; and here too verbal communication is crucial: 'The imperative of open and free communication is the *sine qua non* of the pure relationship; the relationship is its own forum' (1992, p. 194). Although their evaluations differ, from either point of view the love relationship emerges as a 'third', objectified and mediating entity between lovers. It is given shape by means of affective communication for which therapy culture provides the vocabulary, and by capitalism whose markets provide various romantic consumables, including the purchase of various therapeutic 'repair kits'.

In friendship the friends set the terms of that communication; in love these are prescribed and so 'individualized' only to the extent that lovers may *deviate* from extant societal models. Because a given friendship's own normative infrastructure determines the modalities of the relationship, and because its institutional connectivity is relatively weak, it has proven resistant to the reifying pressures of the therapeutic ethos even though it is an *intimate* relationship. Let me illustrate what I mean with just a few mundane examples: while professional relationship counseling – from pre-marital to post-marital, pre-divorce to post-divorce varieties – today firmly belongs to the institutional complex of love, marriage, and partnership (Giddens, 1992; Coontz, 2005), nothing comparable exists for friendship. Indeed, if friends were to arrive at a point where the friendship qua *relationship* is deemed to be in need of expert advice, the friendship is arguably either beyond repair, or the need for guidance itself is an indication that friendship has, by that logic, transformed into 'love' as described in the culture (Guerrero & Chavez, 2005). Advice literature on friendship is typically confined to the variety spawned by Dale Carnegie's *How to Win Friends and Influence People* (2009). Rather than friendship, the genre addresses interpersonal relationships marked by weak ties. Texts in that mode advocate for a thoroughly strategic, calculating attitude oriented to self-interest that by definition cannot apply to friendship as conceived of here. Consider also that there is no equivalent of Valentine's Day, which in a host of countries comes replete with consumable paraphernalia including cards, special vacation, accommodation, and dinner packages, and assorted dating rituals. Cultural representations of friendship generally stress the subversive and flexible character of friendship on the basis of trust and reciprocity (as well as the limits and ambiguities of friendship) rather than reproduce one-fits-all models.

Friendship is not amenable to the kind of self-referentiality that characterizes love and that – amongst other things – posits love as is its own fulfillment and remedy. Love is 'preoccupied' with erotic passion, while friendship typically is not. Love is caught between the promise of mutual, individual self-realization and its status as shelter from the atomizing consequences of individualization – between the threat of total symbiosis and the imperative of autonomy (Burkart & Hahn, 1998, p. 11). But love is also about a common life project, however contingent and precarious individualized biographies may be today (Beck, 1997, pp. 127–138). Again, institutionalization or the lack thereof is important here. Once love was integrated into marriage it became part of an institution that was not only open to connection to other institutional complexes, but in fact provided the very impulse for some of these to come into existence. The modern cultural norm that only love can make a marriage – not to talk about love's imperative exclusivity – augured the development of marriage and relationship counseling; the two entered into a mutually supportive relationship (Gurman & Fraenkel, 2002; Coontz, 2005). The intimacy of friendship neither presents sufficient normative and institutional points of connection for expert systems of that sort, nor are its emotional requirements nearly as precarious. Because interaction can center on limited aspects of the other, friends can offer support and encouragement of some of these aspects to the exclusion of larger life course questions, which romantic coupledom cannot ignore. Love's internal, structurally and culturally reproduced tensions and paradoxes thus make it an ideal subject for expert advice. The same does not apply to friendship; its relational freedom resists prescription and integration into therapy culture.

From a perspective that views private life as worth protecting from organizing principles that are functional to other domains, this freedom is to be positively valued. With reference to expert systems, Markus articulates the potential human costs of systemic incursions into private life:

> therapeutic prescriptions and many other types of advisory activities ... introduce a systemic logic into everyday life, but do it through the language and imagery of the everyday life of the private sphere, blurring the dividing line between the public and private ... [I]mportantly, such activity restricts our creativity in shaping our intimate relationships and attempts to impose a uniform pattern of dealing with a wide range of very specific individual situations, including personal unhappiness, different life tragedies or hurts. (2010b, p. 14)

That is not to suggest that professional therapy doesn't offer important human services, nor that intimate friends self-consciously marshal their relationship to defend a pristine 'realm of freedom'. What it does imply, though, is that dyadic friendships manage to thrive without the kinds of therapeutics offered in the culture and thus lack much of the need for them. So, when Bellah et al. (2007, p. 115) tell us that 'contemporary ideas of friendship are heavily influenced by the therapeutic attitude' this needs to be qualified. As we have seen, early 19th century expressivism predates a general societal therapeutic ethos by a century, and so the kinds of friendships cultivated during that time cannot, by any stretch of the imagination, be subsumed under the therapy culture rubric. None of this means that contemporary friendship is untouched by the therapeutic ethos. Friends may use therapeutic vocabulary in their communications. They may even value each other precisely for their therapeutic mutuality, and the fact that with our friends we can 'be ourselves' points in that direction.

Two provisos need spelling out here: first, as I have argued above, friendship's institutional deficit – its lack of connectivity – means that friendship's intimacy is not subject to cultural imperatives and so may even work as a shelter from them. Secondly, we have today great difficulties in speaking about any intimate interactions without using therapeutic idioms. The therapeutic ethos is so intrinsic to our contemporary evaluation of intimacy that we are inclined to view all intimate relationships through that prism. As far as historical developments are concerned we need to note that the therapeutic ethos owes its rise to societal elaborations of intimacy, of love and friendship, so that our fascination with intimate disclosure is not simply a consequence of the cultural diffusion of clinical practices and nomenclatures since Freud. That process needed the development of modern subjectivities, of concerns with our individuality and authenticity, before it could be focused in psychoanalytic discourse on 'the personality'. Only once the 'talking cures' were sufficiently elaborated on the organizational levels could their take on what it means to be human be diffused back into the culture where it found a ready audience (see also Zaretsky, 2004). Once disclosing intimacy had been given scientific legitimacy nothing could stand in the way of its cultural valorization as the benchmark of what it means to live an intimate relationship. To that extent Bellah and his collaborators are right to suggest a connection between friendship and the therapeutic attitude. But they ignore the differential distribution of social pressures to conform to the trends depending on the type of intimate relationship. Friendship's relational freedom in principle enables the uptake of therapeutic idioms as much as it enables their rejection depending on the specificities of a given relationship. The same is possible in love. But loving couples who decide to opt out of the nexus capitalism–romance–therapy go against a deep cultural grain; and that needs increasingly to be justified, if only to themselves.

Conclusion

The relational freedom of friendship rests on the relationship's institutional deficit. It amounts to considerable space for interacting according to the dynamics of the relationship, unencumbered, that is, by cultural prescription though aware of shared cultural understandings: friends do not hurt or humiliate one another. Support, care, and affection in the context of trust, respect, and justice mark friendship. In so far as this pertains, it is an intimate relationship; if it doesn't it may well be a friendly relation among acquaintances – I can trust and respect even strangers but feel no affection for them – but it is hardly a friendship. As friendship it is recognizable and describable as a specific form of interpersonal relationships; it is legible but it cannot be legislated.

Voluntary, as far as affection and a spontaneous development of liking someone can be considered as such, friendship is relatively obligation-free; it is based on a symmetrical, generalized reciprocity rather than like for like exchange, with the timing of reciprocal acts fairly loose. That free-floating dynamism of friendship 'works' because it is a trust relationship. But, especially when compared to erotic love, the relationship itself is rarely spoken about. The lack of need for articulation is, on the institutional and organizational level, evident in the absence of relationship services and therapeutic-cultural representations, even though friends may, listen to and offer 'therapeutic' advice about things that matter to one another. Situated on the other side of public role relationships, friendship resists integration into therapy culture. The lack of need for articulation of friendship *qua* relationship, the fact that it sits oddly with us to think about having those sorts of conversations with our friends in the way we talk about the relationship with lovers, is symptomatic of its indeterminate qualities. The semantic issues around 'friends' and 'friendship' I discussed earlier in fact speak eloquently to this indeterminacy.

In order not to 'reify' friendship, not to posit it as a relationship that is somehow a self-sufficient reality outside the interactions of friends, we need to discuss the relationship as lived experience. In the next chapter I turn to some thoughts on how friends create the 'little world' of their friendship under modern conditions of complexity and contingency.

4
Friendship, Intimacy, and the Self

This chapter continues to mine friendship's freedom. It approaches that freedom from the perspective of the relationship's internal dynamism, and so hopes to give some clues about how that freedom is constructed by friends and with what consequences. Beginning with describing friendship as delivering a sense of 'home' under conditions of modernity, I turn to the question of how friendship contributes to the making of selves. This question starts from the basic sociological premise that selves are socially constituted, that they are constructed in the business of relating. That is not to detract from the realities of an individual inner life, from an individual 'reflexivity' expressed in 'internal conversations' (Archer, 2003). Nor should a sociological perspective on the self dismiss the unconscious, the '"unthought known", the precognitive and extra-cognitive knowledge without which we would not be ourselves' (Bollas cited in Craib, 1998, p. 10). These areas butt up against the disciplinary boundaries of sociology, and I certainly cannot pretend to have expertise in them. What I can do, however, is emphasize that our humanness cannot be divorced from our sociality. In this chapter I want to focus that perspective on dyadic friendship based on the premise that 'the self in friendship is ... constituted by and particular to the friendship' (Cocking & Kennett, 1998, p. 510). As a particular modality of intimacy, friendship contributes to our sense of self in particular ways and, by extension, contributes to our capacities to negotiate the vicissitudes of living in modernity; and that not just in order to cope with contingency and complexity, but also in order to generate new possibilities for ourselves. Friends may encourage us to realize our potentials, take a new direction in life's journey, and glimpse possibilities of which we may otherwise remain unaware. Friendship's relational freedom enables spontaneity and creativity, and is in this

95

sense *generative*. 'Being oneself in another', Hegel's fortuitous description of intimacy, also happens to be the dynamism that offers the
potential for changes of self. As I will argue further on, that generative
potential of friendship has to do with its structural location between
the private and the public spheres from where friends may 'subvert'
public propriety as well as private secrecy.

Intimacy, modernity, and the need for coherence

During childhood we increasingly engage in arenas where the 'pure
trust' of the mother–child bond is absent, giving rise to 'the tendency to form new attachments in which the aims of pure trust and
equal participation in pristine meaning could seemingly be attained'
(Eisenstadt & Roniger, 1984, p. 40). Through our friendships we
encounter the world outside the family and begin to build a private
life outside the inner sanctum of the intimate sphere. But what kind of
'world' is it we are talking about here? To explain, we can refer back to
and interpret further the notion of modernity as experience I sketched
earlier. As sociologists and social theorists have time and again suggested, the differentiation of spheres of action and individual roles,
and the pluralization and visibility of a kaleidoscope of ways of life,
engender a need for existential footholds. The contingency and complexity of modern life calls for anchorage, which tradition, despite its
many inadequacies, continues to promise. Think of various religious
fundamentalisms and political orthodoxies, for example. The salient
point is that modernity is not simply about linear developments or
advancements, but about tensions; about the call of the old as well
as the promise of the new; about nostalgia as much as hopes for the
future; about opportunity and freedom of choice as much as the persistent truth that 'beggars can't be choosers'; and about tolerance and
openness to difference as much as a dogged refusal to look beyond
one's own backyard. The experience of modernity is suffused with
structural and cultural uncertainties that are shared by all of us, if to
varying degrees and kinds depending on class, gender, age, (dis)ability,
and cultural background.

A number of social theorists have articulated the quintessential modern longing that arises from these uncertainties, or have given context
to it. Anthony Giddens (1991a, 1991b) has referred to modernity's
undermining of our 'ontological security',[1] while Niklas Luhmann
(1995) analyzed social processes leading to the reduction of complexity and so the reduction of existential anxieties. For Zygmunt Bauman

(2013), this 'liquid modernity' of ours has meant a radical detradition-alization of social relations, something that Peter Berger and his colleagues put succinctly some time ago:

> Modernity has indeed been liberating. It has liberated human beings from the narrow controls of family, clan, tribe or small community. It has opened up for the individual previously unheard-of options and avenues of mobility. It has provided enormous power, both in the control of nature and in the management of human affairs. However, these liberations have had a high price. Perhaps the easiest way to describe it is to refer to it ... as *'homelessness'*. (1974, p. 195, my emphasis)

The answer to the question 'how to live an authentic life?' cannot be answered by falling back on a universally valid scheme of interpretation, but has to be self-generated. Various exemplars of modernist literature point exactly to this state of affairs. Take Arthur Schnitzler in *Der Weg ins Freie* (1908): 'Believe me, there are moments in which I envy people with a so-called Weltanschauung. When I want to have a well-ordered world, I always have to create it for myself. This is exhausting for someone who isn't God' (Schnitzler, 1916, p. 308, my translation). Or take Schnitzler's contemporary, the inimitable Hermann Bahr, another *fin-de-siècle* Viennese modernist: 'We have no law other than the truth as perceived by the individual' (1968, p. 38, my translation); or the essay on Rodin in which Simmel, picking up on the transformations heralded by the second industrial revolution in therapeutic mode, asserts:

> The essence of modernity is psychologism, the experience and interpretation of the world according to the reactions of our 'inside', that is, our inner world; the dissolution of fixed contents into the fluid element of the soul, from which all that is substantive is filtered and whose forms are but forms of motion. (1996, p. 346, my translation)

As we have seen, the early Romantics' thematization of subjectivity and self-realization indicated that the gradual diminution of a traditional status hierarchy, with its fixed roles and statuses, ushered in a turn to the personal and private, which, concerning friendship, frequently meant a kind of over-reaching, bare-all intimacy.

What can be garnered especially in modernism, modernity's aesthetic, but also in early sociology, is that existential homelessness engenders a need for coherence of self. That, precisely, is the promise of modern intimacy, with friendship no exception. Siegfried Kracauer keenly observed the connections. The call for individuality, for authenticity, for a life I can truly call my own goes hand in hand with the need '[t]o get away from a dissatisfactory sense of fragmentation instilled in individuals by our economic and social conditions with their countless contradictions and unresolved conflicts', because we 'strive for an integrated form of existence' (Kracauer, 1990, p. 55, my translation). Indeed, Kracauer's writing on friendship can be considered part of his attempt to describe a new world in which ideals of humanity are lost to us moderns and can only partly be recouped in private relations such as friendship (Frisby, 1986, p. 115). Take another one of Kracauer's statements that expresses his belief in the coherence-generating power of friendship: 'While everywhere else I'm compelled to split into thousand circles of life, to take a bit here, to give a smidgeon there, I may approach him [the friend] as fully and whole as I am and how I feel' (1990, p. 46, my translation). With increased chances of anonymity, isolation, and loneliness arise needs 'for communication, for connection and similarity with others' that friendship can fulfill because 'we want to have a home and be home to another' (Kracauer, 1990, pp. 48, 66, my translation). Friedrich Tenbruck echoes Kracauer. For him, too, the bonds of friendship are a panacea to modernity perceived as crisis, for it helps us assuage 'the disorganization which the heterogeneity of the social world threatens' (1989, p. 236, my translation). Not unlike Simmel's approach to differentiation, for both Kracauer and Tenbruck friendship as an intimate relationship can deliver some of the coherence for which moderns yearn. But Simmel was more circumspect concerning the purchase of friendship in the pursuit of coherence:

> Modern culture is constantly growing more objective. Its tissues grow more and more out of impersonal energies and absorb less and less the subjective entirety of the individual. ... This objective character impresses itself upon the sociological structure, so that combinations into which formerly the entire and individual person entered, and which consequently demanded reciprocal knowledge beyond the immediate content of the relationship, are now founded exclusively on this content on its pure objectivity. (1906, p. 448)

Trust in nonintimate personal interactions is now no longer based on full knowledge of the other, as may be the case in small communities, but on 'quantities of knowing and not knowing' with which objective roles are invested. We have knowledge of the other as merchant, as trader, as political leader according to 'what it is necessary to know for the purpose of the relationship in question' (Simmel, 1906, p. 459) . The process of differentiation also effects friendship; 'differentiated friendships' emerge,

> which bind us to one man from the side of sympathy, to another from the side of intellectual community, to a third on account of religious impulses, to a fourth because of common experiences ... They demand that the friends reciprocally refrain from obtruding themselves into the range of interests and feelings not included in the special relationship in each case. (1906, p. 452)

Differentiated friendship does not preclude the possibility of intimacy, though it is constituted by a finely calibrated oscillation between discretion, secrecy, and disclosure, by distance as well as closeness, but not lacking in depth: '[t]he relationship thus bounded and circumscribed by discretion nevertheless has its sources at the center of the whole personality, in spite of the fact that it expresses itself only in a single segment of its periphery' (Simmel, 1906, p. 458). In Simmel, then, friendship retains its central promise of full mutual understanding. But its realization calls for the capacity to sift from differentiated personalities those aspects that give life to intimacy. Similarities alone no longer suffice to strengthen friendships; the recognition of the other as different, and the potential to generate intimate connections from difference, become central to modern friendship. Coherence, then, is something friendship promises; but it can deliver it only to varying degrees. To the degree it does, it can play a vital role in our sense of self, which in friendship is accomplished in specific ways. The precondition for friendship to be able to deliver on the promise of coherence, to offer a home under conditions of homelessness, and to offer the possibility for selves to grow, is that the self be a *social* self.

Social selves, intimate selves, and friendship

Throughout his work Norbert Elias critiqued what he perceived to be the false dichotomy between 'individual' and 'society' in order to argue that the self is in essence relational and therefore unthinkable outside myriad forms of human interdependences. In *The Society of Individuals* (2011) Elias illustrates with a parable the main, and to him incorrect, view of human consciousness that has congealed in Western philosophy:

> On the bank of a broad river, or perhaps on the steep slope of a high mountain, stands a row of statues. They cannot move their limbs. But they have eyes and can see. Perhaps ears as well, that can hear. And they can think. They have 'understanding'. We can assume that they do not see each other, even though they well know that others exist. Each stands in isolation. Each statue in isolation perceives that something is happening on the other side of the river, or the valley. Each forms ideas of what is happening, and broods on the question of how far these ideas correspond to what is happening. Some think that such ideas simply mirror the happenings on the other side. Others think that much is contributed by their own understanding; in the end one cannot know what is going on over there. Each statue forms its own opinion. Everything it knows comes from its own experience. It has always been as it is now. It does not change. It sees. It observes. Something is happening on the other side. It thinks about it. But whether what it thinks corresponds to what is going on over there remains unresolved. It has no way of convincing itself. It is immobile. And alone. The abyss is too deep. The gap unbridgeable. (2011, p. 104)

Elias' statues appear to be made and put in their place by the Western ideal type of the philosopher who, according to Raymond Aron, 'is always starting afresh, as if nothing had been finally established, as if a man isolated by his reflection were questioning himself about the meaning of all actual experiences' (1967, p. 19). The unbridgeable gap these statues face is the gap between inside and outside, individual and society, self and environment, subject and object, which due to our experience of self *vis-à-vis* an outer world is part of our 'natural attitude', as Alfred Schutz (1962) has called our pre-reflexive, 'just so' orientation to the everyday. Conceptually imposed on social life, however, the inside/outside dichotomy, while appearing logically consistent, is false. The *'homo philosophicus'* which the thinking statues represent is a 'closed personality', a *'homo clausus'* that is independent from others as well as fully developed: born as an adult and ontologically static (Elias, 2012a, pp. 512–515, original emphases). So entrenched is this image of the self-sufficient individual in the public imagination that sociologists may find it no mean feat to convince publics otherwise, or even to encourage students to develop that 'sociological imagination' without which we cannot adequately pursue our vocation, and without which, according to C. Wright Mills (2000), individuals can only ever have an inadequate self-awareness.

In order to explain that it is not a closed-off consciousness-box with apertures and a perceiving, calculating processor that is core to our humanness, but the irreducible fact of our sociality, Elias draws on everyday language use, and here on something that is as natural to us as the subject/object dichotomy: our use of personal pronouns. For while in the vocabulary of the thinking statues 'I', 'you', 'she', 'we', 'you' (plural), and 'they' simply reproduce a cognitive separateness on the grammatical level, in Elias' conception there simply is no 'I' without a 'you', a 'she', a 'we', a 'they'. Psychological approaches to child development, especially the object relations paradigm, confirm that perspective. But beyond the maturation process, this holds true for our existence as humans *per se*; it speaks to the reality of our human interdependences. Hence, not only is it 'very misleading to use such concepts as "I" or "ego" independently of their position within the web of relationships to which the rest of the pronouns refer', but 'together, the personal pronouns are in fact an elementary expression of the fact that every person is fundamentally connected to others; that every human individual is fundamentally a social being' (Elias 2012b, p. 119) .

We are, then, both subject and object to ourselves. We are able to imagine ourselves from the standpoint of concrete others. And we orient our thoughts and actions against normative backgrounds – rules and expectations – obtaining in various social environments. Pragmatist philosopher and social psychologist George Herbert Mead called our 'criticizing, approving, and suggesting, and consciously planning' faculty which we always marshal against these backgrounds 'the reflective self' (1964, p. 145). Traversing a long arc that spans modern self-conceptions from the pious subject of the Middle Ages to the inward-turning individual of Romanticism and the analytic subject of the second industrial revolution, Mead mines this reflexive self for its ontology in sociality. From his work onward, there is no more turning back to a philosophical anthropology that could envisage a Lockian pre-social yet conscious individual akin to Elias' statues. For Mead sociality depends on self-awareness, and self-awareness presupposes sociality because it is in interaction that we come to reflect on ourselves. Each individual thinks about their own actions in relation to others' imputed thought processes and actions. Interaction is thus a creative process of mutual interpretations that orient further interactions. Those interpretations rest on our capacity to see ourselves from the perspective of the other and, as we will see further below, in the case of friendship opens us to guidance by friends.

In order to expand on that basic premise, and like Elias drawing on personal pronouns to aid the imagination, Mead proposes an analytic distinction between the 'I' and the 'Me'. The *I* is the seat of our capacity to act creatively both in concert with and against prevailing social norms, be it those that are cognitively grasped, or merely assumed, obtain in face-to-face interaction or in 'the community' or society and culture at large. The *I* acts when interactional 'problems' arise, that is, when habitual action no longer suffices. The normative background to the *I's* activities is internalized in the *Me*, which especially in interaction with others interacts with the *I*. Significantly, Mead does not speak about two separate minds; he makes an analytic distinction of unified thought-processes that are manifest in what he calls the 'inner conversation' (1964, p. 146).[2]

For Mead, the *Me* denotes the internalized will of the general communities to which we belong. What the *Me* internalizes, though, are not only rules and obligations, but also widely held beliefs concerning the way to live a life worth living (e.g. the pursuit of the amorphous American Dream). But on the side of action, the *Me* needs the *I* to marshal its creative powers in order for subjects not to be 'over-determined' and for social change to be explicable. Unlike the provenance of the *Me*, the sources of the *I* are unknown to Mead. They are more or less mysterious, but are expressed in our constant, practical critique of social convention. The tensions between the collective will as lodged in the *Me*, and an *I* that is straining toward individuation, lie at the core of the moral development of individuals, and by extension, that of societies.[3] We might argue that in Mead's rendition of the dialogue between individual and society social norms appear too rigid to do justice to the many contradictory messages to which we are subject in our daily lives; we might argue, as Elias might, that Mead reproduces rather than problematizes the subject/object divide; but we need equally to acknowledge that his was a first comprehensive attempt to conceptualize the human self as emerging from our sociality, from our interactions with the most abstract of institutions to interpersonal relationships with 'significant others'. The self, then, is not merely 'socially constructed'. We can glean from Mead and Elias that our interdependences are what and who we are, because selves are fundamentally relational.

Friendship is one of the many strands that make up that web of interdependences. It gives shape and meaning to that part of ourselves that we perceive as most authentic because it is separate from the public roles and other kinds of private obligations we are asked to perform. As a relationship, friendship has the power to change our relations to self in fundamental ways and, by extension, has the power to change our relation to and position in the world. I want to now begin to draw attention to some of these potentialities of friendship, which emerge from the freedom to be ourselves not because friends allow an unfettered individualism, and not despite the fact that one takes into account another and so is hemmed in by obligation, but precisely *because* there is another with whom we interact in the context of intimacy. In Chapter 3 I discussed the *relational freedom* of friendship as the freedom to relate relatively unencumbered by social prescription, especially when compared to other intimate bonds. Put differently, the freedom *from* publicly imposed norms is also the freedom *to* mutually construct the relationship. In order to explain how that freedom is played out in concrete interaction between two mutually oriented selves, I now go on to elaborate another aspect of friendship's freedom, its *generativity:* the relationally constituted freedom to be ourselves that enables friendship's creativity. In lived experience, of course, the freedom from cultural prescription is inseparable from the creative processes that make, give sense to, and sustain friendship, and so my distinction is purely analytic in order to further investigate central characteristics of this dyadic social relationship. My approach here is phenomenological in a broad sense. I am interested in the intersubjective creation of meaning that orders the 'little worlds' of friendship. Those 'little worlds' are open to the large world in which they are embedded, because friendship straddles both – a peculiar feature of the relationship that, in turn, feeds back into the freedom of friendship.

Generativity: becoming together

If the need for an existential foothold is part and parcel of the experience of modernity, the relational constitution of selves in interpersonal relationships is one of the avenues open to us for gaining a sense of 'home' for ourselves. This theme runs through the sociological literature on intimate life; its best-known figure of thought is that of the family as a 'haven in heartless world' (Lasch, 1995). But in friendship, unlike in the family and also unlike in erotic love, the sense of a coherence is achieved not because prescriptions draw tight boundaries around acceptable actions, but because its relational freedom offers considerable leeway for being ourselves.[4] That freedom of interaction, rather than leading to a kind of free-fall precipitating further existential uncertainties, is grounding precisely because it is bounded by an other; it is a concrete kind of freedom.

None of this is particularly original. Immanuel Kant's call to treat the other as an end and never as a means underpins the modern love ideal, which is thus infused with a morality that 'arrests our self-love', our egotism; freedom of self is found in the willed vulnerability *vis-à-vis* the loved other (Velleman, 1999, p. 360).[5] And following Hegel and Honneth, social recognition in the context of intimacy contributes to our sense of self-confidence because in such relationships the 'limit' that is the other actually constitutes our freedom. Freedom is often envisaged as pertaining to unfettered individual or collective action; this is the principal basis of political and economic liberalism in its crudest forms, for example. It is difficult for us to see any kind of *inter*dependence as contributing to individual freedom, no matter how fictitious the story and achievability of total *in*dependence.

The difference between myth and reality has spurred attempts to rethink the notion of freedom. According to Rousseau, for example, intimacy enables the reconciliation of autonomy and sociability and so saves us from the terrible freedom of loneliness, from being 'condemned to live in solitude' (Todorov, 2002, p. 127). The best-known attempt at conceptual reconciliation is that of Isaiah Berlin's (1969) distinction between a positive freedom *to* fulfill one's own potentials and a negative freedom *from* constraint. In *Das Recht der Freiheit* (2011) Honneth critiques Berlin's negative freedom because it is ideologically wedded to 'a deep-seated intuition of modern individualism' that fails to acknowledge the fundamental sociality of individual freedom (2011, p. 47, my translation). Honneth therefore elaborates a freedom in Hegelian mode. With reference to personal relationships he follows in a tradition of social critique: '[P]ersonal relationships are ... those social relationships in the midst of anonymity and atomization in which the inner nature of humans finds freedom through reciprocal validation' (2011, p. 235, my translation). Following Hegel, Honneth perceives that freedom to be anchored in social institutions because 'the subject is in the final equation only "free" when it meets another in the framework of institutional practices' that enable relations of recognition in the first place (2011, p. 86, my translation).

As I have argued in Chapter 3, however, even on the most abstract level of institutional analysis friendship cannot simply be equated with other intimate relationships, even though it shares common characteristics with them. Moreover, that conflation severely underestimates spontaneous creativity. A small step down the ladder of abstraction, which offers a more differentiated view of intimate relationships, shows that due to its institutional deficit friendship is an extraordinary case. Its relational freedom offers potentials concerning the development of selves, from subtle changes in attitude to thoroughgoing life transformations. I refer to that quality as *generativity*. Let me illustrate what I have in mind by drawing an analogy between the generative freedom of friendship and the freedom obtaining in artistic, creative processes.

I take as my example that kind of improvised music made together by two or more musicians – music that pushes shared knowledge and practices of rhythm and harmony to its outer limits. When all structural boundaries seem to be breached, when polyrhythms brook no 'beat' and harmonic structures allow no center, it is still music – that medium that like no other is able to create, mimic, carry, and directly transmit moods, sentiments, feelings, pathos. That process takes place between musicians, but also between them and actual or perceived audiences. It takes place against the background of musical and social history, however distant – 'original' – the musical expressions may seem. To that extent the creations of a solo musician too are 'social'. Connections to public tastes that have evolved in the history of art, however concrete or tenuous, and interactions with co-creators set boundaries to variety. These connections and interactions make understandable, feel-able, and appreciable that which is 'said'. And hence, however 'free' the music may appear to audiences, it emerges from a freedom of expression that is nevertheless bounded. Even if the musicians decided to give expression to chaos, they still create 'chaos' according to a shared understanding of what it is and isn't, and then hone that diffuse understanding in the creative process itself, that is, through relating. Relating, whether on the immediate level of interaction or on the abstract level of aesthetic history, is in fact inescapable.[6] By extension, total originality, emerging from an individual 'creative genius' who works utterly unfettered by previous or present shared knowledge, is a romantic fiction. The act of creation is limited not only by musicians' technical capacities, but also by the extent to which they are willing to push rhythmic, harmonic, physical, and emotional boundaries. There needs to be a willingness to be vulnerable and take the risk of 'failing' or disappointing others and so to be 'intimate', albeit in highly mediated, artistically expressive form.

All this presupposes trust as a precondition for free, collective expression, although it is qualitatively different from the trust of friendship. Musicians, after all, do not have to be friends in order to create; trust in one another's musicality suffices. But that musicality is multifaceted;

it cannot be reduced to technical prowess (although it is frequently confused with it). Similarities in taste, a fairly equal range of expressive repertoire, an inclination to learn from others, an ability to listen to others while listening to yourself, which requires a nuanced kind of empathy – well expressed by the German *Einfühlsamkeit* – are wound up in that mutual trust, as are an openness to risk rather than the tendency to retreat into the safety of musical platitudes or formulaic patterns. On the basis of a shared trust that all participants will equally contribute their artistic capacities to create freely together, the creative process takes on meaning. The freedom to contribute individually, but always fully alert and spontaneously reactive to the contributions of others, implies to be ready to be guided and interpreted by co-creators who are equally open to being guided and interpreted. These are vital aspects of the interactions' generative dynamism that gives life to the whole.

The generativity of friendship works similarly, although there are important differences. One such difference is that the trust relationship that is friendship operates in the context of affection and care. Instrumental attitudes can thus at times be accommodated *because* of the friendship, although they undermine the friendship when it becomes solely a means to ends. On the basis of that intimacy, vulnerability too takes on a different meaning. Because here intimacy, although it can be mediated by common interest, is aimed at the other as person *qua* person (Suttles, 1970), vulnerability is about the disarming of our own emotional defenses. The stakes then are different when compared to musical collaboration, where risk is more likely to pertain to the fear of judgment concerning musical capacities and artistic contributions. In friendship trust mitigates the risk concerning intimacy, because it assuages the fear of humiliation, shame, or embarrassment.

There is yet another affinity between the generativity of music and friendship, however, that needs pointing out. In artistic endeavors the imperative of authenticity looms large. Amongst musicians (as amongst writers), this is usually expressed as the search for 'your own voice'. Imitation, although an important part of the learning process of any art, is by and large shunned as 'derivative' or at least seen as something to be left behind on the way to authentic expression. In collective improvisation, it is those individual originalities that are supposed to be brought together; imitation ('quoting') may signal *homage* to known artists or works and so can be woven into original material, but cannot be its substitute. If musicians were to continuously mimic one another in a performance, chances are the music would quickly start to sound mundane and uninteresting to most. The mimetic analogue in friendship is the notion that friends mirror one another. That notion, a mainstay in Western conceptions of friendship since antiquity, runs counter to the generativity that marks friendship.

From mirroring to generativity

From Plato and Aristotle to Cicero, Montaigne, and Bacon, and on into the present, the friend has often been described as a mirror self. Indeed, that view cannot be simply dismissed. There are, for example, societies in which it is more than a view: it structures social relationships. Again, relationships among the Swat Pukhtun of Northern Pakistan, which we encountered briefly in the previous chapter, provide an example. The impossibility of trusting, intimate relationships in that society is thrown into relief by a friendship ideal that – logically in the absence of trust – is self-referential through and through. According to Lindholm's psychoanalytic reading, among the Swat Pukhtuns '[n]o other object is available, and love is then displaced onto the realm of the ideal' (1982, p. 269). In reality, only outsiders are possible candidates for friendship, which is further complicated by the fact that this expansionist society 'acts with rapacity to those who are exterior to it' (Lindholm, 1982, p. 244). On the level of the ideal, the relationship is conceived of as essentially narcissistic. Given meaning by the metaphor of the identical twin, one gives everything to the other, but that imagined self-abnegation in fact risks nothing, since the other, just as selfless, doesn't want to receive anything. 'In a very real sense, the friend *is* ego' (1982, p. 242, original emphasis), and in another very real sense that orientation precludes realization of the ideal, so structuring a perpetual cycle of internal distrustfulness, structural impossibilities for friendship formation, and cultural idealization. The Pukhtun case illustrates the mirror view's shortcomings: not only is there the practical impossibility of finding another self; this vision entails an absence of intimacy and so of generativity.

In our own societies there is no firm consensus as to whether similarity is a necessary condition for intimate personal relationships. In Anglophone communities at least, 'like attracts like' is less commonly expressed in everyday speech than 'opposites attract', though the latter usually refers to love relationships rather than friendship as explanation, and sometimes justification, for tensions. When it comes to friends, we are more likely to agree that they are similar to us; that they have similar interests, similar political views, cultural tastes, and dislikes. Since about the middle of the 20th century sociologists have been mainly concerned with similarities in class and status, something that came to be known by the term 'status homophily' (Lazarsfeld & Merton, 1964). The concept refers to the propensity to form friendships with others of similar social position, cultural background, sexual orientation, and the like. We will revisit that concept in Chapter 5. For now I'm concerned with the assumption that friends mirror each other in terms of their interests and 'character' in order to think through the notion that intimate friendship can generate changes in self-perception, interests, and experiences.

Similarities tend to lead to an affirmation of 'what is', rather than pointing to new possibilities. Dean Cocking and Jeanette Kennett (1998) have argued that dissimilarities are much more likely to be generative. To illustrate, they ask us to think about two friends one of whom is 'cautious' and the other 'reckless': '[t]hese friends recognize the contrast between their characters .... Far from being extrinsic to the friendship these dissimilar features are features in respect of which they are friends and which govern much of the interplay between them' (1998, p. 507). The mirror view not only evokes Elias' silent statues, but is commensurate with the tendency in both philosophy and sociology to perceive human beings as fully matured and independent, who, reflected back to us by the friend as an 'objective presentation' of our character, perceive their inherent, already existing potentials which they then only need to activate or actualize. On that view, I might for example acquire an interest in something that my friend finds interesting simply because deep down I already have a nascent interest in that activity or issue, or already possess an as-yet-unrealized capacity. My friend simply helps me become aware of these. To draw on the improvised music analogy, that would amount to saying that musicians bring out in one another what is already there, rather than allowing for spontaneous learning during the creative process because we are receptive to one another. Against that view, the self in friendship is subject to change because friends are 'characteristically and distinctively receptive to being directed and interpreted and so in these ways drawn by the other' (Cocking & Kennett, 1998, p. 503). As a consequence, I am receptive to the other's interests. I might, for instance, agree to go to the ballet with my friend even though I have never been interested in it. I might turn down similar requests by others, and when I agree to accompany my friend I do not 'go begrudgingly or out of an sense of obligation'. I might even learn to appreciate ballet, and 'typically, I will at least be interested in understanding and appreciating it, simply because she loves it'. Even if I do not develop an interest in the art form, my participation does shore up the relationship. Thus we build similarities. What really matters, however, is 'the distinctive kind of responsiveness to the other, which mediates any such move toward similarity, [and] that characterizes ... friendship' (Cocking & Kennett, 1998, p. 504), which is something that common interests alone cannot guarantee. Meeting others with whom we share a lot in common does not simply raise the probability of intimacy. Again, it is the preparedness and inclination to be guided in our interests, a mutual receptivity that makes us want to participate in, or find something out about, what the other likes because, simply put, we *like* them, feel affection and care for them, are attracted to them in some way as *people qua people*, for more, that is, than just what they are 'into'.

But that relationship of mutual 'drawing', as Cocking and Kennett term it, is not like a relationship between leader and follower, nor teacher and student. 'The friend is not a guru who possesses the truth', says Francesco Alberoni. 'The friend's revelation is not a lesson. It is a common arrival at the same conclusion from different viewpoints. It is a convergence in truth' by two equal interactants, each of whom can say, 'yes, it is true; this is who I am and *what I want to be*' (Alberoni, 2009, p. 24, my translation and emphasis). Alberoni lets Henry Miller, who in *The Tropic of Capricorn* reflects on a friendship, make his point: 'Hamilton', Miller writes,

> opened my eyes and gave me new values, and though later I was to lose the vision which he had bequeathed me, nevertheless I could never again see the world, or my friends, as I had seen them prior to his coming. Hamilton altered me profoundly, as only a rare book, a rare personality, a rare experience, can alter one. For the first time in my life I understood what it was to experience a vital friendship and yet not to feel enslaved or attached because of the experience. Never, after we parted, did I feel the need of his actual presence: he had given himself completely and I possessed him without being possessed. It was the first clean, whole experience of friendship, and it was never duplicated by any other friend. Hamilton was friendship itself, rather than a friend. (cited in Alberoni, 2009, pp. 24–25)

Like Cocking and Kennett, Alberoni insists that scholars have overstated similarity as a marker of friendship. In his view '[t]o know means to face the other, to compare, to distinguish', something that cannot be achieved 'through mimetic fascination' (2009, p. 25, my translation). But Alberoni also reminds us that the images we have of one another need in some ways to be compatible; not, however, to the extent that there 'remains nothing to discover'. At the same time 'excessive dissonance' leads to such fundamental reciprocal misapprehensions that friendship is either impossible or wilts (2009, p. 15, my translation). Richard Wollheim's contention that friendship is about 'the exercise of a capacity to perceive, a willingness to respect, and a desire to understand the difference between persons' well expresses attitudes and orientations that go beyond the mutual validation of similarity (cited in Vernon, 2006, p. 148).

Cocking and Kennett do not simply object to the mirror view because it raises the specter of narcissism. What they do object to,

> is simply that the mirror view misrepresents the depth and nature of the engagement which [intimate] friends[7] have with each other and the impact which each has on the other. For you do not passively reflect my own characteristics; what you give back to me is not a reflection, but an *interpretation* of me, and for this you do not need to be like me. The portrait painter does not aim to produce a mirror image of her subject. Though she is appropriately constrained by and sensitive to her subject her role is not that of a copyist. She is not neutral with respect to her subject. Rather, a good artist draws her subject in a new light; she influences and enriches our sense of the person portrayed. So, too, do our close friends *draw* us and so enrich our sense of self through their engaged interpretations of us. ... We are thus, to some significant extent, each other's creators. (1998, p. 509, my emphases)

This mutual 'drawing' is the practical translation of friendship's generativity; and it is, for these authors, also a necessary condition – what they call 'acceptance condition' – for friendship, far more necessary than the much-written-about need for similarity and, as we shall see later, the equally oft-mentioned imperative of mutual disclosure. What we have here is Honneth's first and fundamental form of recognition – love – in action. Engaged in a relationship based on mutual trust, reciprocity, and equality, the drawing account constitutes a description of intersubjective recognition in so far as it enables not just 'being oneself in another', but for each to flourish in that relationship. In cases where the relationship gives impetus for positive life changes, this form of recognition enables the gaining of recognition for (newly discovered) capacities that happen to be societally validated in a given place and time and so generates 'self-esteem' (Honneth, 1996, pp. 121–130). The emphasis is on mutuality. If I am being validated by others – whether associations, institutions, organizations, states or individuals – that I do not respect, no recognition can ensue. Likewise, I can only be interpreted and let myself be guided by my friend in any positive sense if I am open and truthful about myself and the things that matter to me. If not, I will be misinterpreted, or simply have an image reflected back to me that confirms the impression I wanted to give. Rather than recognition, it is simply a validation of my impression management skills and has nothing to do with the will to vulnerability that intimacy presupposes.

Honneth's recognition through 'love' encompasses all intimate relationships, with the parent–child relationship figuring as the original source of (mis)recognition, with fundamental consequences on individuals' relation to self. Some differences between parent–child relationships, erotic love, and friendship are therefore worth pointing out. While it is intuitive that, as has been shown many times over, parental recognition can have lasting effects on the positive development of children that flow on into adulthood, we should note that friendship as a practical relation of recognition can have similar effects throughout the life course, even though the developmental-psychological premises are entirely different because, for one, relations of authority are absent. Whatever the repertoire of parental support, these are not equal relationships. At least for a considerable time, parents by necessity take the lead in emotional, physical, and material terms. Later, a good measure of psychological independence is necessary for children's individuation. In principle, none of this precludes the possibility of the kind of intimacy under discussion here; philosophers have in fact made affirmative arguments for it, although they have narrowed friendship to Aristotle's value-laden conception of friendships of virtue, or 'character friendship' (e.g. Kristjánsson, 2006). Especially when broadened out beyond the intersubjective constitution of a virtuous life, the fact remains that the psychological and social premises are therefore typically very different from friendship (Kupfer, 1990; Jamieson, 1998). In most Western cultural milieux, at least for a considerable part of the earlier life course, teens and young adults are not likely to want to 'hang out' with their parents. Parents are also the least likely people to be befriended by young *Facebook* users because they need space in which they can be and act unmonitored by their guardians (Livingstone, 2008). Consider also that while many parent–child relationships 'sustain lifelong flows of assistance', in friendship support 'is unlikely to be sustained without mutual liking and intimacy', merely on the basis of obligation (Jamieson, 1998, p. 165). Whatever the *individual* possibilities of a given parent–child relationship, *typically* expectations and obligations are structured differently to those obtaining in friendship. To the extent that these have to be negotiated, family and friendship connote different kinds of relationship.

We could argue quite plausibly that guidance and interpretation are essential generative dynamics in erotic love relationships. However, unlike in love, in friendship life trajectories are not centered on a common, 24/7 project that includes shared housework, often centers on children over and above the dyad, and is supposed to include sex (Jamieson, 1998, p. 164). Friendship is not about coupledom. Friends 'never seek to consume each other or fall into a perpetual embrace' (Vernon, 2006, p. 148), and so the relationship does not '"normally" result in a total self-abandon, which is a prerogative of most intensive erotic love' (Markus, 2010b, p, 17) . That does, on the other hand, not mean that lovers cannot, or do not, draw one another. Far from it. But it does mean that the consequences of that mutual drawing will have consequences for the relationship to the extent that both life courses, intertwined as they are, are affected in crucial ways. Whereas in friendship transformations of self can be generated that may or may not affect the practical maintenance of the bond, love relationships center on the relationship as such; individual change is only desirable, therefore, as long as 'the relationship', rather than each separate individual, stands to gain. That is one way to understand Giddens' assertion that in contemporary love 'the relationship is its own forum' (1992, p. 194). Consider also that the generative potential of love is highly circumscribed. 'Public stories' (Jamieson, 1998), about the 'proper' way to live out coupledom, while never determinative, and while they need to be considered across contexts of class, gender and cultural background, do persist as guiding frames of reference (see also, Gross, 2005). Their reality is affirmed by the fact that practices that do not fall within them are interpreted as 'alternative'. So, at the same time as friendship may be a significant part of our lives, there is also less at stake because life plans and projects tend not to hinge on the relationship.

That is not to say that friendship is an unproblematic relationship. Quite apart from the fact that '[t]he greater the intimacy of the pair ... the larger the number of conflicts that can arise' (Becker & Useem, 1942, p. 15), the very fact of friendship's relational freedom, that its modalities differ from relationship to relationship because its 'terms and conditions' lack the institutional frame that gives a certain fixity of meaning to other personal bonds, by force includes the possibility of hurt (Smart et al., 2012). And so it includes the possibility that selves are 'distorted', because in all cases where personal relationships become fraught with tensions, uncertainties, and anxieties, where disrespect and distrust rear their heads, misrecognition can lead to a fundamental questioning of relations to self and undermine people's self-confidence (Honneth, 1996). These realities, in other words, do not so much indicate what is particular to friendship, but rather what is general to all intimate relationships. The intention here is not to gloss over the less than salutary aspects of friendship. Understanding that friendship has the power to change relations to self and so one's life in fundamental ways only highlights the significant psychological and emotional damage that the absence or demise of intimacy can cause.

Generativity and disclosing intimacy

Another common way to think about intimacy is in terms of mutual self-disclosure. According to that view, I express my trust in my friend to the extent to which I am willing to divulge sensitive, personal information and to confide secrets. Surely, then, the generativity of friendship has something to do with how free people feel to self-disclose, and surely under conditions where the therapeutic ethos suffuses all relations self-disclosure here too must be of prime significance. I suggest that, while important, intimacy cannot be reduced to self-disclosure. We could argue, for instance, that the link between intimacy and disclosure is especially tenuous in a culture in which people regularly turn private information into public consumables. The proviso here would be, however, that people do not simply divulge everything about themselves in every context, but for the most part manage to sift what can be divulged without negative consequences from what they need to keep to themselves (Wohlrab-Sahr, 2011). As I will briefly raise in the concluding chapter, the real issue of concern may be the collective lowering of the normative threshold of what counts as private through everyday practices (Blatterer, 2010).

Since publication of Giddens' *The Transformation of Intimacy* (1992), sociologists have more or less agreed that the effective communication of feeling states has become *the* requirement for fulfilling intimate relationships. This essentially middle-class view of what love is all about neatly maps on to such taken-for-granted tropes as 'emotional intelligence', and is blind to growing material disparities, but also differences in cultural background and gender. Jamieson summarizes, and then marshals empirical research against, 'the claim that a particular form of intimacy, "disclosing intimacy" – a process of two or more people mutually sustaining deep knowing and understanding, through talking and listening, sharing thoughts, showing feelings – is increasingly sought in personal life', including friendship (Jamieson 1998, p. 158).[8]

According to Jamieson, friendship based on disclosing intimacy is an ideal; there is no empirical evidence that disclosure is becoming central to friendship. When people were asked whether they have 'true' or 'real' friends, affirmative answers have a strong middle-class bias, with relative access to time and material resources appearing to be significant factors, at least going by the (now fairly dated) UK research she cites (Jamieson, 1998, pp. 89–93). For her, then, disclosing intimacy is only one kind of intimacy that even though ubiquitous in public stories about intimate relationships, intersects with material and practical conditions. Supportive action, on this view, speaks louder than words.

And still. It seems to me that there are culturally shared communicative repertoires that separate the purchase that disclosure has in erotic love relationships from the purchase it typically has in friendship. Again, these differences are also connected to the place either relationship is given, both in the culture at large and in actual interactions: the relationship as project; the 'intervention' of children; housework and the shared everyday, to name some mundane aspects of the love relationship that raise disclosing intimacy to quite a different order of significance than in friendship. Moreover, sexuality is central to erotic love and so it is *passion* as realized and 'consummated' in the relationship that most obviously distinguishes these types of relationships. This is precisely the point that Francesco Alberoni makes, and he explains it by drawing attention to the German for passion: *Leidenschaft. Leiden* is to suffer. Being in love, then, is both ecstasy and torment, the torment, for instance, of inequality because, unlike friendship, love needs no reciprocity; the torment of not knowing, of uncertainty and so the need for questions begging disclosure in order to be reassured of the other's love ('She loves me, she loves me not', as daisy petals fall; 'Where have you been?'; 'Who were you with'?). 'The prayer for love', writes Alberoni, 'is a cry of desperation', and then reflects, '[t]his is the mystery of love: that one can only ask, and never cease asking, even if the other is indifferent or hostile (2009, pp. 14, 15, my translation). The unknowability of love and hence the requirement of continual reassurance positively sanctions jealousy as proof of love, but also repudiates it as an impediment to it. Disclosing intimacy is then to a certain extent built into the modern love ideology, irrespective of whether a certain percentage, or even a majority of research subjects, report not to engage in disclosure much at all. And here it is not simply the disclosure of intimate secrets – or even the injunction that we ought not to have secrets from our partner – that is part of the love ideology; it is, above all, its neat connection to therapy culture and its institutions, and the reproduction of that culture in a range of artifacts, that disclosure takes place, and so makes contemporary love strongly wedded to talk (Illouz, 2007, 2008; Swidler, 2001). As we have seen in Chapter 3, the same does not hold true for friendship.

While it is important to keep in mind the different roles acts of disclosure may play in different types of relationships, it is important not to reduce intimacy to disclosure. Cocking and Kennett agree that this is especially the case for friendship. As we have seen, they mount their argument that mutual drawing is a necessary condition for intimate friendship against the mirror view. But they also dispute what they call 'the secrets view of friendship', a view that, like Laurence Thomas', holds that the idea 'of deep friends not confiding in one another seems almost unthinkable' (cited in Cocking & Kennett, 1998, p. 515). From that perspective, disclosing intimacy as the conveyor of trust is not only the central marker of friendship; people who tend to divulge private information in public forums are incapable of friendship. That trust is conveyed because we make ourselves vulnerable and in so doing put the other in a privileged position to guide, interpret, and comment on our lives. For all the plausibility of that perspective, what's at issue is the significance of mutual disclosure in friends being able to draw one another, and so to generate the potential for developing selves. Is it sufficient, then, to conceptualize friendship as disclosing intimacy?

The answer becomes clearer when we put the question differently: do those relationships that involve the sharing of deeply private information, even information we would tell no one else, qualify as friendship? Firstly, we might share that kind of information not only in one-way situations such as religious confession or therapy, but also engage in mutual sharing with strangers on a plane; and we might do so not because they are friends, but because they are strangers; because we are unlikely to see them again, precisely, that is, because we feel there is little 'danger' that a lasting relationship might eventuate. These are self-contained transactions in hermetically sealed contexts with intimacy either undesirable or short-term and optional. Secondly, while it is true that we take an active interest in what makes our friends 'tick' – what they care about, their views and values, interests and experiences – that is not the same as believing that only the disclosure of those things that are most private, the confession of 'secrets' I hold dearest, is the mark of intimacy. It is something else: that I have chosen to share the things I value and really matter to me with the friend *as a person I like*, as a person for whom I feel affection and for whom I care. And surely that includes many private issues and concerns, albeit as a consequence of intimacy rather than a condition of it. 'For what we value and how we choose to share what we value is also in part determined in and by our friendship' (Cocking & Kennett, 1998, p. 518). Cocking and Kennett's drawing account decenters disclosure both in the sense of disclosure of self *in* an other (mirroring) and disclosure *to* an other, and in so doing shows the generativity of friendship to be its central characteristic.

We should also remember that with intimacy comes a responsibility to protect. Affection and care are not simply expressed by disclosing endless streams of private information, but also by learning and then respecting where the others' boundaries lie; what type of information merely challenges the friends' views, and what type of information may hurt. Albeit in a different context, and as part of another argument, Richard Sennett warned of 'the tyrannies of intimacy', by which he meant the replacement of a 'public realm of impersonal meaning and impersonal action' by an ethos of personality and personal behavior that blocks our ability to see that which really matters in politics: power as its internal logic and chief aim (Sennett, 1977, p. 339). There is something in Sennett that can nudge us to remain circumspect about the cultural ideal of disclosing intimacy. 'The expectation is that when relations are close, they are warm; it is an intense kind of sociability which people seek out in attempting to remove the barriers to intimate contact', says Sennett and then goes on to alert us that 'this expectation is defeated by the act' (1977, p. 338). With a little twisting to bring that statement to bear on the intimate sphere, it contains a warning about a kind of bare-all intimacy that, devoid of discretion, seeks to bulldoze itself into the heart and soul of another. Disclosure for disclosure's sake, even honesty for honesty's sake, does not prove intimacy; it fails the test of affection, care, and respect because it lacks the respect for the other's privacy. Rather, friends are willing and able to bridge differences and, far from having constantly to be brutally honest, have the capacity to balance discretion and disclosure, distance as well as closeness. 'Friendship', according to the German author and playwright Sigmund Graff, 'is an art of distance, just as love is an art of nearness' (cited in Beier, 1997, p. 363). Indeed, the equilibrium of friendship can be seriously thrown out of kilter by unreflected-upon revelations. In order to maintain 'equality and structural balance within friendship', disclosure is calibrated rather than assumed to be bare-all and unconditional (Allen cited in Misztal, 1996, p. 190). The degree of that calibrating 'emotion work' (Hochschild, 1979) differs from friendship to friendship, though it is not subject to public conventions in the way this is the case for acquaintanceship, Simmel's quintessential relationship of discretion. Rather than running counter to trust, balancing disclosure and non-disclosure is possible because friendship's freedom allows for the fine-tuning of mutual sensibilities over time, including the development of no-holds-barred exchanges if the friendship happens to develop in that direction.

To say that disclosing intimacy has been over-valued in friendship is not to diminish the role of disclosure and least of all is it meant to disavow the importance of open communication between friends. Clearly, this is an important part of the relationship. In fact, to repudiate that a mutual opening up, the exchange of private information, of 'eye level' communication is a significant aspect of friendship would be highly problematic from a gender perspective on intimacy, because it would valorize a masculine take on intimacy (see Chapter 5). The point, rather, is to put disclosing intimacy in its place: it is not a necessary condition, but part of an interactional repertoire of friendship that expresses its symmetrical, generalized reciprocity. That 'does not mean that the information must be "exchanged" for information; it requires only an openness and sincerity about the problems that matter to each of the partners' (Markus, 2010b, p. 22, ff. 8) – an openness and sincerity from which disclosing intimacy is *generated* and whose contents and qualities change over time. In that process communication is clearly central.[9] How else do we get to know one another, sort out our commonalities and compatible dissimilarities, whether or not we like each other, and what potential the friendship may promise? What I cannot undertake in this particular context is a detailed conversational analysis of typical friendship communications. What I will go on to do, however, is to place the generative potentialities of friendship in a context that is unique among the variety of interpersonal relationships. For while modern friendship is a private and personal relationship, its relational terrain – to draw on a common spatial metaphor – stretches across the private and the public spheres. That situation is born out in the communicative possibilities of the relationship; and it is therefore decisive concerning the role of friendship *vis-à-vis* other relationships as well as the role it can play in the relational development of selves.

Friendship between the public and the private

We distinguish between what is public and what private by drawing boundaries. Subject to social change, these boundaries are continuously shifting. For this reason sociologists have advocated for a 'threshold analysis' that keeps in view 'a unity of difference' (Wohlrab-Sahr, 2011, p. 37, my translation) by keeping both eyes on either side of the socially constituted boundaries as it were, and by remaining alert to their constant re-constitution on all levels of social interaction, including everyday communication that affirms, challenges, or subverts this 'grand dichotomy' (Weintraub, 1997). For example, limiting the number of individuals that are privy to information is one way to delimit privacy in interaction. In that sense the dyad is the most exclusive of all social relationships. Sometimes boundaries are drawn when two individuals communicate, verbally or not, in the presence of others (think of the 'inside joke'). The entrusting to another person of intimate 'secrets' or personal information creates a sense of privacy, because it obliges interactants to handle information with sensitivity and discretion. Gossip is an example of private communication that lies right on the borders between private secrecy and public disclosure and requires what Bergmann (1993) has called 'discreet indiscretions'. Here privacy is delimited by the act of disclosure of sensitive information about third others to trusted parties. There is a tension here in 'the *discrepancy between the collective public denunciation and the collective private practicing of gossip*' (Bergmann, 1993, p. 21, original emphases). The boundaries run through the gap between the general lip service paid to everyday morality, and the ubiquity of gossiping practices that, far from incidental, also serve to shore up power, establish group cohesion, and reaffirm the everyday moral order.

Communication between friends takes on specific qualities due to its position between the public and private spheres, a position that enables a friend's 'freedom of expression'. The freedom of the relationship is to a significant extent communicative because it is here, in the company of someone with whom I feel at home, someone with whom, as Emerson suggested, 'I may think aloud' (cited in Vernon, 2006, pp. 157–158). Talk (as well as actions) with friends shores up trust and so affirms the relationship, which in turn cannot be divorced from what I suggest to be a central role of friendship: it provides friends with a break from public convention. Intimate friends may express ideas, or vent emotions or sentiments, that are very different from those they present to acquaintances, colleagues, and even family, and find the space to speak their minds not because friendship is a critique-free zone, but because friends do not censor one another. But friendship also offers relief from the potentially claustrophobic self-referentiality of love relationships and so helps to sustain them. Friendship is thus not only 'subversive' of public convention (Suttles, 1970; Eisenstadt & Roniger, 1984), but can also serve to strengthen the shelter of intimacy in erotic love by opening that shelter to the outside. Following long historical developments, friendship, though a personal and private relationship that belongs to the inner sanctum of the intimate sphere, is sufficiently open to the public to be located in a threshold position between the two main spheres of social activity. That position, central to friendship's free-floating status, is borne out in interaction and especially in communication.[10] That at least is the proposition I will now go on to explore in order to further elaborate on friendship's generative possibilities.

Subverting propriety, sustaining intimacy

The relational freedom of friendship contains the potential of subversion. For instance, in the sphere of justice, friendship runs counter to the impartiality that, in modern societies, is seen as absolutely central to the functioning of an equitable, just, legal system (Rawls, 2009). Friendship is antithetical to justice in the public realm and so threatens to subvert due process. In the political sphere, dyadic friendship gives rise to the suspicion of nepotism, and in any case is, like love, perceived egotistical and thus unable to provide political and moral theory with much that can be generalized out beyond private life in order to show what really matters: public utility. So conceived, friendship is antithetical to (public) political life, which by definition is about 'the commons' rather than individual concerns.[11] These are essentially defensive assumptions; they seek to uphold basic principles of democratic governance, that, however imperfectly they may be practiced, are principles worth aspiring to. The suspicion concerning friendship's public utility misapprehends the structural location of friendship, something I will discuss below. It is unlikely, however, that friendship – as a social formation rather than single instances – will seriously challenge the social order. Why, then, the suspicion? One plausible answer is that the increasing rationalization of social relationships that has occurred in Western societies, especially since the late 17th century, and as most consistently theorized by Max Weber, implies that 'the tendency develops in many societies to perceive ... [noninstrumental] friendship in particular as *slightly subversive* to the institutionalized order, to fully institutionalized relationships' (Eisenstadt & Roniger, 1984, p. 18, my emphasis). That 'slight subversion', I argue, is most evident in friendship's everyday alleviating function[12] *vis-à-vis* both public conventions and private institutionalized norms.

Friendship's freedom fills a gap between, on the one hand, formal and informal norms, including that inchoate but strongly assimilated assembly of moral injunctions, sometimes known as 'public standards of decency' or 'community standards', and on the other hand, the myriad feelings, inclinations, desires, hopes, and aspirations especially concerning the contents of individual, self-directed lives. In that in-between space friends may allow each other, and friendship may encourage, 'violations of public propriety' that cement trust, because 'they betray a sort of bedrock reality in individual character', that sends cues concerning that person's 'real self' as 'he has signaled some portion of himself not susceptible to social control' (Suttles, 1970, p. 103). These 'violations' affirm and deepen the sense of trust in the other and, in turn, generate further willingness concerning mutual guidance and interpretation. Just as in the case of disclosing intimacy friendship cannot be reduced to these subversive moments or potentialities. But they signal eligibility as well as ineligibility for friendship to others. 'Where individuals violate the rules of public propriety and find themselves in uncritical hands', says Suttles, 'the first steps toward friendship have already been made'. Once friendship emerges on the basis of the promise that here friends can truly be themselves, they permit the development of 'fellow feeling not based upon a common set of [public] norms and values but a shared attitude expressed *toward* norms and values' (Suttles, 1970, p. 106, original emphasis). For Suttles, then,

> the logic of friendship is a simple transformation of the rules of public propriety into their opposite. Friends can touch each other where strangers cannot. Friends can swear or become exceptionally pious around one another. Friends can entertain subversive or utopian political ideologies that would be laughed at in public circumstances. If, tomorrow, it became publicly proper for strangers to spit upon meeting one another, friends would probably assume that they have the right to neglect this duty. (1970, p. 116)

And it is this shared attitude toward public norms and values that feeds back into the relational freedom of friendship, because '[l]ike partners in crime, individuals find themselves bound together in a *private morality* where the chief guidelines are their own expressed sentiments' (Suttles, 1970, p. 119, my emphasis).

Suttles' account may, at times, overstate the institutional qualities of friendship; not unlike Honneth, he considers the limiting aspects of friendship interaction that exist by virtue of collaborative norm-building on the basis of trust and reciprocity as sufficient to assign friendship a place in the raft of social institutions. As I have already argued, such approaches underestimate friendship's institutional deficit. Also, Suttles' account is overly 'functionalist' in the sense that it sees friends' violations of public propriety as contributing to societal equilibrium: violations are contained and thus non-threatening to the social order. That argument is tautological. If it was true that friendship is society's way to guard against potentially destructive forces, by Suttles' own logic we might expect friends to challenge those societal quarantining propensities. Others have argued the exact opposite. For Alberoni (1984), for example, intimacy is a 'nascent state' of social movements for change. The point to take from Suttles, however, is that friendship's subversion of public norms and conventions generates the construction of a private morality that pervades this 'little world'.

The private moralities of given friendships are, to invoke Emerson once again, built on the knowledge that here we 'may think aloud'. But thinking aloud is risky, because we may at times think the unthinkable. But because it personifies trust, friendship allows us to speak the unspeakable, to say what not only from the standpoint of the public, but even against our own better judgment, may well be considered indecent, questionable, problematic: the feminist may, for a time, become sexist, the leftist conservative, the tolerant intolerant, the open-hearted mean-spirited. Friends will make these allowances because they recognize one another's human fallibility. It is the existence of such possibilities that, beyond the Aristotelian notion that intimate friendship is only possibly between the virtuous, marks 'the beauty of friendship' (Heller, 1998).

That alleviating function of friendship is not only confined to the sense of control we might feel about *public* norms, values, and conventions, but includes other intimate relationships. In fact, the notion that friendship can subvert love rests significantly on a shared understanding that not only lovers but also friends are confidants, and that confidants may offer counsel to one another not only regarding work and common interests, but also about their respective partners. Add to that the self-referentiality of love that goes hand in hand with culturally reproduced uncertainties, the weakening but persistent pressure that couples ought to head down a relatively narrowly conceived path of marriage, children, and mortgages, and we get a fairly claustrophobic image of 24/7 love. Being able to provide a window out from those confines, friendship can diffuse the psychological and emotional intensity of the intimate sphere.

But friendship too needs a web of affiliations. According to Markus, friendship's threshold position is shored up in so far as 'the intimate sphere alone is much too narrow for friendship':

> Friendship does not really thrive here, it wilts. It not only suffocates in the enclosed atmosphere of the intimate, but its exclusive restriction to the sphere of intimacy contributes to the further overloading of the intimate sphere itself. For such a full inclusion of friendship leaves the intimate sphere without a channel which could provide relief and which, at the same time, would be able to transmit the innovative impulses from this part of life into the public occupied by another type of personal relationship, by love, which needs shelter in order to thrive. (Markus, 2010b, p. 19)

The threshold position of friendship, then, may 'subvert' love. Jealousy concerning a friend, for instance, is most likely motivated when more than friendly attraction is suspected. This is a persistently effective barrier to the formation of cross-sex friendships, as we will see in Chapter 6. But friendship may also be seen as subversive when the 'secret' life of lovers is discussed or problematized. But that subversion may well turn out to be a blessing:

> Erotic love has its own pathos streaming from its own emotional and sensual intensity. But because erotic, sexual love is satiable, it needs friendship in order to sustain and to renew itself, by opening to new impulses from outside, which friendship ... is able to transmit. (Markus, 2010b, p. 18)

All this points to the fact that assigning friendship a place on either side of the shifting boundaries between the public and the private domains is no easy task. Friendship is a private, personal, and intimate relationship that needs 'outside' stimulus; the stimulus of common interests, of conversations about what's going on 'out there' in the world, rather than 'in here' in the relationship. And it is this openness to the outside that not only nourishes friendship; so nourished, it is also able to play a sustaining role in love. More concretely, we can think about those instances where friends periodically spend time with each other away from their partners, and so break the routine aspects of coupledom. Friends may lend a willing ear to some issues that have emerged between lovers and may give advice or offer a new perspective. Or, they might regularly socialize with the couple, and include their own partner, which opens the love relationships out to interactions that diffuse love's inward focus.

Friendship in love

But there is a more complicated case, though it is also the one that is most settled in the public imagination: the notion that a fulfilling love relationship needs to be underpinned by friendship. 'My husband/wife/ partner is also my best friend', is therefor a fairly common statement. In fact, Giddens' pure relationship model is often read as friendship with sex added on. Again, this ignores the many issues couples have to deal with, and that friends do not as a rule have to negotiate. From a perspective that recognizes the practical differences in obligations, expectations, and activities, the commonsense ideal sits oddly with realities. But even when, as Giddens has it, justice, equality, respect, and reciprocity, which are integral to friendship, have become part and parcel of a pure model of love, there are legitimate doubts that can be raised about the extent to which these ideals are realized. In this respect Jamieson's (1999) critique is significant indeed; and it can be both updated and extended by reminding ourselves of issues such as intimate partner violence, or the unequal division of household labor and child-care across the so-called 'developed' countries (OECD, 2013; Raley et al., 2013; Magaraggia, 2013; Magaraggia & Cherubini, 2013).

The common sense notion, then, that love needs friendship to sustain it thus appears to originate in a felt (if not always articulated) sense that erotic love is somehow deficient; that the sexual component of erotic love, which in the heteronormative imaginary divides lovers from friends, is recognized as insufficient for the maintenance of fulfilling relationships, notwithstanding the mid-twentieth century combination of therapeutic discourse and feminist struggles aimed at liberating sexuality. That 'new cultural model of intimacy' is explicit in films, such as many of Woody Allen's, which portray women's journey through dysfunctional relationships only to find freedom, and invariably sexual freedom. Masters and Johnson's *The Pleasure Bond* has been singled out as canonical in a transformation of intimacy that moved sex center stage (Illouz, 2007, pp. 27–28).

Jagose, taking her cues from Seidman's cultural history charting the eroticization of romantic love, and the eventual valuation of sex for its own sake, delivers important critical insights on the matter. Seidman argues cogently that, for instance via an increasingly available marital advice literature, sexual techniques were raised to central status in the catalogue of learnable strategies whose correct deployment promised marital bliss. Sex came to communicate love, and rather than emotional and spiritual connection came to signify its presence. This valorization of love led, by the 20th century, to its increasing autonomization. Becoming ever more important as a highly personal mode of expression, it also became steadily impersonal, and as recreational sex came to figure as an end in itself, 'accru[ing] an independent worth as a vehicle for pleasure and self-actualization' (Jagose, 2012, p. 84).

What Seidman interprets as a 'double bind' whereby a public debate vacillated between the sexual and spiritual accounts of love depending on who was speaking – reformers or Puritans – Jagose perceives 'a single logic [that] structures the double bind of modern sex', namely 'the alienation of the historical Western subject under the well-known and affectively bruising conditions of modernity that makes sex newly available as a compensatory technology of recognition.' Fixing her gaze on the atomizing and alienating aspects of modernity, Jargose holds that

> no matter how much sex is imagined as a privileged practice for the alleviation of the anomie that characterizes modern social relations by dint of its being apprehended as an intimate act, both particularizing and privatizing, it is equally available for the experience, whether depressive or euphoric, of the same impersonal intimacies it is normatively understood to counter. (2012, p. 85)

Sex as intimacy, in other words, might do its work as an idea, but falls short of expectations in practice. Love, while not the same as friendship, needs friendship to describe that part of the relationship that *is* intimacy. Sex – the defining feature distinguishing love from friendship for much of Western history, and conflated with intimacy rather than seen as one intimate possibility among others – does not suffice to describe the need for intimacy, because autonomous sex, practiced for its own sake, is also easily divorced from dynamics of care and support on the basis of trust and respect – dynamics, that is, without which friendship cannot exist.

All this raises the suspicion that the wish for friendship as the intimate bedrock of the love relationship is based on a persistent dissatisfaction with what therapeutic culture dishes up as the crux and nub of erotic love: a 'good sex life'. The cultural apotheosis of sexuality as *the* indicator of intimacy in love is not only remarkable because 'love has often been ignored in the histories of sexuality' (Haggerty, 2007, p. 71), but because it cannot live up to needs for intimacy as 'shared solitude' on the basis of mutual trust, reciprocity, and respect (Markus, 2010b, 11).

And so, if there is a 'problem' with love it seems to center on sex. No matter how 'liberated' our societies may appear – sex is, after all, everywhere – Michel Foucault (1980b) was undoubtedly right when he showed what tremendous difficulties we have dealing with it on the societal level, and that at a time when the trope of the 'prudish' Victorians is supposed to highlight our own sexual enlightenment (see also Gay, 1999). As we will see in the next chapters, our persistent uncertainties about it, the fact that we position sex as central not only to our identities, but as a practice normative to intimate fulfillment while at the same time regarding it as a threat to friendship, has consequences for friendship, and for cross-sex friendship in particular.

None of this is to say that lovers cannot be friends; to disavow that possibility is to repudiate people's capacities to make sense of their relationship through the available cultural vocabulary, and to make sense of it creatively. On that count we could argue that just as 'family' is a stand-in metaphor for intimate relations in friendship (e.g. usage of 'bro', or 'brother' among male friends), and especially in the nonheterosexual contexts of 'families of choice' steeped in the notion that 'blood is thicker than water', 'friend' is a stand-in metaphor in erotic love relationships. The sociological point here, then, is that while it is true that lovers can be friends, that is markedly different from saying that erotic love relationships are or can be friendships. This, at least, is the conclusion we arrive at when we attend to interpersonal relationships in a conceptually differentiated way.

Conclusion

In Chapter 3, I discussed friendship's relational freedom and its prerequisite: friendship's institutional deficit, which arose from the slow, bifurcating development of love and friendship in the course of Western history. In this chapter I was concerned with the internal dynamics that are both results and drivers of that peculiar social relationship. Again, modernity as mode of experience embedded in social and cultural transformations looms large here. Existential uncertainties under conditions of contingency and complexity also rouse the search for anchorage, for spaces in which we can be 'at home'. Friendship is one such space; its intimacies permit interactions that are subject neither to rules of public propriety nor to the private secrecy of other intimate bonds. At the same time, friendship holds the potential to nourish and sustain intimacy in relationships other than itself while, perhaps, also holding up an unsettling mirror to a culture that continues to valorize the distinguishing marker of sexuality in matters of love. There is, then, much room in friendship to develop a sense of self beyond our public performances and duties. Friendship has the power to fundamentally change our relations to self, and can do so because our selves are fundamentally social, and so irreducible to individual psychologies, to egos. The 'I' relies on the 'we' but also on Mead's 'Me' to understand itself fully. Relationships that are lived, practiced, 'done' differently according to different contexts, environments, and milieux, 'make' us just as we remake them in interaction. Through our friends we may even discover capacities, talents, and interests we never knew we had. Those possibilities exist in the first place because rather than simply mirroring each other's characters, friends draw one another in a process of interpretation and guidance. Rather than simply mirroring one another, friends open potentialities; 'new' selves may arise from and in interaction, much like the creations that emerge in admittedly more condensed and circumscribed contexts of improvised music creation. The drawing account of friendship gives concrete substance to work in critical theory that alerts us to the potential for human flourishing when processes of social recognition do their work.

With this installment, my analysis of friendship's freedom comes to a close. Like all human relationships, friendship too is lived, practiced, and experienced in more than the confines of private life, granted even that it straddles the boundaries between those interactions we classify as private and public at any given time. The freedom of friendship does not simply break through the social order, but still finds formidable obstacles. And while we could name a few obvious candidates that may hinder the formation of friendships, such as race and ethnicity, and age, there is in my view no greater obstacle, no greater 'normative barrier', to it than gender. The next chapter will begin to attend to the issues that emerge when we view the freedom of friendship as embedded in the contemporary gender system, and in so doing I will draw the contours of one – and I believe it is the most persistent – limit to friendship's freedom.

5
Gender and the Love–Friendship Paradox

Having surveyed the relationship's institutional deficit and its unsettled position on the boundaries between the private and public spheres, I have in the preceding chapters elaborated what others too have suggested: that of all interpersonal relationships friendship provides us with extensive relational freedom of interaction, with all the generative potential that entails. But I have also intimated that this freedom isn't total, because of friendship's embeddedness in the social order. For example, as I have shown by way of contrast with some anthropological literature, modern friendship has developed as a private and personal relationship. To that extent, friendship's embeddedness in a modern social order is enabling. Private and personal, it is unscripted, contingent on friends' capacities for intimacy, and on their very own practical construction of a specific relationship ethic. But friendship's embeddedness also means that it is constrained. For one, it is semantically 'constrained' to the extent that we partake in the collective construction and reconstruction of its meanings. Thus there is the constraint to interact like friends, and not like lovers or parents and children, because there is a cultural understanding – partly contested as we shall see – of what friends typically do or say, or refrain from saying and doing, and how they think about each other. This is simply part of a sense-making process by which friends construct the relationship against the background of societal understandings to which they, in turn, contribute.

Now, there is a theoretical strand in sociology that assumes that a general loosening of cultural norms of sociability, including those underpinning intimate practices, somehow automatically translates into an 'individualization' of everyday interactions; that just about any relationship is such that individuals who identify themselves as belonging to, living outside, or sitting in between social categories simply choose with whom and how they live, play, and work (see especially, Beck & Beck-Gernsheim, 1995, 2002). And in fact they do, although that needs qualification: just as no interactions and relationships take place in a structural vacuum that somehow dissolves class, gender, race, and other differentiating markers, neither do they take place in a normative vacuum. Both structural and cultural contingencies saturate the space of relating, and saturate it thoroughly. That goes for friendship, especially when gender is thrown into the mix.

Friedrich Tenbruck (1989, p. 240) noted that gender relations deliver the single most important indication that friendships are connected to the social organization of a society. The task I have set myself in this and the subsequent chapter is to take Tenbruck's assertion seriously, and to mine its validity from a conceptual angle that is consistent with my approach to friendship. And that means to elaborate the other side of friendship's institutional deficit as it were, namely that side that connects to the institution of heterosexuality. I argue that gender – even when class, race/ethnicity, age, and (dis)ability are bracketed and left to one side – constitutes a formidable limit to friendship's freedom.

Despite the reality that men and women share fulfilling friendships, my aim is to show that among the heterosexual mainstream, gender norms constrain the formation and maintenance of these relationships to the extent that people have to overcome cultural barriers that do not apply to same-sex friendships. The reality of those barriers regarding what is ostensibly the 'freest' of all interpersonal relationships tells us something about the gendered constitution of our societies and the gendered distribution of power in intimate dyads. This illustrates the inextricability of dyads and the social environment.

I begin in this chapter with a general discussion of gender as a social organizing principle and then turn to the one institution to which friendship connects most explicitly, namely heterosexuality and its normative infrastructure, to what is commonly referred to as 'heteronormativity'. I am particularly interested in those widely shared, mostly unspoken and inchoate norms that deliver a sense of what kinds of intimate interactions are considered 'normal' and therefore 'ought' to obtain between women and men. I show that 'normative homosociality' is crucial to the practicalities of cross-sex friendships. Pursuing that thread, I go on to discuss social categorization, stereotyping and what I call *presumptive prioritization* – processes that order interactions between and among men and women according to hierarchical cultural schemes. At least in the heterosexual mainstream, these processes help anchor in everyday life the societal association of friendship with homosociality and love with heterosociality. This 'love–friendship paradox', I suggest, lies at the heart of normative barriers to cross-sex friendship that, although challenged by everyday relationships, continue to present challenges to the formation and maintenance of cross-sex friendship, a topic that will be more concretely discussed in the next chapter. The present discussion, then, is intended to lay some conceptual groundwork.

Gender and heterosexuality

It is a sociological commonplace that age, race, (dis)ability, cultural background, religious affiliation, class, and status play a role in the likelihood of friendship formation. Summarized by the term 'status homophily', that take leans on commonsense notions such as 'like attracts like', 'birds of a feather flock together', and the reality that contexts in which similar types of individuals tend to interact are conducive to strong ties (Lazarsfeld & Merton, 1964). Being 'on the same wavelength', holding the same values and worldviews, having similar interests and 'personalities' makes friendly interaction more 'efficient', especially when the relationship is reduced to communicative processes (e.g. Rogers & Bhowmik, 1970). Those whom we perceive to be like us are simply easier to talk to; conversation is less likely to be strained. That story seems a little too straightforward, however. Its plausibility, lodged in commonsense, obscures the complexities of everyday life. As exemplified by research on interracial friendships, given opportunities for socializing among diverse populations there is today quite a measure of inclusiveness concerning difference (Moody, 2001; De Souza Briggs, 2007). But findings always depend on how researchers conceptualize homophily, what kind of shared attribute is given weight or, to use social science terminology, what 'independent variables' are selected in studies on the likelihood of friendship formation. Whatever friends' cultural or class backgrounds, for example, common interests tend to trump them to the extent that race and class may have little or no impact. This is not to say that social categories and backgrounds don't matter; it is simply to point out that the selection of research questions is vital and that therefore the significance of difference should not be underestimated, especially with a view to the generative potentials that it may help foster.

A universal schema of difference is that between biological reproductive systems, which are interpreted and socially structured in different ways depending on time and place. That notion of 'sex' differences is, according to Goffman, 'at the base of a fundamental code in accordance with which social interactions and social structures are built up, a code which also establishes the conceptions that individuals have concerning their fundamental human nature (1977, p. 301). The cultural interpretation and social structuration of the perceived differences, the codification of practices, attitudes, and behaviors as 'male' and 'female' is what we generally understand by the term 'gender'.[1] Sex differences are a fact of nature; gender is an artifact of culture. In fact, so deeply etched are the gendered interpretations of human nature in our sense of self; so riven is the world in which we live with gendered assumptions; so imbued are all manner of small and large-scale interactions by gendered ideologies and practices that gender inarguably constitutes a universal social organizing principle.

The codification of interactions, behaviors, and attitudes according to tacit as well as explicit principles of what is held to be normative about gender means that societies, however 'advanced', are still divided and sex-segregated despite challenges to division and segregation. The normative cultural attribution of gender differences, which has its basis in minimal biological differences that people, societies, and cultures have rendered extraordinarily significant, is visible everywhere: in the gendered assumptions about and allocation of child and home-care responsibilities; in the segregation of educational institutions, public restrooms, and locker rooms; and the feminization of some jobs and the masculinization of others, just to name some random examples. Goffman refers to this translation of sex categorization into forms of social organization as 'institutional reflexivity', and explains that 'segregation is presented as a natural consequence of the difference between the sex-classes, when in fact it is rather a means of honoring, if not producing, this difference' (1977, p. 316), thus legitimizing what Connell has called the 'gender order'.[2] For Goffman that institutional reflexivity provides a part answer to the question: 'How in modern society do such irrelevant biological differences between the sexes come to seem of vast social importance?' (1977, p. 316).

In *Masculine Domination* (2001), Pierre Bourdieu explains how social organization results from the classification of objects, activities, and bodies as 'masculine' or 'feminine'. For Bourdieu, the cultural translation of biological differences into categorical differences is manifest in our embodiment of gender. Internalized as 'habitus' – as the habitual, pre-reflexive orientation to the world that drives our practices – the symbolic gender order is natural to us to the extent that all gender divisions, including the division of labor, are literally embodied. It is, then, via that symbolic order that we come to learn, understand, embody, and inhabit gender divisions. 'With this bodily reference', states Krais in her explanation of Bourdieu's work,

> the social division of labour between the genders anchors itself in the habitus as deeply and firmly as possible. And, by pretending to be the 'natural' order of the world, it – like no other social structure – makes us forget that it is itself a *social structure*, produced and reproduced by humans themselves. (2006, p. 121, original emphasis)

Feminist, gender, and queer studies literature – a literature too vast to canvass even in a cursory manner here – has grappled with the social and personal consequences of processes that institutionalize, and thereby naturalize and so legitimize what are in fact mostly artificial differences. In these divided societies, economic, social, and political power is distributed unequally between that sector of the population we label 'men' and that which we label 'women'.[3] In turn, that inequality turns on the relentlessly hammered-home notion that men and women are in essential respects different creatures of habit, proclivities, physical and emotional capacities, and needs. In public discourse the extent of everyday inequalities is largely obscured by such (uneven) developments as women's integration into labor markets, or by the relative extension to women of sexual agency and autonomy concerning their reproductive futures following their own collective struggles from the middle of the 19th century. Under such conditions, and precisely because some structural change is constantly drawn upon in the public domain to repudiate the need for a political feminism, it pays, I think, to take into view the normative assumptions and the *modi vivendi* that take their lead from them – assumptions and expectations that orient the everyday interactions between women and men who are practically implicated in the mutual reproduction as well as transformation of codes of femininity and masculinity. These codes, moreover, deliver models that not only distinguish men from women, but also establish hierarchical categories among women and among men who are perceived to be more or less feminine and masculine, and whereby a perceived lack of stereotypically feminine characteristics, practices, and behaviors in women, and masculine traits, practices, and behaviors in men, attract a range of negative social sanctions (e.g. Deaux et al., 1985;

Prentice & Carranza, 2002; Kimmel, 2004, 2009; Connell, 2005; Green et al., 2005).

All this matters in friendship, because friendship too is part of a gender order whose normative infrastructure is encountered, sometimes reproduced, and sometimes challenged by friends. This might seem curious, since I argued earlier that friendship, especially when compared to erotic love, resists commodification and reification and so is only imperfectly integrated into a culture of capitalism that has, by way of a therapeutic ethos, saturated interpersonal relationships. So, how is it possible that friendship resists commodification even under capitalism, which surely 'organizes' our social lives, but cannot do so in the same degree regarding the constraints delivered by the gender order? To address that question, we need to revisit and further elaborate my suggestion that while friendship's institutional connectivity is comparatively weak, it does connect to one institution: heterosexuality.

Heterosexuality as institution

The conceptualization of heterosexuality as an institution can be traced back to the influential works of Adrienne Rich (1980) and Monique Wittig (1992) who explored the constitution of heterosexual norms of conduct with the identification, labeling, pathologization, and marginalization of homosexuality. Rich's polemic took aim at the more or less inadvertent reproduction of 'compulsory heterosexuality' as 'a beachhead of male dominance' not only in mainstream discourse but also in feminist writing, thus highlighting the hegemonic nature of heterosexual norms across sexualities and ideological positions (1980, p. 633). Drawing on Jean-Jacques Rousseau, and partly in reference to Rich's work, Wittig elaborated what she called the heterosexual 'social contract' as,

> precisely the rules and conventions that have never been formally enunciated, the rules and conventions that go without saying for the scientific mind as well as for the common people, that which for them obviously makes life possible, exactly as one must have two legs and two arms, or one must breathe to live ... For to live in a society is to live in heterosexuality. In fact, in my mind social contract and heterosexuality are two superimposable notions. (1992, p. 40)

For both Wittig and Rich, and for a number of writers following their lead, heterosexuality goes beyond sexual orientation, desire, and practices: functions as the taken-for-granted basis for the organization of social arrangements *in toto*. Reminiscent of Durkheim's (1966) 'collective representations' – components of the ideational dimensions that lend a measure of integration to modern societies – for Wittig heterosexuality is 'an ideological form which we cannot grasp in reality, except through its effects, whose existence lies in the mind of people, but in a way that affects their whole life, the way they act, the way they move, the way they think' and thus is 'an object both imaginary and real' (1992, pp. 40–41). That social force of the heterosexual contract can only be maintained if, whatever its contestations, it holds widespread legitimacy. Writing in a French context where heterosexuality 'has no juridic existence' in family law, Wittig thought that '[a]nthropologists, ethnologists, sociologists would come to take it for an *institution*, but as an unwritten, unspoken one' (1992, p. 41, my emphasis). In that conception heterosexuality orientates, as well as being reproduced and maintained by, a whole raft of social practices, cultural representations, and structural arrangements that are organized around norms of 'appropriate', normal, and legitimate social interactions – sexual and otherwise – between and among men and women. For political reasons Rich and Wittig treated heterosexuality more or less exclusively as the marginalizing benchmark of 'non-conformist' or 'alternative' sexualities, which for Rich has the power to intervene even in alternative social and sexual arrangements. As a logical conclusion, only two political options remain in order to escape the overweening power of institutionalized heterosexuality: (lesbian) separatism or a kind of inner exile: 'If ultimately we are denied a new social order', states Wittig, 'I will find it in myself' (1992, p. 45).

Writers who have taken important cues from the likes of Wittig and Rich in their analyses of heterosexuality have broadened the approach (e.g. Seidman, 1997; Richardson, 2000; Jackson, 2006; Katz, 2007). For them, heterosexuality figures not only as an assembly of ideas that marginalize nonheterosexual identities and practices, but also describe, define, and delimit those ways of being in the world that heterosexuals can legitimately claim for themselves *qua* heterosexuals – ideas, actions, and experiences that are neither the same nor can be reduced to heterosexuality as 'sexual orientation' or preference (Jackson, 2006; Jackson & Scott, 2010, pp. 74–100).

The central concept in this approach, one that sensitizes us to the institutional constitution of heterosexuality, is *heteronormativity*. Heteronorms constitute the normative infrastructure of heterosexuality to the extent that it 'defines not only a normative sexual practice but also a normal way of life', and as such goes beyond mere heterosexuality as sexual orientation (Jackson, 2006, p. 107; Jackson & Scott, 2010, pp. 74–100). To say that heteronormativity is the term connoting the normative infrastructure of heterosexuality is not to conflate the structural organization of gender (access to labor markets, child care policy, etc.) with everyday negotiations of the gender order and subjective identifications with a range of genders, but to recognize a distinct dimension of norms we habitually draw upon in our individual and collective efforts to make sense of a world that is *a priori* structured along the binary distinction male/female. Those norms are not merely given, monolithic, and unchangeable, but are constituted, challenged, and changed over time by social action.[4]

At the same time, while it may be possible to analytically separate the normative dimension of heterosexuality from the structural dimension, in real life macrosocial conditions, everyday interactions, and self-perception are certainly intertwined (Jackson, 2006). For instance, keeping in mind considerable variation between jurisdictions, in many countries parental leave entitlements are distributed unequally between men and women, even though work entitlements are at least formally on par. There are clues here concerning the normative dimension of heterosexuality, that dimension, that is, that organizes meaning.[5] Commonsense assumptions tend to give priority to maternity over paternity leave because women's caring capacities are assumed natural. By extension, men who take on care responsibilities are often feminized. In countries where paternity leave is comparatively generous, uptake may among other things be impeded by gender stereotypes around masculinity that discourage men's uptake of leave provisions (Hobson, 2002; Bittman et al., 2004; Magaraggia, 2013).

Heteronormativity thus connects the institution of heterosexuality to other institutions, especially by way of cultural assumptions that affect structural exigencies and everyday interaction, including friendships, as we will see. As always when social norms are at play, we need to keep in mind that as they 'operate as the normalizing principle in social practice, they usually remain implicit, difficult to read, discernable most clearly and dramatically in the effect they produce' (Butler cited in Jackson, 2006, p. 114). Again, heteronormativity does more than simply define normative sexual practices; it provides coded scripts for the meaningful interpretation and experiences of 'ways of life' lived in the gender order. That situation can be explained without falling into the trap of positing the norms underpinning the institution of heterosexuality as 'so entrenched as to be unassailable' (Jackson, 2006, p. 117). In that endeavor it is apposite to include

Berlant and Warner's now well-known take on heteronormativity in our conception:

> By heteronormativity we mean the institutions, structures of under-standing, and practical orientations that make heterosexuality seem not only coherent – that is, organized as a sexuality – but also privileged. Its coherence is always provisional, and its privilege can take several (sometimes contradictory) forms: unmarked, as the basic idiom of the personal and the social; or marked as a natural state; or projected as an ideal or moral accomplishment. It consists less of norms that could be summarized as a body of doctrine than of *a sense of rightness* produced in contradictory manifestations – often unconscious, immanent to practice or to institutions. Contexts that have little visible relation to sex practice, such as life narrative and generational identity, can be heteronormative in this sense, while in other contexts forms of sex between men and women might not be heteronormative. Heteronormativity is thus a concept distinct from heterosexuality. (1998, pp. 548ff, my emphasis)

Heteronormativity is conceptually distinct from heterosexuality, while in practice neither can do without the other. And it is by way of het-eronormative assumptions, rather than statutes, acts, and laws, that heterosexuality connects to friendship. That institutional connectivity between friendship and heterosexuality is implicit in 'a sense of right-ness' that attaches to the gendered organization of sociality, to the expected repertoire of affiliations between men and women, to the gendered construction of homosociality and heterosociality.

Homosociality, heterosociality, and social judgment

Recently, Australia's largest brewery screened TV commercials advertis-ing one of their beers; they illustrate well the central place of (male) homosociality in Australia, something that can be unproblematically generalized to other Western societies. The commercials depict a hetero-sexual couple on holidays and are themed around the 'coincidental' – but obviously planned – 'intrusion' of the male protagonist's 'mates' on the couple. In the first of these, the couple lounges at a pool. One of the male protagonist's friends, accompanied by his female partner, walks into the scene. Both men fake utter though pleasant surprise, when yet another 'mate' appears in the pool – and upon seeing the others duly drops his female companion into the water. Yet another couple appears, and the clip ends with the men happily congregating away from the women, enjoying the advertised beverage. A second advertisement revolves around the same theme. This time adjacent hotel rooms booked by male friends enable their faux coincidental meeting and necessitates, it seems, their spending time together on their own. Both advertisements end to the tune of Jackson Browne's version of *Stay (Just a Little Bit Longer)*.

We can hardly speak of 'subtext' here, so blatant is the message, but a few words about the context need to be stated upfront. These advertisements were shown during the 2013–2014 cricket season, and especially the matches between Australia and England, which were sponsored by the brewery. The ads were aimed at a male audience. The particular beer advertised is not a 'boutique' choice, but a kind of standard brand, much like Budweiser in the United States; it has, in other words, fairly broad appeal, just as cricket attracts fans from all social classes and a wide range of cultural backgrounds and genders, although it is commonly portrayed as a sport of choice for the 'Aussie' male, which is just as commonly portrayed as Caucasian, with the advertisements cited here being no exception.[6]

The message is this: men, or 'real men' in any case, prefer to hang out with each other rather than with women. The 'naturalness' of that assumption is not only represented by the acquiescence of the women (in both clips the gullibility and passivity of the female characters are striking), but is most strongly legible in the 'tongue-in-cheekness' of the scenes; the plot is intended to be comic. The fact that it is confidently aimed at eliciting laughter speaks to the common sense notion that 'boys will be boys',[7] that exclusive (male) homosociality is expected, that preferring to spend time with their mates rather than with women is simply what heterosexual men do, or that at the very least men need time out from women (see also, Lyman, 1987). The naturalness of that assumption is thrown into relief when we imagine the advertisements made up of a different cast: if the women were to be substituted by Australian Aborigines, for instance, or Hindu Sikhs, not only would the humorousness of such representations be presumably lost on a majority of viewers, the ads would be censored by media legislators, and if not would give cause to public protest. In any case, such productions would today be close to inconceivable. Gendered stereotyping rarely causes that type of public concern. We are simply supposed to get the joke.

But cultural representations as well as real practices of homosociality are not confined to men. There are, for example, not only 'bucks' or 'stag' nights', but also 'hens' nights'; there are not only 'boys' nights out', but also 'girls' nights out', not only fraternities, but also sororities, just as there are still gender-segregated educational institutions, and so forth. As we will see, women too tend to prefer same-sex to cross-sex friendships, although this is linked to culturally reproduced styles of intimacy; emotional support is feminized and thus both expected and more likely to be offered by women. Homosociality is distributed across genders, but that is in itself a function of gender divisions. Male homosociality is, for historical reasons, privileged because women were, and sometimes still are, barred from male-dominated public and organizational life. In the public domain woman have to aspire to membership by emulating masculine ideals and are frequently used as 'currency' to shore up male heterosexuality and homophobia (Lipman-Blumen, 1976; Kimmel, 2004). Female homosociality is thus to a significant degree a consequence of power and resources accruing to men. As a result, the social organization of gendered arrangements is such that homosociality is normative and thus intrinsic to and reproductive of heteronormativity. Homosociality orients and structures social interactions between and among women and men, both on the cultural level according to what counts as 'proper', 'appropriate', and 'normal' attitudes, practices, and behaviors, and on the structural level as far their spatial and organizational arrangements are concerned.

Normative homosociality continues to impact on the formation and maintenance of friendships between men and woman. In order to lay some foundations for thinking sociologically about the cultural obstacles to these friendships, I now turn to social processes of categorization and stereotyping through which we identify self and others in the lead-up to discussing what I call the process of *presumptive prioritization*, a process whereby we attribute social identities to others and make judgments about them. I then go on to argue that in love and friendship we attribute types of intimacy according to the perceived gender composition of dyadic relationships.

Categories, stereotypes, and presumptive prioritization

In order to make sense of the social world, human beings need to cognitively minimize the complexities of social life, something that in modernity becomes acute. One way by which we achieve this is to order the world and its myriad occurrences into categories. At least according to Luhmann (1995), the differentiation of separate subsystems of action both causes further complexity while at the same time promising to reduce it. Thus, categorization, for one, occurs on the institutional and organizational levels. Think of census categories that inform policy formation, but also of scientific sub-disciplines that create, categorize, and label phenomena of the natural and social worlds and in so doing may distinguish between individual and social normalcy and pathology (Foucault, 1980a). But categorization also takes places in everyday interaction. We categorize others and ourselves according to mutually constitutive similarities and differences. This aids us in identifying self and others because, again, '[w]ithout categorization the complexity of the human social world might not be manageable at all' (Jenkins, 2000, p. 8). We can, therefore, view processes of categorization and identification of self and others as belonging to certain social groups with certain shared characteristics, attitudes, values, practice, statuses, entitlements, etc. as sense-making dynamics that are fundamental to our sociality.

In some sense we are dealing here with a sociological variant of the perception and categorization of objects that, following a long line of philosophical investigations from Kant to Mach, Brentano, and Husserl, was elaborated in *gestalt* psychology from the 20th century (Sternberg, 2008, Heinämaa & Reuter, 2009). Simply put, that philosophical approach is interested in our perception of forms and ensuing inferences about their types and categories which we make based on minimal information (e.g. seeing the end of a cat's tail disappear around a corner is all that is needed for most of us to perceive a cat rather than, say, a rat). We share those neurological processes with other animals; they are universal. For sociologists, on the other hand, these cognitive processes depend on cultural scripts, schemas, and heuristics. These are themselves products of culturally and historically specific modes of social life. They orient attitudes to and assumptions about social identities, roles, and situations, including what situations and interactions are appropriate for whom.

Cognitive processes that serve our need to abstract from observations in order to make sense of the social world are central to phenomenology. A branch of philosophy founded by Edmund Husserl (1859–1938), phenomenology is concerned to explain how we make the world meaningful through acts of consciousness; it seeks to 'analyze the presuppositions of daily life' (Natanson, 1970, p. 3). The 'world' here denotes our 'life world', by which Husserl understood the realm of experiences and actions to which our consciousness brings the 'natural attitude' of taken-for-granted common sense. Alfred Schutz (1962) sought to bring phenomenological principles to bear on Weber's interpretive or meaning-centered approach to social science in order to distinguish between, and bring into mutual interdependence, the unreflected-upon experiences of the everyday and their 'second order' interpretation in the social sciences (see Hughes & Sharrock, 1997). Going on with the business of living, being able to manage the mundane, routine aspects of the everyday is, according to Schutz, only possible because we collectively construct our understanding of the social world; its meanings are shared, rendering the world and our experiences 'intersubjectively valid' (Natanson, 1970, p. 5). We inherit our 'stock of knowledge' in the practical, routine engagements with others, but also collectively produce and, over time, modify that knowledge. Central to these processes is what Schutz calls 'typification': our largely unconscious appraisal of objects, situations, and actions according to what is typical about them (Schutz, 1962). That pertains to knowing how to post a parcel without having to know the intricacies of the organizational dynamics of the postal service as much as to our shared assumptions about the 'how' and 'what' of intimacy among friends, family, and lovers, as much as to the differentiating categories of gender, class, age, and disability, and so on. Conceivable as a reduction of complexity, typification lies at the center of social interaction because it is both an expression of unarticulated social norms and the intersubjective process by which they are produced, reproduced, and altered over time. For Schutz these are first and foremost social expressions of the unreflected-upon life lived in Husserl's 'pre-predicative realm of experience' (Natanson, 1970, p. 6), without which social life is inconceivable. Reflecting upon these is the task of the human and social sciences (see especially Schutz, 1973). Schutz's conceptualization has informed a range of interpretive approaches in sociology.

Taking the social constitution of norms as a sociological given, sociologists have sought to understand and explain processes of typification particularly in the context of institutional, organizational, but also face-to-face dynamics of categorization. Classic treatments are Goffman's (1963b, 1990) work on stigma and our need for 'impression management' under conditions where control over our own social identities is limited (because how others perceive us is inaccessible to us) (Jenkins, 2000). In a paper whose nuanced take on social categorization and identification cannot be rehearsed here, Jenkins (2000), ever mindful of the dialectic dynamics between self and external conditions, puts into perspective sociologists' ('fashionable') overemphasis of self-identification, the self-determination and malleability of identities, and of difference, which became particularly prevalent from the 1990s. Just as self-identification and self-determination are to be given less analytic weight in favor of powerful institutional forces that continue to categorize and 'identify' people, so too is the malleability of identities highly dependent on resources and thus cannot be divorced from social dynamics of recognition. Difference, on the other hand, needs to be considered as limited, because 'socially and epistemologically categorization involves the invocation of similarity *within* categories, as the basis for differentiation *between* them. ... Difference does not make sense without similarity (any more than individual identity does without collective membership)' (Jenkins, 2000, p. 22, original emphasis). In these processes stereotyping plays a central role.

First used in Lippmann's classic *Public Opinion* (1922), the term 'stereotype' has become a central concept in the study of prejudice and has become firmly integrated into the Anglophone vernacular. The study of stereotypes has over the decades moved from the investigation of discriminating attitudes and practices – at first chiefly concerning racial and cultural minorities, and only later concerning gender – to an appreciation of stereotyping as part and parcel of cognitive processes that minimize sense-making complexities. On that view, stereotypes are schemas that aid perceivers in the processing of information. Rather than assuming them to be simply erroneous thought processes, researchers have more recently come to think about stereotyping as functional and dynamic to social life. A defining characteristic of stereotypes is that they *'imply* a substantial amount of information about people beyond their immediately apparent surface qualities and generate expectations about group members' anticipated behavior'. That is, stereotypes *appear* to deliver valid knowledge about people because, 'transmitted through socialization, the media and language and discourse', they are widely held, constantly reproduced, and so confirmed; they appear legitimate, pending evidence to the contrary (Dovidio et al., 2010, pp. 7–8, my emphases). How do these processes unfold?

In all social contexts we presume the existence of certain types of relationships in accordance with social identities and roles[8] that we expect individuals to enact appropriate to a culturally 'agreed upon' definition of the situation. For example, if as naïve passers-by we were to look into a classroom and spot an adult among a group of schoolchildren, we would likely presume the adult to be performing the role of teacher and the children to be students at their school. That would most likely be our *first*, intuitive guess according to the immediately available evidence. That 'evidence' need not be correct; it can be arbitrary and spurious, but will seem logical and plausible as long as it fits the prevailing cultural scheme of interpretation concerning specific social roles and identities in specific contexts. Whatever the truth-value of the evidence, in all instances of social judgment – whether it is about a generalizing attribution of traits and characteristics to members of a social group, an appraisal of a social situation, predictions about one's own emotional reactions – an 'if X then Y' logic is at play, irrespective of those processes being consciously thought through or 'automatic, associative' (Kruglanski & Sleeth-Keppler, 2007, p. 117). Alternative inferences concerning social identities, roles, and interactions require additional evidence to replace commonsense interpretations with alternative explanations (e.g. in the above example it could be a parent looking for her child, or a janitor holding a sermon about restroom cleanliness).

There is, then, an important temporal dimension to these acts of social judgment; they are processes. We are most likely to *first* presume stereotypical categories, identities, and situations *before* we make alternative inferences. Thinking moves from an intuitive, unconscious 'first-order' set of assumptions to 'second-order' presumptions only once further evidence gives cause for reflection. Following the pioneering work of Allport (1954) and Tajfel (1969), unconscious, 'knee-jerk' judgments about groups and individuals are today widely recognized in the field as 'implicit' stereotyping (Banaji, 2001, pp. 15103–15104). In an elaboration of the theme, the process of 'automatic stereotyping' has been tested on a variety of social phenomena, including stereotypical assumptions about gender (e.g. Eagly & Steffen, 1984; Banaji & Hardin, 1996; Green & Ashmore, 1998; Glick & Fiske, 2001; Rudman & Glick, 2001; Irmen, 2006; Rudman & Fairchild, 2007). Recognizing the temporal dimension of these types of cognitions, researchers attempt to measure automatic social judgments using so-called 'response latencies': the faster the response to cues, the less conscious and therefore more spontaneous and automatic judgments are supposed to be. For instance, Banaji and Hardin (1996) have shown that, when presented with word combinations consisting of a recognizably female first name ('Jane') and a stereotypically consistent profession ('nurse'), measured response rates were significantly faster than when subjects were presented with an inconsistent combination ('Jane'/'doctor').

Social psychologists recognize the reliance of, intuitive judgements upon cultural, 'general knowledge structures' (Smith, 2001, p. 9689). In his survey of developments in the field, Smith states: '[s]tereotypes were found to be activated automatically, and to affect impressions of individual group members as a "default" condition unless perceivers are particularly motivated (e.g., by a conscious desire to avoid using stereotypes) and cognitively able (e.g., through freedom from time pressure or distraction) to overcome these effects' (2001, p. 9689). I call the temporal movement from pre-reflexive, unconscious cognition processes (first-order assumption), by which we make 'automatic' sense of a situation, to a 'change of mind' according to further evidence (second-order presumption) *presumptive prioritization*. Intuitive, unconscious judgments have temporal priority over reflected-upon judgments. And they have temporal priority because an unspoken consensus concerning the definition of a situation provides the default position, and so, because culture aids cognition, is immediately available for a cognitive reduction of complexity. Presumptive prioritization does its ordering work in relation to the gendered constitution of intimate sociality, as I now go on to explain.

Gender and the heteronormative love–friendship paradox

Automatic stereotyping has an important role to play in the presumptive prioritization of audiences' judgments concerning others, especially in cases where readable biological differences serve to legitimate them. This is especially the case when physical attributes are made to do the work of essential distinction to the extent that the reality of overwhelming similarity is erased from the interpretive scheme. Here gender is the cardinal case in point. Gender attribution is foundational to the self; as soon as we are born we are subject to a 'crucial act of social categorization' by which 'we are ascribed a gender' (Jackson & Scott, 2010, p. 95). The power of gender categorization is clearly evident in transgendered identities because they frequently cause considerable consternation not only on the part of outsiders, but also on the part of transgendered people themselves: there is a need to attribute to self either one or the other social identity, 'woman' or 'man'; and those who can live with ambivalent self-identification will, in one way or another still have to constantly deal with the fact that others – whether individuals, organization, or institutions – will categorize them (for a personal account see Bornstein, 2013; for a critique of Bornstein see Califia, 2003).[9] Constantly reproduced notions of what counts as masculine, effeminate, feminine, butch, or camp orient interpretations, which unless they are disproven, strengthen the cognitive efficacy of the stereotype.

These processes are also at play when audiences witness interactions between and among women and men, and especially when they witness *dyadic* interactions. Cultural scripts about gendered interactions support general assumptions concerning homosociality and heterosociality; these are marshaled in intuitive, first-order descriptions of intimate relationship types. It is here, in processes of presumptive prioritization, that we can detect the persistence of heteronormativity and institutionalized heterosexuality and thus the still-firm foothold of the binary gender order. Heteronormativity not only assigns normalcy status to heterosexuality, it encourages the patterned distribution of interactions between women and men. What's more, it does so differently depending on whether love or friendship is the issue. Presumptive prioritization, according to the hypothesis, is likely to unfold in the following way. When a (perceived) man and woman are witnessed together by a stranger, that stranger is more likely to intuit a romantic love relationship than a platonic friendship. The inference 'friendship' requires further evidence and so is subject to a burden of proof. The reverse obtains if the dyad is made up of either two (perceived) men or women. Lacking evidence to the contrary, audiences are more likely to intuitively judge the relationship type to be friendship rather than love. I call this phenomenon the 'love–friendship paradox'.

There are several conditions that need to obtain for these automatic judgments to be facilitated. For the 'love' judgment to be made, the individuals in question need to be of similar ages. In societies such as ours where informal age norms are fairly settled (Settersten, 2003), 'love' will have priority especially if the man is perceived to be older, which also reflects the reality that the great majority of heterosexual woman are in relationships with men who are older than they (Darroch et al., 1999). A significant age difference in same-sex dyads may signal a father–son or mother–daughter relationship. Judgment is also *context-dependent*. If a heterosocial dyad is witnessed in explicitly nonheterosexual contexts, such as a gay bar for instance, it goes without saying that the 'love' inference may not be automatic, while the opposite applies to the same-sex dyad. The same goes for culturally produced signifiers that align with what kind of *appearance* counts as 'camp' or 'butch', or with *behaviors* that signal romantic intimacy. But all things being equal, it is fairly uncontroversial to suggest that regarding cross-sex dyads the first-order assumption will be that of 'love' rather than friendship, while regarding same-sex dyads the first-order assumption will be that of friendship. Table 5.1 schematically represents this cultural phenomenon.

Table 5.1 Presumptive prioritization and the heteronormative love–friendship paradox

Gendered sociality	First-order assumption (heteronormative)	Second-order presumption (nonstandard)
Homosociality	Friendship	Love
Heterosociality	Love	Friendship
Time	→	→

Heteronormative first-order assumptions that perceive homosocial dyads as friendship and heterosocial dyads as love relationships rest on two interrelated cognitive foundations, one probabilistic the other cultural-normative: it is a simple fact that there are more heterosexual-identifying and other-sex attracted than nonheterosexual-identifying and same-sex attracted people in our societies, with the latter hovering anywhere between the 4 and 10 per cent marks (Gates, 2011; Gates & Newport, 2013a,b). However, statistical 'facts' are connected to normative standards which may, for instance, inhibit identification as non-heterosexual and so keep same-sex attracted individuals 'in the closet' (Stephens-Davidowitz, 2013). Beyond a purely probabilistic argument that says 'we tend to perceive things we are most likely to encounter', prevailing heteronormative assumptions indicate not only what we ought to be perceiving, but also how we ought to feel about and engage with the same or opposite sex, and whether or not we ought to own up to self and/or others should nonstandard attitudes or desires be present. And here the temporal dimension implicit in the concept of presumptive prioritization is significant; it explicitly conveys what automatic stereotyping implies, namely that second-order presumptions denote literally second-order *priorities*, because we are dealing with 'second-class' situations – situations, that is, that are in some ways 'deviant' or at least unconventional, but definitely nonstandard. Their nonstandard quality is shown up by the fact that they are invisible, unreal, nonexistent unless we receive additional information that, once processed, changes our perceptions. Presumptive prioritization, the process describing how the love–friendship paradox works in everyday life, thus captures and names the hierarchical ordering dynamics inherent in the taking up of the default position. These processes indicate that a simple norm typically applies: *in respect of 'love', heterosociality is normative while homosociality is nonstandard; in respect of friendship, homosociality is normative while heterosociality is nonstandard.*

Viewed through the prism of the love–friendship paradox it isn't difficult to understand why in the public imagination love trumps friendship, and especially heterosocial friendship. We value friendship in all contexts, homosocial and heterosocial. But we value it in homosocial contexts in general, while we value it in heterosocial contexts only as an ideal underpinning love, which takes priority. That is, we valorize friendship as an ideal, as a value, but collectively reconstruct normative barriers to its practical realization in heterosocial interaction. In heterosexual love, 'friendship' and 'friend' function as metaphors connoting intimacy, just as 'family' functions as a metaphor for intimacy in friendship. That 'family' cannot function as a metaphor for intimacy in sexual love can be traced back to the incest taboo. That 'friendship' does that work in love relationships has to do with the Western over-evaluation of sexual practice as the quintessential marker of intimacy.

The centrality of sexuality is particularly problematic in heterosexual male friendships, where it may figure as a barrier to intimacy. Miller (1992) speaks eloquently to the problem. It arose especially when the author canvassed his research intentions with other academics:

> Everywhere I have gone there has been the same misconception. The bizarre necessity to explain, at the beginning, that my subject is not homosexuality.

> The fear of homosexuality and how it affects the possibilities of male friendship in our times are topics that need contemplating ... The point here, however, is that the estate of male friendship – indeed, of nearly all human relationships – is sufficiently sunk that mere sex remains at the center of people's imaginations. The only moving human relationships that people seem able to conjure up are erotic ones. (Miller, 1992, p. 3)

The reduction of intimacy to sexuality, or the valorization of one part of a much larger repertoire of intimate possibilities, then, has deleterious consequences for both male friendships and cross-sex friendships. In male friendship it may work as a negative foil against which stoic, straight masculinity can assure itself in the often unspoken but taken-for-granted reproduction of homophobia. In cross-sex friendship the narrow version of intimacy is the normative justification for the patina of unusualness that covers the relationship in the public imagination. And in both heterosocial and (male) homosocial variants it considerably strengthens the normative barriers to their formation, inhibits the living out to their fullest intimate possibilities and their sustainability, and hence surely accounts, if not for their impossibility, at least for their relative uncommonness. This is only one effect that the institution of heterosexuality has on intimate relationships; it turns out to be decisive for friendship.

Conclusion

Sexualities are inferred and attributed to dyads according to their (perceived) gendered composition, with heterosexuality the default norm. By extension, alternative sexualities and nonstandard relationship types are subject to a burden of justification. Relationships that question the authority of the scheme simply by virtue of their existence are nevertheless subject to its reality as a cultural heuristic. None of us are immune to the typifications and categories that make the social environment we inhabit legible, manageable, and livable. The love–friendship paradox not only does its work from the 'outside' so that all we might need to do is barricade ourselves inside the citadel of friendship; the paradox orients expectations among friends and therefore, to whatever degree, is always already present on the 'inside' as an interiorized reality and, as we shall see in the following chapter, has to be negotiated by friends. The sociological point here is that in the practical experiences of personal relationships the dyad cannot be divorced from the culture writ large. Its interactions refract social arrangements and the assumptions that give them life. I now elaborate that point by turning to the intersection between the personal and the social in cross-sex friendship.

6
The Love–Friendship Paradox and Cross-Sex Friendship

This chapter discusses the symptoms and consequences of the normative assumptions I condensed in the love–friendship paradox (Chapter 5) with specific reference to cross-sex friendship. While we might assume that today intimate relationships are free from social convention, that turns out to be true for cross-sex friendship only to a limited extent. The social construction of different types of intimacy for men and women, and the norm of sexual attraction, impede these friendships. Platonic heterosocial friendships challenge these norms but may also reproduce them. It is under these conditions that 'friends with benefits' relationships seem to offer the best of both worlds: casual sex in the context of friendship. But taking the benchmark of intimacy to these relationships shows that they fall short of realizing what they promise. Others construct 'erotic friendships' in an attempt to reconcile sex and friendship without partaking in the cultural staging of romance, but without having to forgo to generative potentials of intimacy. The reality of heteronormative barriers regarding what is ostensibly the 'freest' of all interpersonal relationships yields insights into the gendered distribution of power in and the gendered constitution of our societies.

The problem of cross-sex friendship

In a recent article in the online magazine *portable.tv*, Cora Quigley writes,

> 'Can men and women be friends?' has been an oft asked question for as long as I can remember, and one that has never actually applied to my life or the lives of anyone else I know, because it

has never needed to be asked. Because, you know, in our lives men and women are friends. Believe it or not, nobody's running around screaming, 'Wait? Is this happening? IS THIS REAL?! WHY AREN'T WE ALL HAVING SEX ARGGH', as that would be very silly indeed. The possibility of romance definitely isn't a given when it comes to friendships between men and women, not by a long shot [*sic*]. Unfortunately, this sort of thing isn't a very common theme across the different forms of media, though I must say TV seems to fare a bit better in that respect (Quigley, 2013, original emphasis).

Quigley then goes on to list some examples of successful heterosexual cross-sex friendships portrayed in popular culture: Ron Swanson and Leslie Kope in *Parks and Recreation*; John Cusack's character Lloyd Dobler and 'his lady friends' in *Say Anything*; Peggy and Don in *Mad Men*; Elaine, Jerry, and George in *Seinfeld*; Harry and Hermione of the *Harry Potter* series; Andy and Maggie in *Extras*. Quigley points to a perceived discrepancy: on the one hand everyone seems to have platonic friendships with the opposite sex, and on the other hand there are few media representations of them. And when they do appear, such as most famously in *When Harry Met Sally* (1989), but also in *Friends With Benefits* (2011), the plot invariably ends with those friendships turning into romantic attachments. The heterosocial love norm, briefly threatening to create thematic tensions, is re-established and that presumably to the satisfaction of audiences. So, at least as a part answer to Quigley, we might say that cultural representations of platonic friendships between heterosexual men and women are rare because they fall outside the norm. Cultural artefacts, as much as they may transgress mainstream norms and expectations, especially as products of large-scale culture industries, are also supposed to turn a profit by satisfying emotional needs, and perhaps none more so than the need for whatever sells itself as romantic love at any given time (Adorno, 2005; Fromm, 2013). Quigley also errs on the optimistic side when it comes to the prevalence of these relationships. When close, intimate friendships rather than the catch-all term 'friends' are taken as the benchmark of analysis, these friendships are relatively rare. That rarity is connected to normative assumptions about gender and 'appropriate' personal relationships between men and women – from which the pop-cultural reproduction of romance cannot be divorced. Thus, the answer to the question 'Can men and women be friends?' is a resounding 'Of course!', and in fact sociologists often celebrate its realities (Monsour, 2002). That might be qualified, I suggest, with 'and they often do so against the odds'.

A focus on popular culture may give the impression that all this is relatively new. And indeed, public discourse turned to the phenomenon mainly from around the 1990s. But we should not forget the past to give some context to the present. Take, for example, the friendship between Abigail Adams and Thomas Jefferson, the republic's third President, as insightfully analyzed by historian Cassandra Good (2012). Both Abigail and Thomas seemed to have had a particular aptitude for friendship, and in Jefferson's case that is most explicit in his at once tumultuous and touching friendship with Abigail's husband, John Adams (Shklar, 1998). The friendship between Abigail and Thomas was lived in a context that made privacy as impossible as it was undesirable, for the gossip and rumors that would inevitably follow suit would have been detrimental to the friends' reputation and as a consequence to the relationship. Though salons and civil society associations had begun to facilitate interactions between women and men, the possibilities for private interactions were severely curtailed. The friends' social standing added a further dimension to these restrictions. And so, to the degree that their friendship was – and had to be – public it was also constrained.

If friendship as a noninstitutionalized relationship is relatively free from cultural prescription, this is the case to an extraordinary degree in heterosocial friendship (see also Booth & Hess, 1974; Argyle & Henderson, 1984; O'Meara, 1989; Rawlins, 1992; Felmlee, 1999; Felmlee et al., 2012) – not because here society turns away from the relationship and leaves it free rein, but because these relationships threaten the heterosocial love ideal. In the context of the early American republic, and especially for the intellectual and political elite,[1] the 'ambiguity of the boundaries between friendship, romance or sexuality and marriage left heterosocial friends particularly open to gossip and charges of impropriety' (Good, 2012, p. 19). Gossip easily and frequently 'blossomed into scandal' at a time in American history, 'which idealized companionate marriage and domestic tranquillity' (Kierner cited in Good, 2012, p. 19). In the absence of cultural scripts for cross-sex friendship – neither guides to etiquette nor letter-writing nor novels thematized these relationships[2] – and in the presence of public fears that these bonds were little more than male ruses to seduce women, not only Abigail and Thomas had to put in place strategies that put the purely platonic quality and hence the relationship's propriety beyond doubt.

The most common strategy was to embed the friendship in other social structures and environments such as literary salons or religious communities where heterosociality was accepted. Testimony to the then already ambiguous connotations of the term 'friend', the language of family – friends would refer to each other as 'brother' or 'sister', or depending on age differences even 'father', 'daughter', 'mother', or 'son' – served to situate these friendships in a better delineated intimate structure. Embedding heterosocial friendships in the language of family was more than rhetoric; it signaled 'permanence, loyalty and affection' to the other, as well as 'the propriety of the relationship to those around a pair' (Good, 2012, p. 23). That example shows the usefulness of the 'family' label across time and different forms of intimacy: back then, it was a useful as a descriptor of appropriate heterosocial relationships; in the contemporary context of 'families of choice' it is useful as a descriptor of intimacy and communal solidarity; in both cases the label is appropriated in the service of *nonstandard* forms of intimacy.

'Triangulating' the relationship by including spouses in social interactions or by addressing them in letters between the friends was the most common strategy to assuage any notion of impropriety (see also Sedgwick, 1985). At a time when a woman's status was inseparable from that of her husband, when she had little say about their social interactions and especially their socializing outside the home, husbands had the power to decide with whom their wives could and could not socialize. And so marriage could either cement the friendship or expose it to the lethal prohibition of an intolerant or jealous husband (Good, 2012, pp. 23–29). According to Good,

> The sheer frequency of friendships between men and married women suggests that husbands often permitted their wives to enter such relationships or simply did not exercise their authority by interfering. The existence of the protocol here did not prevent friendships between married women and men, suggesting the constant tension between rule and reality. (2012, p. 25)

The need to embed heterosocial friendships in other social relationships in order to align them with norms of public propriety, and the fact that in the case of married women husbands had the authority to condone or prohibit these, meant that the voluntarism, egalitarianism, intimacy, and freedom to self-construct the friendship were severely truncated. The valorization of male friendship as the model friendship also depended on the limitations that male authority placed on heterosocial interactions (Good, 2012, p. 25). This historical example illustrates that while normative homosociality pertains to men and women alike, male authority plays the crucial role in the construction of what is a general social reality.

And yet marriage needed friendship; it could not stand alone very easily, at least as a fulfilling relationship according to the ideal of the companionate marriage, especially when legal prescriptions erased women's identities and legitimized husbands' authority over them. Thus the satisfaction of intimate needs encountered institutional barriers that were compensated for by seeking care, support, and companionship in friendships. Just as heterosocial friendships needed to be embedded in fully recognized social relationships in order to bolster their viability, marriage frequently needed to be embedded in friendships – homosocial and heterosocial – that could deliver the intimacy that marriage may have promised but could only fulfill if couples went against the normative injunctions of patriarchal power (Good, 2012, p. 29).

Clearly, then, during nascent modernity friendship – and none more so than its heterosocial variants – both challenged public norms of gendered propriety and relieved marriage from tensions. Before the advent of Giddens' pure relationship ideal, before the diffusion of the therapeutic ethos, at a moment in history when the notion of friendship as underpinning successful marriages began to emerge as part of the companionate ideal, ideals clashed with legally shored-up male authority. A sense emerges here that the human longing for free association eventually (and with considerable effort on the part of early feminists) won out. But before we might be tempted into a triumphalist stance that relegates these gendered realities to the distant past, we need to take history to the present to fathom the extent of the changes.

Contemporary challenges to cross-sex friendship

The contemporary literature on heterosocial friendship tends to conflate friendships and friendly relations. This can be especially misleading when the frequency of these relationships is at issue, when interview subjects are asked about their preparedness to make friends with the opposite sex, and when they are asked about their behavioral expectations (Afifi & Faulkner, 2000; Fuhrman et al., 2009). The majority of research is focused on platonic friendships between heterosexual women and men. A broader approach is exemplified by that of J. Donald O'Meara, for whom cross-sex friendship denotes 'a specific type of friendship – a nonromantic, nonfamilial, personal relationship between a man and woman', and who qualifies the nonromantic aspect of the relationship 'in the sense that its function is purposefully dissociated from courtship rites by the actors involved. *Nonromantic does not mean, however, that sexuality or passion are necessarily absent from the relationship*' (1989, p. 526, my emphasis). As we shall see further below, that qualification is not only important but prescient, because it was only some time later that the topic of nonplatonic friendship among heterosexuals emerged in the culture to an unprecedented degree.

Sociologists often emphasize structural changes that have led to greater opportunities for the formation of cross-sex friendships. For example, Werking (1997) and Monsour (2002) stress that women's increased labor market participation and a blurring of traditional male and female forms of work have been conducive to friendships between women and men. Add to that the advent of online communication, which has opened new spaces for intimate interaction across the range of gender identities (Lambert, 2013). However, some of the literature overestimates the enabling facets of these changes while underplaying normative constraints (see especially Monsour et al., 1994; Monsour, 2002). Among those researchers who are interested in the normative, sense-making dimensions of heterosocial friendship there is a consensus that it is marked by an absence of cultural scripts that help define and orient, and so give stability of reference to, interactions, whether in the past or today (e.g. Booth & Hess, 1974; Adams, 1985; Rubin, 1985; O'Meara, 1989; Swain, 1992; Fuhrman et al., 2009; Halatsis & Christakis, 2009; Good, 2012). For example, some time ago Booth and Hess (1974) showed that despite structural opportunities these 'anomalous' relationships remained relatively rare because of confusions concerning their relational boundaries. As Swain (1992, p. 169) has argued, these boundaries are strengthened by a 'lack of societal expectations of men's friendship with women, and by the resulting attempts by audiences to interpret them in terms of heterosexual coupling relationships'. In other words, significant structural transformations have not precipitated an equally significant transformation in cultural norms, and of heteronorms in particular:

> Cultural messages provide scripts for how men and women should interact with each other, and therefore, not only gender, but also the gender composition of a friendship influences a platonic relationship. Women and men regularly face a host of media images that romanticize and sexualize their routine encounters and confront an array of societal expectations and constraints that make a rewarding friendship with someone of the 'opposite sex' challenging. Yet males and females now routinely interact within environments that bring them into close contact, such as college, the labor force and other

societal institutions. Cultural scripts have yet to catch up with the times, however. (Felmlee et al., 2012, p. 520)

O'Meara (1989) points to the main challenges that heterosocial friends face, the first three of which – emotional bond, sex, and gender inequality – fit well with the gendered distribution of sociality in the contemporary imagination I have sketched with the love–friendship paradox. The fourth challenge O'Meara highlights is the relationship between the dyad and its 'relevant audiences'. On that view, the constitution of the relationship occurs not only between friends, but also in their interactions with third others 'for the purpose of conveying relationship authenticity' (O'Meara, 1989, p. 537). Rawlins stresses that friends may need to 'adopt a strategic position *vis-à-vis* those who would threaten the relationship with rumors and attributions', and thus 'orchestrate social perception of their relationship' (cited in O'Meara, 1989, p. 537). The embedding of friendships in other, more legitimate private relationships is cited as one strategy and points to historical continuities.

And yet, we might argue that today there is much greater acceptance of cross-sex friendships, and that a greater range of intimate activities is accepted than might have been the case not only in the 18th and 19th centuries, but even only a few decades ago, although that would depend on specific social environments, on the friends' social and relationship status, age, and cultural background. The very fact that these relationships exist at all is testament to individuals' capacities to negotiate public convention, and the judgments or suspicions of significant others, colleagues, peers, or a wider public. They may or may not orchestrate strategies to signal relationship authenticity; they may not care and so ignore others' attributions; but they may also defend their friendship *vis-à-vis* others or terminate interactions with some of them, just as they may 'begin to question their shared reality' and reassert, redefine or terminate their bonds (O'Meara, 1989, p. 539). Culture orients but doesn't determine practices, behaviors, and attitudes; but it also goes deep and reaches the internal dimensions of the dyad, and to a significant degree orients the construction of friendship along gendered lines.

Heterosocial friendship, gendered intimacies, and sexual attraction

If interactions between men and women continue to be informed by assumptions that shore up the institution of heterosexuality, how is that reflected in heterosocial friendships? How does their embeddedness in the gender order manifest in everyday realities? And what strategies might dyads use to bridge the gap between a normative order and the reality of their bonds? The place from which to begin the attempt to answer these questions is a research consensus: the gap left by the absence of cultural schemes that could orient interactions is filled by an orthodox gender scheme that serves as heuristic background to interactions. At a fundamental level, the scheme attributes one set of intimate capacities and typical ways of 'doing' intimacy to men and another to women, and in tandem with a raft of other stereotypes, this intimate essentialism is legitimized on the basis of biological differences. biological differences. The fact that individual men and women *are* able to forge fulfilling intimate, nonromantic bonds with one another might be taken as a sign that they are less likely to buy into stereotypes, since the reality of their relationship is already unconventional. But not only does the literature on automatic stereotyping show that even the most aware and self-consciously inclusive individuals are not immune to stereotypical thinking and prejudice (Allport, 1954; Banaji & Hardin, 1996; Smith, 2001; Irmen, 2006); the literature on cross-sex friendship shows how ever-available gender scripts are played out even in these relationships. Add to that sexual attraction, and we get a fairly confusing mix of scriptlessness and normative prescription, personal sentiments, and desires – of public as well as private ambiguities – that in one way or another have to be negotiated by heterosocial friends. Research on gender norms demonstrates that in the absence of cultural scripts for heterosocial friendship, 'people invoke instead well-known cultural gender schemas' because 'friendship represents a place where gender ideology and inequality are enacted on a regular basis (Felmlee et al., 2012, pp. 527, 519).

A gendered division of intimate modalities is most explicit in the notion that in friendship men 'stand side-by-side', while women are 'face-to-face' (Wright, 1982); that male friendships are characterized by instrumentality; that male intimacy is mediated or sublimated by common interest and shared activities while women's friendships are said to be marked by sharing and emotional connection (Caldwell & Peplau, 1982). These assumptions are constantly reproduced in the cultural formation of model, 'hegemonic' masculinities (Connell, 2005). Although few men manage to embody and live up to them, these models set benchmarks to which men are encouraged to aspire. They invariably include the stoicism of the in-control 'alpha male'. The constant drumming home of normative male homosociality as providing the space for men to be 'real men' sometimes resonates with the timbre of unemotional 'male bonding'. To illustrate: the motto of the *Australian*

Men's Shed Association – a not-for-profit organization whose aim it is to prevent 'social isolation by providing a safe, friendly and welcoming place for men to work on meaningful projects and to contribute to the wider community' – is 'shoulder to shoulder' (AMSA (Australian Men's Shed Organisation), 2014). Especially because this is a well-intentioned, important initiative, it is interesting to note that the sublimation and mediation of intimacy, which a 'shoulder to shoulder' stance infers, is assumed to suffice in diminishing men's sense of social isolation. 'Eye to eye' connection, or 'heart to heart' intimacy between men may be a side-effect of relationships built on common activities; they cannot be directly named. The organization thus seems to recognize that direct appeals to intimacy are likely to discourage men from joining.[3] Such instances do not simply indicate different, gendered modalities of intimacy for men and women, but illustrate the often subtle workings of homophobia.

As Michael Kimmel (2004) has argued, anything that smacks of stereotypically feminine traits devalues masculinity among men, raising the specter of the 'sissy'. Thus men learn from a young age to erase those behaviors, practices, and attitudes (gestures, vocal inflections, interests, appearance, emotional expressiveness, etc.) that are considered effeminate or hint at femininity. Sexism, misogyny, and homophobia are linked. Homophobia is not simply a prejudice against men who are 'homosexual', but a prejudice against femininity (with the 'camp' stereotype the most explicit example), and so cannot be divorced from heterosexism and misogyny. Men, consciously or not, use women as 'currency' in the mutual self-assurance of straight sexuality and stoic masculinity (Kimmel, 2004). Against common sense perception, women only count in masculinizing processes in so far as their essential devaluation as status-conferring signifiers is concerned. On a less controversial level perhaps, the mere fact that some men feel the need to refer to their 'feminine' side when talking about instances of feelings of care, nurturance, and support, and in doing so actually reiterate their essential manliness, shows how deeply etched the cultural norm of stoic masculinity is in individual psyches, despite frequent self-perception to the contrary.

A fairly uncritical approach on gendered intimacies holds that men simply 'do' intimacy differently (Messner, 1992; Davies, 2011). Others argue that especially in America intimacy has been 'feminized' so that the privileging of an expressive female style has ignored the more instrumental male approach (Cancian, 1986, 1990). Without entering into further semantic dissections about what intimacy is, both takes are insufficient: Cancian's because – other than coming close to essentializing gendered intimacies – it underestimates those elements of 'male' intimacy that are significant in friendships between women (Bank, 1995); and the former because it ignores a pressing fact: men increasingly suffer from a lack of intimate connections in their lives (McPherson et al., 2006). And while it may be true that men learn the 'shoulder to shoulder' repertoire of intimate interaction, it is not true that men do not want the kind of intimacies that are generally attributed to women (Burleson, 1997; Greif, 2009). Rather, the characteristics of one 'hegemonic' model are generalized to include all men. It would therefore be highly problematic to suggest that when men's intimate lives are at stake we ought not to use a yardstick by which female modalities of intimacy are measured. Such a stance seriously misjudges a general human need for intimacy and takes a cultural product with potentially harmful consequences as simply an essential part of the male experience. Intimate connections that go to the heart of the human experience ought to be available to everyone regardless of their gender. However, the possibilities for those experiences are differentially distributed along lines of gender in societies where ideals of male stoicism and homophobic and misogynous attitudes are thinly veiled realities. Thus, intimacy in emotional and spiritual terms is for men mostly available only if they are able to foster such connections with women. Among men it appears still to be uncommon.

The rarity of intimacy between men is illustrated by the emergence of the so-called *bromance* in popular culture.[4] Importing the intimacy-signifying semantics of family, and (with a good dose of irony) the semantics of romantic love, it is significant that '[o]nly heterosexuals can have a bromance', that these relationships are therefore strictly platonic (Chen, 2011, p. 248). If a bromance is simply 'a close nonsexual friendship between men' (Sargent, 2013, p. 23), it is interesting that it is in the early 21st century that the label emerges. Let's assume that naming intimate male friendships reflects a need for intimacy that younger generations of men are able to express; that they are able to own up to 'fellow feelings' in a way that older renditions of men's friendships couldn't. We know, for example, that younger cohorts of men are more likely than middle-aged or older men to express emotions, even if they are as yet far from seriously challenging the 'shoulder to shoulder' ideal (Butera, 2008). So, if no other criterion of analysis is brought to bear on these dyadic friendships than the presence or absence of close connections, the emergence of bromance can be seen as a positive development. What is less positive about them, however, is that they also affirm heteronormativity in the context of male homosociality. Rather than evincing a broadening of repertoires of intimacy among men, I suggest the opposite: it shows the depth of normative homosociality and the lengths to which men go in order to signal their heterosexuality. Let's assume that alternative interpretation as our starting position.

Normative homosociality is reproduced in so far as the cultural representations of bromance invariably center on their priority in a hierarchy of men's personal relationships. Take as an example an online article for women that lists, among *10 Signs your Guy is in a Bromance*, 'He has more nicknames for his best guy friend than for you', 'He spends more time getting ready for his bro's night out than for your Friday night date', and 'He answers his buddy's call ... in the middle of sex' (Smith cited in Chen, 2011, pp. 246–247). The tongue-in-cheek tenor of such statements is clear. As in the TV commercials depicting male homosociality I discussed in the previous chapter, humor is again necessary because men can today no longer claim homosociality as an entitlement, or publicly announce their greater estimation of men's company as confidently as other generations still could. Humor obfuscates; it masks normative injunctions, deeply held beliefs, and attitudes behind irony and good-natured 'fun'. Humor can thus be a formidable defense against critique and can work in the service of justifying self-rationalization: critical interpreters can be charged with an inability to take a joke, or to understand the 'real' intentions of actions and statements. One's own utterances and actions can be justified to others and self as 'harmless fun'.

Bromance reproduces heteronormativity not simply by boundary drawing, by spelling out injunctions against whatever behavior may be deemed 'gay' at any given time. It is already instantiated by the very emergence of bromance as a labeled cultural phenomenon. Its representations keep male intimacy resonating in a register that doesn't cause much public dissonance: here we can be 'intimate' but not 'gay' and definitely not 'sissies'. In the handful of American movies and TV sitcoms that have thematized bromances from the early 2000s, any dissonance that could be breaking through the heterosexual boundaries of platonic relations is smoothed by the ironic handling of intimate scenes (Sargent, 2013). Physical intimacy can be mimicked or played at, but never seriously acted out. The boundaries between heterosexuality and its others remain intact. The issue here is not with heterosexuality. Most men, after all, identify as heterosexual and are entitled to signal their sexuality. The issue is another: that over the last decade Anglophone societies especially have carved out a cultural genre, and created a label and language for the relationships that the genre both conjures and describes, so that a need for intimacy among men may at the same time be given rein and be contained within the margins of hetero acceptability. I would suggest that these processes of cultural containment, first and foremost, reflect a cultural unease about male intimacy; an unease about the fact that some younger cohorts may indeed be pushing against traditional boundaries.[5]

There are, then, hopes as well as less salutary continuities with the past. For now it should be clear that there are persistent gendered norms; they are social facts; they are not only challenged, but also drawn upon by many to orient everyday interactions, and this is explicitly the case in cross-sex friendship. The themes of (natural) male stoicism, or lack of emotional expressivity, and (natural) female care and emotional support are evident in the literature on heterosocial friendship, where the consequences of their enactments are shown. For instance, in a study of the mutual support offered by platonic friends, Buhrke and Fuqua (1987) show that in situations of personal stress both men and women are more likely to seek support from their female friends. The authors explain this finding with reference to masculine norms which limit (heterosexual) 'men's same-sex relationships' by discouraging the disclosure of feelings', while 'it may be more socially acceptable for women to be approached for support than men'. They add that social learning processes may be at work in these dynamics: 'given that women are more frequently sought out for support, it may be that women have learned to be better supporters', but they also have 'been socialized into the nurturant role' and thus 'are more likely to be supportive than men' (Buhrke & Fuqua, 1987, p. 349). The women reported that they felt generally 'closer' to their female friends, and so preferred their homosocial relationships. Again, men found intimacy in cross-sex friendship rather than their friendships with other men. But they also tended to overestimate the closeness their women friends felt toward them. Buhrke and Fuqua suspect that women and men may 'apply different standards of closeness so that what may constitute a close relationship for a man may not be considered such by a woman' (1987, p. 350). Differentially distributed expectations about care and support also mean that women are simply more likely to be supportive. Thus it is men, rather than women, who reap the emotional benefits from the relationship (see also Rose, 1985; Rubin, 1985).

Far from signaling that heterosocial friendships are simply enriching for everyone (Monsour et al., 1994; Monsour, 2002), research suggests that men tend to devalue women relative to other men. While men are inclined to value their women friends for the emotional support they can give them, they also hold them to higher relational standards: men are more forgiving toward their male friends should they cancel plans; they use fewer normative expressions ('shoulds') in conversations with male friends than with female friends; and their judgments are particularly harsh should women disclose personal information about them, while they are relatively forgiving toward their male friends in similar circumstances (Felmlee et al., 2012; Felmlee, 1999). Accordingly, 'women are often held more responsible than men for the expression of behaviors in interpersonal relationships that promote emotional closeness, social companionship and overall [relationship] positivity' (Fuhrman et al., 2009, p. 578). It seems as if women are reduced to their attributed emotionality; that even in what is ostensibly an equal, just, and fair relationship of trust, 'emotion work' (Hochschild, 1979) is mostly expected of women, while what they *typically* get in return is not of the same order; of a different order, perhaps, if we think of a feeling of physical safety that women may experience, or if we consider that these friendships can teach us about 'the opposite sex'.

Discrepant experiences and perceptions of intimacy between women and men were reiterated when respondents were asked to report whom they thought they 'knew better', same-sex or cross-sex friends. Men thought they knew their women friends better than same-sex friends, and thought they were better known by their women friends, who in fact did not corroborate such assumptions. Men, while consistently valuing their cross-sex friendships more highly than their same-sex friendships in terms of mutual support and knowledge of one another, just as consistently overvalued how their women friends perceived them in these terms. This might well have to do with the fact that women and men are socialized and encouraged to form divergent senses of self, especially concerning intimate relationships. Citing research on gendered constructions of self, Felmlee et al. (2012) reiterate that women's sense of self is highly contingent on their sense of relatedness to others, to the extent that their sense of independence is correlated to their sense of situatedness in a web of social relationships. For them, independence and interdependence are two sides of the same coin. Men, on the other hand, tend to stress independence and conceive of it in rather individualistic terms (see also Cross & Madson, 1997). These are fundamentally different notions of freedom: one recognizes the generative potentials that inhere in interdependence, in relationships; the other perceives of the need to defend freedom as total independence. The first variant recognizes the fact of our interdependencies; the second clamors for the realization of a fiction, and seeks to have it all – freedom, support or companionship as needs arise, on tap.

But before we jump to essentialize women's intimacy and recommend it as the cure-all for contemporary ills in relationships, we need to remember that the supposed warmth of women's affections is as artificial as the supposed coolness of men's; that the normative edifice we have built around the trope urges women to act accordingly, and silences those among them who don't feel that they can embody the standards of care and affection that are meant to be lodged in their cells. The differences, therefore, exist in reality because they are supposed to exist; and they are supposed to exist because they serve men better than women. On the aggregate level, these culturally embedded differences negatively prejudice the likelihood of cross-sex friendship. Once entered into, these relationships call for considerable communication skills to meet the challenges. Among the range of challenges, none is greater than that of sex.

Sex troubles

Heterosocial friends come up against the love–friendship paradox as a scheme by which people 'develop a generalized readiness to encode all cross-sex interaction in sexual terms and all members of the opposite sex in terms of sexual attractions' (Bern cited in O'Meara, 1989, p. 529). Even if we are for the moment only concerned with 'straight', platonic friendships, cultural expectations and the resultant need to justify the nonsexual nature of their relationship *vis-à-vis* third others, as well as potential sexual attraction on the part of one or both friends, indicate that it has to be contended with as a social fact and individual reality.

Researchers have investigated the challenges that sexual attraction may pose for heterosocial friends and whether women and men tend to think differently about them. Especially in the initiation phase, sexual or romantic attraction between cross-sex friends, whether mutual or one-way, is common. The long-term success of the friendship depends to a considerable degree on the negotiation of guidelines that, in platonic friendships, disallow sexual activity (Fuhrman et al., 2009). In the Greek context, Panayotis Halatsis and Nicolas Christakis (2009) set out to test whether sexual attraction, as one among a variety of possible types of attraction (see Reeder, 2000), actually is a challenge in cross-sex friendship, if so why, and how it is managed by friends.[6] It is important to note here that the authors are pointedly concerned with close friendships, with intimate bonds rather than friendly relations; they are among the very few who recognize the distinction and qualify their choice of sample in this manner. The majority of Halatsis and Christakis' respondents held that while their friendships were not primarily initiated owing to romantic, sexual interest, sexual attraction could emerge out of the intimacy that marks the relationships, but also due to social pressures: 'Even if the two of them don't feel it', states a 37-year-old woman, 'those around them will bring it to their attention and influence them' (Halatsis & Christakis, 2009, pp. 925–926). Real or perceived audience attribution here clearly plays a role.

Research highlights the gendered dynamics of sexual attraction embedded in the heterosocial erotic/romantic imperative, that other half of the love–friendship paradox: men are more likely to be sexually attracted to their women friends than women are to them, irrespective of their own or their friends' relationship status; men rate sex as more beneficial to the friendship than women do, and generally rate sexual attraction higher than women, although everyone seems to think that the costs of sexual attraction – let alone actual sexual activity – out-weigh the benefits; women are mostly aware of men's sexual desires for them, partly because men are also more likely than women to express that attraction (Abbey, 1982; Rose, 1985; Rubin, 1985; Bleske-Rechek et al., 2012; Felmlee et al., 2012). Setting cultural specificities to one side, Halatsis and Christakis (2009) explain some of the differences: 'men's psychosocial role', or in our language social norms to do with mascu-linity, 'requires or justifies a more assertive sexual pursuit, which results in an ambivalent predisposition toward women friends, revealing a vacillation between viewing women as potential sexual partners, on the one hand, and social companions, on the other' (Halatsis & Christakis, 2009, p. 932). This may explain why men are more likely to initiate dat-ing, and women are more likely to initiate friendships (Buhrke & Fuqua, 1987). Another interpretation, which takes its cues from earlier work by Rubin (1985) and Abbey (1982), centers those 'predispositions' more strongly in differentially constructed modalities of and capacities for intimacy. Stoic masculinities – masculinities, that is, that raise emotional non-expressivity to the level of virtue and assign that expressivity along with nurturance and care to women or 'effeminate' men – encourage masculine subjectivities whose experiential repertoire of verbally and physically expressed intimacy is truncated when compared to women. Men are thus more likely than women 'to misconstrue their cross-sex friends' freer expression of intimacy as indication of sexual attraction'. Whether or not this can also be led back to 'a generalized tendency of men to perceive the world in sexual terms' (Halatsis & Christakis, 2009 p. 932) is, however, to tread the line of critique somewhat lightly. I suggest that a generalized tendency of men to perceive women not only as potential companions, but also as currency that shores up valorized male homo-sociality and straight masculinity, ought at the very least be included in social scientific interpretation (for an excellent example see Flood, 2008).

Halatsis and Christakis show that sexual attraction plays an ambivalent role. Confirming other research, they not only echo O'Meara's (1989) and Rawlins' (1982) view that cross-sex friendship can accommodate sexual activities, but that in some cases it may enhance the relationship. In the main, however, sexual attraction is perceived to pose a threat to the friendship. And it is perceived as a threat because, according to the respondents, 'it increases the probability that the friendship will be harmed by the ensuing complications and conflicts' (Halatsis & Christakis, 2009, p. 922). Indeed, most of us are familiar with statements that express the fear that sex and/or romance could destroy a friendship. These 'complications and conflicts' are suspected to emerge from the transformation of friendship into romantic love. That transformation is perceived as migrating the relationship into the much more fixed and highly prescribed terrain of love where 'sexual activity entails commitment, exclusivity, and possessiveness that do no befit a friendship' (Halatsis & Christakis, 2009, p. 923). The fear that sex may diminish the friendship has nothing to do with sex as pleasurable activity. Rather, it has to do with the cultural significance that sexual practice has been made to carry. In this particular context emotional intimacy plus sex signifies erotic love as described and prescribed in the culture. Lacking alternative scripts to draw on, the 'love' script is readily available, as is the newer script of the strictly sexual relationship (e.g. 'friends with benefits', see below); neither, however, suffices to fulfill the needs for friendship for these respondents. In romantic relationships 'partners must constantly monitor their behaviors so as to be mutually likeable, and to monopolize their partner's attention. Thus, they end up not being as authentic as they think they ought to be in a "real friendship"'. Romantic relationships are seen as too 'self-serving' and thus as 'incompatible with the ethical ideal of friendship'; but romantic relationships are also 'associated with more relationship talk, thus affecting the quality of friendship' (Halatsis & Christakis, 2009, p. 926). This accords with my earlier elaboration of love as self-referential, as institutionally connected to a therapeutic ethos and apparatus (Chapter 3). The authors conclude that sexual attraction, whether 'potential or real', does in fact constitute a challenge for cross-sex friends. 'This is likely to be the case, because it causes confusion concerning the relationship's definition and nullifies the benefits of the cross-sex friendship' (2009, p. 926).

For the majority of the participants, emerging sexual attraction did not lead to the termination of the friendship (see also Reeder, 2000). In order to maintain their bonds, different strategies were adopted. About half the respondents did not disclose their sexual attraction to the other, because they wanted to preserve the friendship and to avoid rejection. For about a fifth of the sample, mutual disclosure of attraction led to the formation of romantic liaisons, a minority terminated their friendship (16%), and about a quarter successfully integrated sexual practices into the friendship and found this to be an enhancement of the relationship (Halatsis & Christakis, 2009, p. 933). The study confirms that due to the lack of scripts concerning cross-sex friendship,

> every close friendship between a man and a woman alludes to a latent sexual attraction. Cross-sex friends have to affirm the non-sexual and/or the nonromantic nature of their relationship intrapersonally, interpersonally, and with their social networks ... [W]hen [sexual attraction] is expressed, however, friends need to explicitly or implicitly negotiate that nature of their relationship. (Halatsis & Christakis, 2009, p. 934)

Intersectional friendships

The need to describe, label, and categorize the relationship, to create clarity about what it is and what exactly it represents, is then ever at the forefront of those types of heterosexual, cross-sex friendships that transgress the normative scheme of the love–friendship paradox. But the issues do not stop with heterosexuality. While the literature on homosocial friendship among same-sex attracted individuals points to far more practical fluidity between the 'love' and 'friendship' categories, and to greater acceptance of that fluidity in nonheterosexual communities (Nardi, 1999; Foucault, 2000; Bray, 2003), friendships between straight men and lesbian women, and gay men and straight women, constitute less clear-cut cases. Anna Muraco's *Odd Couples* (2012) is, to the best of my knowledge, currently the only research into what she calls 'intersectional friendships'.[7] That research is particularly interesting because at first glance we might assume that the mismatch in sexual identities renders heteronormative imperatives null and void.

Intersectional friends 'police' stereotypes of sex, gender, and sexual orientation, but according to Muraco also act as 'gender outlaws' who challenge mainstream norms (2012, pp. 78–100). For example, friends 'police' situations where gay males turn straight women friends into mothers, or when straight women turn gay friends into paragons of masculinity while simultaneously valuing their feminine qualities. The evidence supporting 'outlaw' behavior is thin, however: women engaging in shared activities that are traditionally assigned to masculinity (playing pool), and gay male friends raising their straight women friends' esteem by commenting favorably on their bodies and encouraging 'sex positive' attitudes are taken here to signify acts of defiance. Actually, 'outlaw' behavior is virtually absent, leading Muraco to conclude that 'the straight men and straight women ... reaped the greatest benefits in terms of support for gender nonconformity in intersectional friendships' (Muraco, 2012, p. 99). This, I would suggest, says more about the triumph of heteronormativity – and heterosexuals – than norm-breaking innovation.

Muraco also turns to the problem of sexual attraction. She shows how for some friends the absence of sexual attraction fosters closeness, but also how the irreducibility of sexual orientation to a straight/gay dichotomy conjures erotic desire as 'both a nuisance and a threat to friendship' (2012, p. 116). Again, the absence of a script specific to these friendships leaves a void that is frequently filled by heteronormative scripts. For instance, straight women friends of gay men may interpret intimacy as romance, and some men fantasize that their bonds will turn lesbian women straight. Aside from showing that sexual tensions may be present in these friendships, Muraco convincingly marshals them as evidence for the fluidity of sexual identities, the efficacy of heteronormative assumptions across genders and sexualities, and the cultural depth of the platonic friendship norm. Despite the tensions between cultural rules and reality, these friendships not only problematize sexual practices because of their very intersectionality, but because sexuality is either sidelined or quarantined, while intimacy is by and large preserved.

The nonstandard quality of and cultural unease about these relations are evident in the need to name them, and what's more, often name them derisively. When it is general knowledge that a woman prefers to associate with gay males, for example, the term 'fag hag' is sometimes used (although whether it is intended pejoratively or not depends on who does the designating) (Moon, 1995; Muraco, 2012, pp. 95–96). The point to be reiterated here is this: heteronormativity, especially as lodged in the love–friendship paradox which prescribes the normative terms of engagement in heterosocial and homosocial contexts, while most explicitly efficacious in heterosexual cross-sex friendship, makes its presence felt even in those heterosocial bonds where seemingly non-complementary sexualities may be assumed to disallow the challenge of sexual attraction and gendered attributions of intimacy.

Romantic others

In her historical analysis Cassandra Good shows how cross-sex friends would seek to affirm the authenticity, respectability, and propriety of their relationship by actively embedding them in marital relationships. Whatever the historical differences, these third, significant others continue to matter. At least one study shows that people tend to have higher expectations of their romantic partners than of their cross-sex or same-sex friends regarding emotional closeness, social companionship, and overall relationship satisfaction, although participants had significantly higher expectations of their cross-sex friends if they themselves were not in a romantic relationship. Apart from showing that the participants perceived cross-sex friendships to be fundamentally different from romantic relationships – the latter has at least notionally to do with long-term commitment – the study confirms that cross-sex friendships are especially vulnerable to romantic relationships, not least because 'individuals who have a romantic partner tend to shift away from [especially cross-sex] friends as the primary source of emotional support' (Fuhrman et al., 2009, p. 585; for a study of attachments among young people see Markiewicz et al., 2006).

Although the psychological literature rarely offers explanations for these findings, we can interpret them against the backdrop of the love ideology's lynchpin: monogamous exclusivity. That need for exclusivity rests on the need to be validated as authentic, unique, and therefore irreplaceable – as 'special', something that friendship can fulfil to a limited extent only because here inclusivity rather than exclusivity is the rule. The emphasis on exclusivity in love makes a degree of jealousy highly functional to couple relationships, despite popular advice against it (e.g. Bevan, 2009). Jealousy is functional in love because it signals emotional attachment to and desire for the other; it is a sign of love that is time and again reiterated in popular culture and is, for all its pathological aspects (Fromm, 2013), particularly potent because the question 'Does s/he really love me?' is as central to the experience of passionate love as it is unanswerable. Now, 'the existence of [cross-sex] friendship can generate a great deal of suspicion and jealousy', to the extent that often 'the only viable or "safe" cross-sex friends are relatives or those who are nested in couple relationships' (O'Meara, 1989, p. 539). Thus, friendships can not only enrich couple relationships by adding social support (Monsour, 2002), and by opening coupledom to 'outside' impulses, but also because it can serve as the foil against which jealousy is projected and love's passion affirmed.

To view this from an admittedly coarse-grained historical perspective, I suggest that while once the legally enshrined right for men to possess women gave institutional legitimacy to jealousy, and therefore to the curtailment of women's freedom of association, from about mid-20th-century exclusivity was 'democratized': now women too could insist on adherence to the exclusivity norm, and eventually could seek legal remedy should their spouses transgress it. But with the equalization of exit options from marriages, and the call for more equal participation in the intimate sphere, its terms not only shifted in the legal domain; they shifted also from (male) ownership to the shared psychological and emotional *entitlement* to a fulfilling love relationship. And commitment to another and to a shared life, even if 'until further notice', remains the anchor for exclusive monogamous love, whether in marriage or not. That ideology does not go unchallenged; it is the main logic against which proponents of alternative, nonmonogamous relationships pit themselves – and in so doing highlight its persistence (Klesse, 2014).

Moreover, coupledom is imbued with the notion of a shared life-project that typically contains plans to do with kids and mortgages, and increasingly calls for the synchronization of asynchronous work trajectories, but also entails having to deal with the mundane realities of shared living and the 'gripes' it may foster (Blatterer, 2009; Kaufmann, 2009). On that view the freedom of friendship looks attractive indeed. But friendship does not simply trump, or win out over, these banal realities of love. The love ideology, after all, promises that love can conquer all that lies in its way, and that conquering the banal realities of the everyday is simply more easily done together with shared aims to focus solidarity. Cross-sex friendship 'promises' nothing. Thinly represented in the terrain of popular culture, their plots in any case mostly turn out to be love stories, and love stories of the most conventional kind. Here heterosocial friendship is either merely a phase people go through, or a challenge that needs to be met in order to test the power of love. Love remains, as an ideology and desired set of practices, the central benchmark to heterosocial intimacy, whatever its 'structural' organization, in marriage, cohabitation or otherwise. A partner's friendship with someone of the opposite sex may thus be perceived as a threat or challenge to the relationship, because these friends threaten or challenge the hope of one's irreplaceability in the eyes of the other, and threaten or challenge the promise of the relationship as a mutual project – a project whose success is measured in the collaborative achievement of tangible markers that are highly valued in our society.

Friends with benefits and erotic friendship

Tomas, protagonist of Milan Kundera's *The Unbearable Lightness of Being* (1984), 'desired but feared' women.

> Needing to create a compromise between fear and desire, he devised what he called 'erotic friendship'. He would tell his mistresses: the only relationship that can make both partners happy is one in which sentimentality has no place and neither partner makes any claim on the life and freedom of the other. To ensure that erotic friendship never grew into the aggression of love, he would meet each of his long-term mistresses only at intervals. He considered this method flawless and propagated it among his friends: 'The important thing is to abide by the rules of threes. Either you see a woman three times in quick succession and then never again or you maintain relations over the years but make sure that the rendezvous are at least three weeks apart.' (1984, p. 11)

What Kundera describes as 'erotic friendship' clearly has a sexual dimension, but has nothing to do with friendship. Highly strategic, these kinds of relationships are mutually agreed upon and ultimately self-serving relationships of sexual needs fulfillment. Care and support need only be present to a very limited extent, if at all. Trust may or may not confine itself to issues around sexual health. The other's life as such, her relationships, dreams, desires, hopes, and fears need not matter. While relationships of a sexually 'intimate' nature, they are devoid of intimacy. The most common descriptor of these relationships, whether in everyday discourse or in cultural productions such as Hollywood movies, blogs, online and offline magazines and in the research literature, is 'friends with benefits' (Afifi & Faulkner, 2000; Eisenberg et al., 2009; Lehmiller et al., 2011; Vanderdrift et al., 2012).[8] The literature tends to conflate these relationships with the strong ties of friendship, or differentiates them only insufficiently along the lines of intimacy. Once differentiated along lines of intimacy, we can glean friends with benefits relationships' (FWBRs) strategic rather than intimate rationale not only in Kundera's fictional account but in everyday attempts to delimit and bed down the relationship category by setting out rules. Much like Tomas, Hartley (2010), for example, offers up rules to a presumably male audience, which include:

(1) *Don't hang out with her.* ... Take the 'friend' part of that phrase lightly. Just because you are friends doesn't mean you have to go out to dinner, even if she's paying for herself.

(3) *Limit your time to less than 2 hours.*

(4) *Talk on the phone one to two times a week.*

(5) *No email allowed.* Whether one of you is in a committed relationship or not, it's best not to put anything in writing.

(7) *Don't do pillow talk.* If you want to remain friends with benefits, and nothing more, don't reveal your dreams and ambitions after you get laid.

(9) *No sleep overs.*

(10) *Run at the first talk of becoming more than friends with benefits.*

Likewise, Kwateng (2010) urges women to 'REMEMBER you're not his girlfriend', that '[a]ll the common relationship courtesies don't apply' and that 'being F.W.B. with a close friend' is to be avoided in favor of '[h]ooking up with acquaintances', which is 'an ideal situation because you don't run into them on a regular basis.' Intimacy is to be avoided at all costs, or is at least considered a real threat to these opportunistic – though presumably often sexually satisfying – encounters. Thus FWBRs can be assigned to the range of friendly relationships and, do not meet the criteria for friendship.

Of course, whatever the rules and whatever the sociological categorization pursued here, in practice dyads will always find their own way of negotiating interactions, whether or not lines into the romantic terrain are crossed, whether or not and to what degree intimacy is permitted to enter. But at least as far as the cultural representations and collective ways of talking about these relationships are concerned, we are not dealing here with friendship in the intimate sense. When they are reduced to episodic 'hook ups', these relationships are instrumental, are geared toward the fulfillment of sexual needs and therefore need not involve the mutual trust, care, and respect we can expect from friendship. In their study of the first-year college experience, Wade and Heldman (2012) show that FWBRs in the context of a prevailing 'hookup culture' are little more than pretexts for instrumental sexual encounters in which young men call the shots and young women feel enormous pressure to conform. Actual friendship is almost impossible.

Female students 'believed that all men wanted sex from all women and, despite the "friends with benefits language" often used to describe friendship that included sexual activity, sex and the potential for sex seriously undermined friendship' (Wade & Heldman, 2012, p. 136). As one student states:

> They all have sex on their minds. Every guy I connect with here on a purely friendly level has sent me numerous texts around 2 am asking, 'Hey you. What are you up to?' … straight guys rarely want to be just friends with women. Even if the girl is ugly, he could drink enough to make her pretty.

FWB experiences at college include what the authors call 'the normalization of masculine coercion'. What appear to be frequent and mostly alcohol-fuelled instances of psychological and physical coercion were only with difficulty understood by the women in those terms because in the cultural context those actions appeared normal. Just as the women felt they needed to comply with a highly sexualized set of practices – some women, for example, made sure to lose their virginity before entering college in order not to be marginalized from the start – so the men too felt pressure to prove their masculinity by having sex, even if that meant the application of undue pressure, or engaging in behavior that by any other standards is assault or rape (Wade & Heldman, 2012, pp. 137–138).

This is not to simply write off FWBRs. Time and context clearly matter. While they have probably been with us for a long time, the very fact that they have required a label and have become culturally represented only very recently marks a further differentiation of private life in the emergence of a distinct, autonomous sexual sphere in step with historical processes that saw the increasing eroticization of romantic love from about the 19th century. Recreational sex is 'freed' not only from the mutuality of intimacy, but is also 'freed' from the market place (e.g. sex work) and 'freed' from social opprobrium. Viewed positively, FWBRs may indicate an increasing flexibility concerning the range of friendships as they may evince the broadening scope of the relationship driven by everyday practices (Allan, 2008). Viewed more skeptically, we might point out that these dyads are not only *not* required to enact the characteristics of friendship, but are encouraged to shun the interdependencies that come with caring for another. In that vein, Kundera's account speaks eloquently to (male) freedom as the denial of interdependence.

But the mutual abnegation of intimacy also implies something else, namely that the doors are wide open to unjust and disrespectful practices, attitudes, and behaviors. Rather than merely indicating a democratization of sexual relations between men and women, these relationships may just as well constitute realizations of masculinizing fantasies among males that give priority to serial, casual hook-ups with a minimum of emotional fuss that, for that very reason, are probably quite rare in their pure form (Epstein et al., 2009). We may also wonder who in these relationships, as far as they are realized, actually 'benefits'. While the term 'fuck buddies' may not resonate well with producers of large-scale cultural productions and standard-bearers of community values, it is at least a more honest and to the point descriptor of the content and function of these relationships. It seems, then, that Kundera's 'erotic friendship' label needs to be reserved for relationships where intimate friendship and sexual play are conjoined, while the orthodoxies of romantic coupledom are declined.

These erotic friendships sit squarely on the boundaries we have collectively drawn around (platonic) friendship and (erotic) love. They are mainly discussed in nonheterosexual contexts (Nardi, 1999; Foucault, 2000; Bray, 2003) – in contexts, that is, where heteronorms do not apply and are therefore subject to different 'community' values and standards (Weeks, 1996; Weeks et al., 2001; Heaphy et al., 2004). Whether or not heterosexual relationships of that kind augur 'the end of homosexuality' (Bech, 1997) in so far as they successfully mimic the more open possibilities of gay friendships and so diminish the latter's extraordinariness remains to be seen. Clearly, those who construct 'straight' erotic friendships are likely to find historic precedent and contemporary realities in nonheterosexual relationships, while at the same time having to negotiate their friendships against the background of institutionalized heterosexuality.

In straight as well as queer contexts, 'open' or polyamorous relationships approximate erotic friendships. To various degrees of political commitment, polyamorous relationships are self-consciously nonmonogamous or anti-monogamous; they shun the strictures of romantic exclusivity and thus seek to rework a central promise of the Western love ideology: to be recognized by the other as authentic, special, and irreplaceable. Instead, only perceived parts of various individual selves are affirmed as unique. Partners are therefore no longer expected to be irreplaceable as far as the totality of their being is concerned, but because there are *some things* about them that are seen to be irreplaceable, something that resonates strongly with Simmel's thoughts on the differentiated personality (Chapter 4).

In times of a burgeoning need for the justification of traditional forms of intimacy, the increasing cultural visibility of polyamory – see for instance self-help literature and TV series (Taormino, 2013) – has also translated into growing academic interest. What is as yet on the margins of research are those heterosexual, cross-sex friendship dyads that more closely than polyamorous relationships approximate romantic coupledom and yet eschew its central characteristics. Unlike polyamory, this kind of erotic friendship may or may not be open to third or more others; it may or may not, therefore, include the political motive to challenge monogamy. Unlike many polyamorous relationships, and unlike more traditional romantic relationships, they do, however, eschew romance and the construction of a life-project consisting of socially validated tangibles (e.g. mortgages, cohabitation, family, children), and so sit squarely in the terrain of intimate friendship.

We don't know how common and how successful such erotic friendships are. Little beyond anecdotal evidence is available (e.g. Halatsis & Christakis, 2009). But going by the realities of the normative barriers to cross-sex friendship in the heterosexual mainstream that I have discussed at length, they are likely to be rare. Where they exist they need to be negotiated in a semantic vacuum. There are no publicly available stories to guide interaction. The relationship has to be self-constructed to an extraordinary degree and makes communication about the 'terms and conditions' of the relationship extraordinarily important, something that friendship in the orthodox sense does without, but love needs. Communication in order to maintain the relationship is so important in heterosexual erotic friendship because the only available scripts are those that devalue heterosocial friendship, or in any case recommend platonic interactions, and those that center on the orthodoxies of romantic coupledom. These friendships deserve research attention. We need to ask: how common are they? Who engages in them? How do people negotiate them? What obstacles do these friends encounter, and what do they gain? What tensions do these relationships create or help alleviate? To the extent that they exist, these erotic friendships are limit cases, dyads that 'subvert' heteronormative sociality in the intimate sphere. I suspect they are subversive not because they build cultural enclaves inside a mainstream from which they hope to 'queer' the institution of heterosexuality, but because they are doing it 'just so' – in the suburbs, mostly without political motive, unmarked by the accouterments of sexual identity politics, or the deconstructive zeal of an intellectual elite. They expose the persistent power of heteronormative assumptions around friendship and love, and the irrepressibility of human agency and creativity as we strive to realize intimacy.

Conclusion

The thesis that friendship as a noninstitutionalized relationship is relatively free of cultural prescription and may even be immune, resistant to, or subversive of cultural norms, conventions, and social trends stands corrected when the light falls on heterosocial friendships, particularly in the heterosexual mainstream. Here the limit of friendship's freedom is explicit. While in all friendships cultural norms have only limited prescriptive power, in cross-sex friendships that freedom does not pertain, or in any case has a different source. Heterosocial friends need to carve out their freedom of association against the realities of the love–friendship paradox; against heteronormative ideals that allot to heterosociality the 'hot' passions of erotic love, and to homosociality the 'warm' bonds of friendship. Heterosocial friends are free to shape their personal relationship according to their own desires. But they also have to contend with heteronormative barriers that do not pertain to homosocial friendships. The void left by the absence of cultural scripts concerning interactions between cross-sex friends, whether platonic or sexual, is filled by gendered assumptions concerning normative forms of sociality. These assumptions limit more than the freedom of friendship, however; they limit also the possibility to imagine these relationship in other than gendered and sexualized terms, that is, simply as friendships between individuals who are more than their genders and sexual proclivities and identities.

Several cultural phenomena, then, converge to render heterosocial erotic attraction and romantic ideals the order of the day, with the love–friendship paradox its fitting frame of reference. Against its heuristic background, platonic heterosocial friendships challenge received notions about normative sexual attraction and the gendered attribution of intimacy. But they do so not because they simply repudiate expectations in practice. As we have seen, they may just as well reproduce deep-seated cultural norms. They challenge common sense above all because they highlight the *contingency* of relationship categories, their social constructedness, and therefore their changeability. The normative barriers that heterosocial friends face and the common sense descriptions and prescriptions about the 'natural order' of things intimate they encounter, recreate, or change are the stuff of these relationships.

More than that, however, cross-sex friends point beyond themselves. From the small enclave of dyadic intimacy, their practical engagements in the world tell us something about the persistence of a gender order that 'orders' indeed; that reduces complexity and in so doing distorts interactions between women and men, because that reduction is always premised on another: the reduction of people to physical markers that have been made to figure as insignia of such fundamental difference that even in the intimate sphere – in that terrain of life where the soul, the heart are supposed to live in good accord with reason – the gap between them is barely bridged in modes of sociality so as to affirm our similarities while giving space to that which may be different. And that goes to show that the study of dyads can tell us much about the societies in which we live. In this particular case, it is this: if even the freest of all interpersonal relationships, the freest of all human associations, is marked by the limiting dynamics of gendered relations, the societies in which they are lived continue to be marked by an unequal distribution of gendered power, not only in market and polity, but also in the everyday interactions between men and women who care for one another.

Conclusion: Friendship's Embedded Freedom

Freedom is a universal human value. And among all social relationships friendship holds the greatest potential for it to be realized. But it's not the kind of freedom that those who can only conceive of it as an unfettered independence from others hold as their central creed. It's not the kind of 'live and let live' freedom that some think suffices to make for a 'good society' simply because we refrain from encroaching on the freedoms of others. It's not the kind of 'freedom of choice' we are asked to (literally) buy into, although the freedom to choose a life of our own is a significant achievement for those who are able to actively do so. Those versions of freedom either de-emphasize or ignore its very wellspring: our sociality, our need and capacity to exist and to create, in concert with others, the conditions for an autonomous existence. The web of interdependences we weave together delivers its basic conditions; it holds us and frees us in holding us. Without its hold we fall, while the exercise of power constricts it, strangling freedoms large and small. The kind of freedom friendship can deliver is the freedom to be yourself. Not despite others, but because of them. Not because in these others you may find a willing audience that listens to your concerns and opinions, but because together you can create intimacy that allows the continuance of what Arendt, while critical of a modern retreat to the intimate sphere, with reference to Rousseau, has called the 'rebellion of the heart' (1958, p. 39).

Intimacy has the potential to 'rebel' against those dynamisms of modernity that since the Enlightenment have been valorized but also critiqued by social thinkers. Especially friendship retains that potential. Exchange relationships that objectify others for their use value have no place in friendship. Adam Smith's hope to integrate friendship into the contractual exchange relations of commercial society remains unrealized even in full-blown capitalist market society. The hope to integrate friendship into law, to make the relationship subject to formal norms that could govern obligations and distribute rights (Leib, 2011), is based on a fundamental misjudgment of intimacy. Rights and obligations can be legislated, intimacy cannot. Those aspects of the popular therapeutic ethos that seek to address the pain and hurt that often accompany relationships, by way of reifying emotions and objectifying relationships, have little to offer to friendship. Whether or not it is 'therapeutic' for friends to have one another in their lives is beside the point. The real point is that friendship cannot be reduced to 'the relationship' as a topic of endless talk about it, to be dissected, weighed, and measured for its mutual benefits. When the relationship itself, and not the other, becomes the subject of discussion, it is either a sign of trouble, a sign that friendship may have changed form and become 'love' in the orthodox sense, or that it may simply no longer exist. Intimate friendship between men 'rebels' against the reproduction of a masculinity that can perceive of itself only in enactments of stoicism, homophobia, and sexism and so averts its eyes from the other. But by breaking through the artifice and rules of male homosociality it also has the potential to question and to resist the normalcy of heteronormativity, and little by little challenge the taken-for-grantedness of the love–friendship paradox that, beyond friendship, casts intimacy in a differentiating and ultimately marginalizing light. All friendships hold the potential to realize the experience of freedom. Its value is most starkly visible in friendships between women and men where sex may or may not serve the relationship, but does not determine it, because intimacy cannot be reduced to it. In friendship, then, freedom and intimacy are inseparable.

But, as we have seen, the freedom of friendship has its limits. There is a difference between what friendship does and what it promises. While intimacy and freedom together in this relationship have resisted the encroachment of exchange relations – have resisted bureaucratization, but also the psychologization of the relationship – it is also an arena in which gender relations are not merely challenged but reproduced. The friendship dyad – the smallest of all social relationship, and so the smallest of all available sociological prisms – contains *in nuce* gender relations in the culture at large. That may well be the most significant sociological yield of the previous chapters. For, as Simmel well knew and urged us to take seriously, sociologists cannot afford to neglect any type of relationship, no matter how 'large' or 'small', in our efforts to investigate, understand, and explain central aspects of our sociality. And part of that work must surely be to make connections between private experience and public life, even between the ephemeral and fleeting instances of human interaction and social-cultural trends, because neither can be well understood without the other. In our particular case that connection is as follows.

Friendship is the least prescribed and scripted of all interpersonal relationships. As such it can be conceived as the freest. But in this freest of all relationships unequal societal gender relations are manifest; they are not merely 'sedimented' in friendship but actively made, as well as reworked, and challenged. To put it with a different emphasis: since the freest of all relationships refracts the normative injunctions of a gender order that continues to posit women and men as fundamentally different and unequal, the power of that order in the everyday lives of 'ordinary' people is great indeed; its strength is so great, in fact, that there are 'terms and conditions' concerning gendered interactions that are largely unquestioned, as the persistence of the love–friendship paradox shows. In the heterosexual mainstream at least we continue to make assumptions about the natural order of gendered sociality: friendship is homosocial, love heterosocial. The ideational persistence of that scheme, its normativity, despite far messier realities, leaves no doubt that heteronormativity continues to hold tremendous orienting power concerning the formation and lived experience of intimate relationships, and that not only in the realm of erotic love, but in the more open terrain of friendship. Our 'advanced' societies are thus gendered through and through. Friendship too is part of that gender order. Its social freedom is therefore an *embedded* freedom.

But what does it mean, to say that friendship is embedded in the gender order, takes part in its differentiating dynamics, but is untroubled by, say, capitalism? After all, the commercialization of intimate life with respect to love, but also love's openness to the therapeutic professions, does not obtain to friendship according to my argument. Gender is a universal differentiating category, while capitalism is an economic, political, and cultural organizing principle of social relations that is particular to some societies, and depending on context takes on particular form. That capitalism – or socialism for that matter – also structures gender relations was already explained by Friedrich Engels' *The Origin of the Family, Property and the State* (2010 [1884]). And in fact, because women were for such a long part of our history confined to the household, it was extraordinarily difficult for them to establish friendships on the cusp of the public and the private spheres; friendships, that is, as lauded from Aristotle to the Enlightenment and beyond. Gender cuts deep into the fabric of individual identity. So do 'the hidden injuries of class' (Sennett & Cobb, 1972). The gender order organizes relationships between the socially constituted categories 'man' and 'woman'. The economic order organizes social relations, attributes status and prestige, and awards tangible and intangible resources along lines of class. But in terms of *individual identification* these are also different orders, whatever their interrelations. That is not to say that friendships are somehow disembedded from the economic order. It's simply to suggest that processes of gender attribution are more immediate because sex categories, pre-reflectively assigned, appear more obvious than class differences. Once gender is attributed all sorts of normative behaviors, attitudes, and practices are called in, monitored, and policed by self and others. Sexualities, character traits, body movements, patterns of speech, cultural tastes, and so on, are expected and performed; gender is embodied in a sense that class belonging and political and economic persuasions are not. There is no equivalent to social mobility in gender, at least not in terms of scale and bodily and representational consequences if we take various possibilities of gender performance or gender reassignment into the equation.

The embodiment of gender, the carrying in us of the cultural schemes that typify and differentiate between that which counts as masculine or feminine, makes the 'crucial difference between the symbolic order of gender and other social classifications such as class' (Krais, 2006, p. 121). Carving out a personal sense of identity against the attributions and expectations of audiences is therefore in most cases an extraordinarily difficult and courageous undertaking, as 'coming out' stories and transgender (auto)biographies attest. That embodied sense of what it means to be a woman or man, a 'sense' that is usually shored up in the most fleeting of encounters, in the 'just so-ness' of the everyday, and is honed again and again in relation to our own bodies, our own selves. The freedom of friendship is embedded in the gender order and thus limited to the same degree to which normative notions of (heterosexual) masculinity and femininity are embedded in social and psychological processes of gender identification.

To speak about friendship's freedom as an embedded freedom is not only to highlight the normative force of the gender order, but also to realize that women and men are able to construct fulfilling friendships despite societal barriers to heterosocial friendship. This is not simply a statement about 'structure vs. agency', that perennial conceptual bugbear in sociology, the center of a debate that seeks to understand how exactly individual action links with structural and cultural conditions. It is an indication, rather, that human creativity and learning are not simply stymied by limits, but that the limits themselves can constitute the stuff from which creative action is made. Not unlike the overturning of status barriers by 19th century lovers, as depicted by Jane Austen and others, although with less momentous consequences, the overturning of the love–friendship paradox by heterosocial friends speaks to the power of intimacy to subvert public norms. Norms of gendered sociality are especially stubborn. It is one thing to read about strategies marshaled by cross-sex friends among the 18th and 19th century elite in order to retain public respectability, but it is quite another to ponder the persisting unease about intimate relationships between men and women that do not fit the scheme of erotic coupledom at a time when intimate life is said to be up for grabs, its vicissitudes made to appear personal business only, while its orienting cultural matrix seems hopelessly out of date. To that extent, research on cross-sex friendship speaks more eloquently about the reproduction of normative forms of gendered interaction than barrier-breaching innovation. But when it does turn to the latter it tells us that people learn; that they learn not only about the other, but also about the others' social category, about them as men or as women. Thus there is at least a potential that inheres in the generativity of friendship – a generativity that thrives on difference.

The notion of generativity combines a sense of generosity with that of creativity, and illustrates all that is life-affirming in personal relationships. But is all that not merely so much idealization? Is it not simply the continuance of an Aristotelian take on friendship that sees in its virtuous variant all that is beautiful, good? And of course the answer must be 'yes'. Not all friendship is generative, because not all friends, however intimate, 'draw' each other. Friendship can just as well be a resting place in which to be, a 'home' in which to put your feet up and let go; it can be regenerative as well as generative, with neither excluding the other. Whether or not it leads to a development of self is surely specific to the relationship in question. But to say that something is ideal is not to say it cannot be real. We can, of course, measure instances of its reality, research design methods that help us sift the ideal from the real. We might then come to the conclusions that the ideal of friendship is seldom borne out in reality, or that friendship the way I have discussed it here is very rare indeed – so rare in fact that it is hardly worth writing about in a social science context concerned with generalities. None of this ought to be dispiriting for the simple fact that such friendships do exist. And so what we can glean in the relationship – the way it has been written about and experienced, in the cultural layer of collective understanding that has congealed around it – is the difference between an ideal and a utopia. Friendship is not utopian. Its potentials are also always real. It changes lives.

Love revisited

None of this is impossible in love, because here too, with our lovers and spouses and partners, we are able to discover hitherto hidden aspects of ourselves. Our lives take new directions, and given that there is commitment to common life-projects, given that we are able to negotiate not just the big questions of a life together, but also the banal incommensurabilities of everyday life, erotic love, like friendship, provides a space for self-reflection, growth, and learning. Love, like friendship, allows us to extend ourselves out to another, and in that mutual extension we may generate possibilities for change in the context of care, affection, and respect. It is in this sense that Erik Erikson (1994) wrote about 'generativity' as a stage in adult ego development. And while we could debate the merits of the 'ages and stages' approach to human development (Blatterer, 2009), there is a recognition in Erikson's conception that a reconciled relation to self crucially depends on the ability to extend the self to others with genuine care.[1] That the capacity to extend that care, and its fruitfulness, depends on the same capacity for intimacy in the other is to give a sociological spin to his approach.

The issue with love, then, is not whether or not individual relationships can be fulfilling. Just like there are fulfilling cross-sex friendships, there are of course fulfilling love relationships, because we cannot account for the specificity – the ingenuity, creativity, loving capacities, and compatibilities – of single individuals. After all, it is social scientists who detect relationship categories and give life to them via 'second-order' interpretation. People's individual interactions constantly confound the artificial constructs we create in typifying work. And so it is decidedly not the case that romantic coupledom is somehow 'lesser' than friendship. The issue is another: the image of (heterosexual) love handed down to us from a time when intimacy moved to the heart of love, when marriages began to be forged on the uncertain basis of feelings, has for all its emancipatory moments also bequeathed us tremendous uncertainties and contradictions. Erich Fromm (2013), for example, recognized that the dream factories' relentless construction of love as romance, as a sentimentality that could ultimately be *purchased*, had very little to do with generativity, but had everything to do with the self-sustenance of various industries. The constant reproduction of love as irrationality, the repetition of the ever-same mantra that says that only an irrational love is 'true love', justifies not only the sweetest moments of tenderness, but also the most vile and destructive actions.

At the same time, the maintenance of gushing sentimentality and of the erotic energies that usually accompany the beginnings of relationships is expected to be sustained infinitely as the central signifier of intimacy. These expectations, fuelled at every turn by cultural representations, take on particular significance in societies where the very reason for relationships is the fulfillment of emotional and sexual needs. The problem is thus not with love as a set of emotions. After all, as such it pertains to friendship as well. The problem lies with how that set of emotions has been culturally framed, with the expectations with which it is loaded, and with what human realities its ideology may hide. Mary Evans comes to the point:

> The West ... endorses and validates romance, and yet cannot recognize that the encouragement of this set of feelings places a terrible burden of expectation on its participants. To be 'romantic' has always been associated with turning away from reality. In relations between men and women our apparently overwhelming need for romance would sometimes suggest that the reality of these relations is too awful to be allowed. (2003, p. 18)

What might Evans mean by 'the reality' of love, by that which romance promises to overcome or least help us forget for a while? Perhaps that loving coupledom is mostly about the mundane, routine interactions of everyday life; that love is in the shared *doing* of those ever available fifty per cent – half the housework, half the childcare, half the organization of leisure pursuits and social events, of caring for the other; and doing it with a full, respectful orientation to the other. Perhaps love has something to do, then, with the shared engagement in the banal necessities of life as well as extraordinary moments in the shelter of intimacy. For it to become a reality on a massive scale – let alone supersede that repertoire of romantic representations that replaces the sharing of the mundane with the mundanity of consuming – gender relations would have to be dramatically different, and that would, among other things, necessitate a major social redefinition of masculinity. For as long as independence rather than interdependence remains the model of masculine freedom, and as long as therefore women are called upon to muster their 'natural' capacities to make love work, nothing much is going to change. The issue with love then is not its individual problems or successes, but its cultural frame *against* which intimacy needs to be constructed.

Psychologically, emotionally, materially, there is simply less at stake in friendship than in love. While it is desirable to have close friends, and while in the social media age the practice of 'friend farming' indicates that there is some status to be gained in the popularity stakes from increasing your number of *Facebook* friends, this is in no way comparable to the valorization of love relationships. Besides being regarded as central to the organization of domestic, economic, and social life, coupledom has been invested with meanings that go to the core of our individuality. It promises an authentic inner life, and a sense of emotional and material security, respite from the threats or realities of alienation (Langford, 2013, p. xi). Commitment to the other is synonymous with commitment to a chosen life together, and so to continuous negotiation and communication with all the pressures that may bring.

For couples, friendship can indeed have an alleviating function, because it opens love out to the world. But friendship can have that function also because relative to romantic couple relationships it is fairly obligation-free. It is rarely, if ever, a 24/7 relationship; absences by and large do not jeopardize the relationship, even if years intervene between encounters. But there is something else that needs to be taken into account, and this again speaks to friendship's embedded freedom, this time from a different perspective. Friendship has been called a 'flexible' relationship, because it is able to cope with the many uncertainties of contemporary life (Allan, 2008). Not only are love relationships riven by uncertainty and failure. For a growing number of people everywhere, precarious work (or from the side of employers 'flexible' work) is the order of working life. The *en masse* entry of women into the labor market after the Second World War has not only lead to 'emancipation', but has enabled the expansion of unregulated, poorly paid part-time jobs that are mainly filled by women. Add to that increasing time poverty and it soon becomes clear that even if we narrow our view to economic life only, the perfect employee is the unencumbered *single* individual who is able to maximize mobility and time. '[W]e might consider', writes Evans, 'that the single life is the only *possible* way of life which makes participation in the workplace feasible. Relations with others demand time and commitment (for intangible rewards) and those relations, in a sexually liberated culture, no longer have any particular scarcity value' (2003, p. 139, original emphasis). While the contemporary love ideology heavily invests in sexuality as the signifier of intimacy, sex as recreational pursuit is available without the commitments whose rewards are in any case 'counterproductive', viewed from the standpoint of work and career. And precisely here is the fit between friendship and the demands of contemporary work: friendship can cope with structural demands more readily because its commitments are less binding, its own demands less diverse, its obligations more easily negotiable; and yet it can provide the benefits of company, trust, intimacy, and sometimes even sexual intimacy. Thus, while friendship highlights structurally induced 'unfreedoms' in the intimate sphere, and remains resistant to the reification and the logic of exchange relations, it is also highly compatible with an economic and political order that turns to a significant degree on the 'liberation' of the historically most 'flexible' variable – labor (Gouliquer, 2000).

Nonheterosexual friendships and heteronormativity

Heteronormativity is situated on the cultural side of societal dynamics that limit the social freedom of the intimate sphere because, as I have tried to show, it is to that institution that friendship can be envisaged as connecting most prominently. Clearly, then, friendships in nonheterosexual contexts do not come up against the same normative barriers, and to that extent their freedom must be greater. And in fact it is. As historical work and social research have shown, the platonic friendship ideal does not nearly have the normative force in nonheterosexual relationships that it does in the straight mainstream. That relatively greater openness to sexual possibilities does not indicate an absence of jealousies or a greater preparedness to more completely include others – as companions and confidants, as well as sexual partners – as if nonconformity to heterosexual norms somehow automatically translates into a greater propensity for personal inclusiveness. It points to something else, however: that different ways of life logically include different ethics of intimacy. Such differences may threaten a given intimate order. From the standpoint of the institution of heterosexuality, that 'threat' renders the marginalization of nonheterosexual intimacies legitimate, which in turn shores up heterosexuality as the norm. But what does it mean for difference to 'threaten' dominant modes of intimacy?

In so far as marginalization legitimizes the status quo we ought not to overestimate the subversive powers of nonconformist ways of life. Cultural subversion is therefore not simply to be understood as a radical undermining of majority attitudes and practices, but as a subversion of the world's taken-for-grantedness (Markus, 2002). Fundamental to the experience of modernity, cultural pluralism, which results in the inexorable confrontation of people who are different, with modes of thinking and doing, of living that are different to my own, cannot but relativize my way of life as merely one among other possibilities. Pluralism 'subverts' because it disturbs and problematizes. That it doesn't necessarily translate into an enlightened openness *vis-à-vis* the new and different is illustrated by attempts to conjure traditions, to find pristine collective selfhoods in an imaginary past where the cohesion of a pure community unsullied by the presence of unwanted others is exaggerated to an extraordinary degree (Anderson, 2006; Hobsbawm & Ranger, 2012). Regarding sexual identities, legitimacy for the institution of heterosexuality is not so much found in a mythical, collective straight past – let's leave aside the odd statement about those days 'when men were real men, and women real women' – but in nature 'out there' as well as embodied, 'in here'. That ideological basis of heterosexuality is far from fractured, although pluralism furnishes the conditions for political and everyday challenges to it.

It seems to me that Foucault's statement on friendship needs to be understood in that measured sense of 'subversion', which he in fact evokes in his reflection on the relationship between (male) alternative intimacies and heterosexual society:

> One of the concessions one makes to others is not to present homosexuality as anything but a kind of immediate pleasure, of two young men meeting in the street, seducing each other with a look, grabbing each other's asses and getting each other off in a quarter of an hour. There you have a kind of neat image of homosexuality without any possibility of generating unease, and for two reasons: it responds to a reassuring canon of beauty, and it cancels everything that can be troubling in affection, tenderness, friendship, fidelity, camaraderie, and companionship, things that our rather sanitized society can't allow a place for without fearing the formation of new alliances and the tying together of unforeseen lines of force. I think that's what makes homosexuality '*disturbing*': the homosexual mode of life, much more than the sexual act itself. To imagine a sexual act that doesn't conform to law or nature is not what disturbs people. But that individuals are beginning to love another – there's the problem. The institution is caught in a contradiction; affective intensities traverse it, which at one and the same time keep it going and shake it up. (2000, pp. 136–137)

The 'homosexual mode of life' Foucault speaks about, and hence the title that was given the interview, is 'friendship as a way of life'. We need to add here, I think, that the friendship model offered itself as *the* model of intimacy because no other model was legitimately available. Just like 'families of choice' came to stand in for genetic or 'involuntary' ties that in so many cases cannot brook difference, friendship was available as a descriptor for intense erotic love relationships not only because it was associated with choice, but also because, commensurate with the love–friendship paradox, same-sex relationships were and often still are *a priori* attributed friendship status by a straight majority culture. These attributions have to be contended with in some way or another because nonheterosexual relationships are not divorced from society; even enclaves of difference are still embedded in the social structure writ large. Of course, to what extent individuals bother to engage with mainstream expectations is a matter of individual psychology, but also of age, class, and cultural affiliation. But we can at least speculate that on the collective level, claiming the friendship label to denote an extensive range of intimate practices may be a strategy of contestation; it buys into the attributions nested in the love–friendship paradox at the same time as it 'subverts' heteronormativity in the intimate sphere, in love as well as friendship.

It is here then, in the tensionful relationship between nonheterosexual practices of intimacy and mainstream expectations that the paradoxical qualities of the love–friendship schema are fully developed. In an imaginary, entirely autarkic, and closed nonheterosexual society the schema would be meaningless. And in a heterosexual world that *perceives* of itself as independent of its actually co-constitutive 'others', the paradox is invisible: the expectations and normative attributions that the schema depicts are merely integrative as a normative reflection of how the world always was, is, and ought to be. That there are significant continuities between these 'worlds' is evident in the political movement toward same-sex marriage (often critiqued for its approximation of a problematic heterosexual institution) and the all-encompassing reach of the nexus capitalism–romance–therapy beyond heterosexuality. To what extent intimate cross-sex friendships between self-identifying heterosexuals that include sexual practices take their lead from nonheterosexual intimacies, because orthodox notions of friendship are insufficient, is a matter for further research.

Friendship and sociology

From the perspective offered here, we cannot speak about growing sociological research on friendship. We continue to marshal it in research as a sinkhole concept that is made to contain all sorts of friendly rela-tions (e.g. Smart et al., 2012). In a thought-provoking polemic, Michel Eve (2002) charges sociologists with having unduly conflated sundry personal relationships within the category. He also critiques the 'general tendency within sociology to subsume information on friendship into a framework of debate about community, less communal or more com-munal, insufficiently communal or too communal forms of relations', because 'community' is a central concept of the discipline tempting sociologists to subsume all personal ties under its semantics (2002, p. 390). I share Eve's concerns, and have been at pains to explain the need for a differentiated view of friendship and thus a methodology that distinguishes intimate from friendly relations.

Equally interesting is Eve's observation that social psychology is mainly interested in dyads that, due to their personal dynamics, are seen to be 'based on the exchange of "emotional support" and on pure individuality', with little or no attention being paid to the connected-ness of friendships to other relationships, or the '"social" traits of the persons involved' (2002, p. 387). Again, I share Eve's concerns. They lie at the heart of my endeavor to take a sociological lens to dyadic friendships. But at the risk of swimming against the tide of a new orthodoxy, I need to invoke the specter of 'disciplinarity' in response. Eve, in conflating *disciplines*, does not admit that *sociology*, largely due to the conflation of personal relations we both take issue with, has in fact had very little to say about close friendship dyads. And in sociol-ogy the 'social traits' of comrades, colleagues, acquaintances, and even friends have definitely not been sidelined. I need, among others, only point to Graham Allan's pioneering work on friendship as one salient example of research that neither ignores dyads nor networks, nor class, age, gender, or cultural background.

The present work has confined itself to gender because it is here that I see the most obvious dialogical connection between the little world of friendship and the big world we collectively build, share, and rebuild. But during my research a problem emerged: the need for empirical research, and for qualitative research especially. The initial thought process went something like this: if it is true that the relational freedom of friendship allows for an extraordinarily great range of interactions as long as they are pursued in the context of intimacy, then the work of describing 'how people do friendship' struck me as an endeavor that would add very little to existing work. It is, however, the case that quali-tative research on gender as a limiting case for friendship's freedom is very thin on the ground indeed. While there is some work on cross-sex friendship, the complexities of heterosocial and heterosexual friendships that attempt to integrate sex into the relationship while drawing relational boundaries to traditional erotic love are almost impossible to disentangle without access to lived and reflected-upon experience. That work needs to be done. For now what I offer in this study will have to suffice.

To what extent I have succeeded in drawing out the links between the dyad to the macro-structures of the social shall be judged by the reader. To view the dynamics of gendered power through the prism of this intimate dyad was the task I have set myself. Sociological and feminist writing on love has done so for eons. But here the constraints, the prescriptions, the 'whats' and 'hows' are thickly given. Not so in friendship, where its freedoms tend to obscure its embeddedness in, and so the constraint by, the social order; a social order that is etched into our very being, and that, marked by its injunctions and ready-made manuals for acting and thinking, we tend to shore up, re-invent, and reproduce – just as some may overcome them and slowly, step by step and only ever together with others, may change its dominant *modi vivendi*. But for all my efforts to show that which is typical in friendship as a modality of intimacy; for all my engagements with the literature on friendship in my field and sometimes in others; for all the contextualizing ground I have prepared in order to breath sociological life into friendship as a truly puzzling relationship type, I am unconvinced that there is much of a case for a dedicated 'sociology of friendship' (for a debate, see Eve, 2002; Pahl, 2002).

The subdivision of sociology into different areas of expertise may have its professional merits. But it also tempts us to lose from sight a lesson to be learned from Durkheim, but also from Elias, namely that the differentiation of social life that characterizes modernity – whereby its parts appear as discretely marked, and which we are sometimes encouraged to perceive as such because it serves power to divide the personal from the political, the intimate from the public, the systemic from the individual – needs to be seen, understood, and then explained as *interdependent*. That is a formidable task to be sure; but it is also where sociology's relevance is arguably situated. That in itself is no argument against subdisciplinary differentiation. But it seems to me that at the very least we need to pay close attention to the inextricability of what are ostensibly disparate social and cultural conditions and trends. And so, rather than expending energy in the creation of a sociology of friendship, it might be better to channel our sociological imagination to continue to integrate intimate friendship into the purview of sociology *per se*. And that means to continue to explore the connections between different types of personal relationships, their various relationships to public life, the normative and practical spillages that occur between differentiated spheres of action, and their consequences for people's everyday lives.

Similar concerns may be raised about a 'sociology of personal life' (Smart, 2007; May et al., 2011). Owing to the problematization of the concept of 'the family' by real-life complexities, there is a growing interest in extrafamilial relationships. Advocacy for a 'sociology of personal life' thus finds traction in changing practices and understandings of personal relationships. Apart from my reservations about subdisciplinary division, a critical stance toward such a project has cautioned that a focus on the personal detracts from the 'relational' aspects of individuality (Ribbens McCarthy, 2012). The suggestion I want to offer is to retain a focus on 'privacy' in such an endeavor. As briefly discussed in Chapter 1, the modern notion of privacy is unthinkable without the historical differentiation of public and private spheres of action. We value privacy because it is central to the notion of freedom, conceived as autonomy to live self-directed lives. I would like to highlight a further aspect pertaining to the issue of autonomy in personal relationships that resonates with Rössler's (2005) conception: the constitution of normative disclosing behavior about self and intimate others through everyday interaction.

As I have argued elsewhere with specific reference to social networking sites (Blatterer, 2010), both the individual need for public or semi-public visibility in the pursuit of recognition, and the moral force of the 'nothing to hide' argument, when brought together in a collectively shared set of practices, have the potential to change the normative understanding of privacy from the ground up; to change reasonable expectations about what constitutes informational privacy and so weaken its legal defensibility; to make disclosing behavior the default position. Because intimate relationships, including friendship, depend on a mutual trust that certain types of information be protected from access by third others, changes to the normative understanding of privacy can undermine confidentiality and discretion as necessary conditions for intimate relationships. To such changes friendship is – emphatically – *not* immune. In fact, its comparative openness to public life may expose it to such dynamics more readily than, say, erotic love or parent–child relationships. Keeping privacy central to sociological studies of personal life enables us to learn how the personal articulates with emerging normative notions of privacy. This, moreover, enables us to retain the *critical* ambit of sociology – not as a discipline that prescribes how things ought to be, but as a discipline that reflects on the social and cultural conditions necessary to enable flourishing, autonomous lives and thus doesn't shy away from pointing out those relations of power that exact real costs undermine the basic social conditions for human decency.

Friendship and 'the decent society'

To live in a *decent* society is to live in a society whose 'institutions do not act in ways that give the people under their authority sound reasons to consider themselves humiliated' (Margalit, 1996 pp. 7–8). That take on humiliation is one of the conceptual platforms from which Markus (2001) ponders the complementarities between a 'decent' and a 'civil' society. She aims to reconcile them in a vision we may aim to realize in order to create the best possible conditions for freedom and autonomy.[2] Her reflections are the platform for some final thoughts on friendship and its embedded freedom.

The notion of 'civil society' is highly contested. Depending on approach, it may encompass collective attitudes of civility, of civil manners, of civic-mindedness, or – and this is the approach Markus offers – a society that rather than *being* civil actually *has* an organizational infrastructure, that enable the contestation of political issues and norms. Civil society so conceived is essential to functioning democracies; and so we 'could say that civil society exists when there is a sustained attempt by people to be in charge of shaping their own life conditions and influencing actually and visibly the relevant decisions of various public bodies and institutions' (Markus, 2001, p. 1014). But for civil society to be effective in political will formation it needs an ethical logic. And it is here that civility connects to civil society. The shared semantics are not incidental. For Philip Selznick (1994), for instance, civility works because it is impersonal, and 'as a norm of behavior toward nonintimates and even strangers, it is '"cool, not hot; detached, not involved" and therefore "not a morality of engagement"' (cited in Markus, 2001 p. 1019). This is the point with which Markus takes issue. Although she recognizes its importance, civility alone cannot integrate a plurality of civil society perspectives and agendas because its coolness cannot 'generate an interest in the interests of the others', let alone foster solidarity. 'Thus, while a thriving civil society has to be civil, not all societies that are civil necessarily have a flourishing civil society'. Here Markus, taking her lead from Margalit, introduces the concept of 'decency':

> [C]ivility is cool, almost depersonalized. Decency, however, implies something more or at least something different: a respect for the

'dignity' of each person and some interest in, and commitment to, promoting the ability of all members of society to lead a dignified, humanly meaningful life. It involves not only the toleration of other views and convictions, but also an interest in and openness toward what they say, along with an attempt to understand the reason why it can be meaningful to hold such a view. (2001, p. 1021)

From that perspective, a decent society is not only one in which (negatively formulated) the institutional and organizational conditions for humiliation are absent, but one in which an engaged respect for the fundamental dignity of others – insiders as well as outsiders – is present.

What shape a decent society should take is subject to civil society debate; it is, as a normative concept, 'vague and empty', open to be filled with contestable content, thus preventing the 'essentialization of any particular social arrangements as the only possible form of a decent society' (Markus, 2001, p. 1023). General principles – nonhumiliation, the right to autonomous, dignified, and meaningful lives – serve to orient public debate concerning the requirement for the concrete realization of decency in specific contexts. As a 'moral orientation' it provides, above all, a 'utopian horizon' orienting the societal realization of decency by way of civil society mechanisms central to democracy (2001 p. 1027).

The question I want to ask in conclusion is whether there are any fruitful connections that can be made between the notion of a 'decent society' and friendship. One way to approach the issue is to come at it from the side of democracy. We can think about the affinities between democracy and friendship in a number of ways. We could, for instance, take our lead from Giddens (1992), for whom the 'transformation of intimacy in late-modern societies' is above all a democratization of personal relationships, which is most evident in the 'pure relationship' ideal, of which friendship is itself a pure form. For Giddens, the contemporary ideal of intimacy mirrors contemporary ideals of political democracy. With its appeal to justice, equal participation and autonomy in personal relationships that argument is cogent. Less convincing may be Giddens' assertion that these 'advancement[s] are rich with implications for democratic practice in the larger community', even extending globally. For to say that a 'symmetry exists between the democratizing of personal life and democratic possibilities in the global order' (Gibbens, 1992, pp. 195–196) is to describe the potential reach of democratic ideals into different spheres, but does not explain the mechanisms by which one interacts with, influences, or learns from, the other.

Neither is decent society simply a 'friendly society'. To imagine a society in which predispositions toward feelings of amity are simply generalized as a political organizing principle not only betokens a 'naïve hope' (Markus, 2010b, p. 20), but such a model is in fact undesirable because the personal norms of friendship would undermine the regulatory impersonality at the heart of liberal-democratic bureaucracies. The normative incompatibility between democracy and personal friendship has a long tradition in political philosophy. For Arendt (1958) the personalization of friendship was symptomatic of a modern retreat from public life into the inner sanctum of the intimate sphere. And already for Tocqueville only friendly relations in the contexts of political institutions and democratic associations – 'political' rather than intimate friendships – were conducive to democracy, because they are able to eschew 'the dangers of the privatized, narcissistic friendship of democratic despotism' (Mallory, 2012, p. 33). The problem of friendship *vis-à-vis* political democracy as critiqued in political philosophy is essentially the twin problem of partiality and narcissism.

We can, however, rather than ask what friendship can bring to democracy, ask what democracy can do for friendship. We can make the argument, for instance, that democratic societies are conducive to the intimate bonds of friendship, just as authoritarian societies are disadvantageous to their formation. For people to be able to form relationships of easy, relaxed sociability where little thought needs to be given to discretion, where they don't have to watch what they say, social trust needs to be a general societal characteristic (Misztal, 1996). In other words, 'political freedom and personal freedom mirror each other' (Shklar, 1998, p. 16).[3] This does of course not mean that there cannot be intimacy under nondemocratic political conditions; but they are not conducive to them, although they are definitely conducive to other solidarities, to camaraderie in the face of despotic power, for example, as the history of political revolutions attests.

It seems to me that the affinities between the 'utopian horizon' of a decent society and friendship can be drawn out differently, namely by seeing that utopia already, and at least partially, realized in friendship in the context of private life. I have proposed that mutual trust and respect, justice and equality (in the context of care and affection), are more than norms of friendship: friendship personifies its own necessary conditions. A friendship that needs to orient itself on norms in order to exist is not (or no longer) a friendship. That orientation to shared norms can be learned, of course, as the literature on social networking for personal (usually monetary) ends illustrates. But that is not about friendship; it is about learning how to act *as if* the trust and respect, the justice and equality, of friendship were a reality. Friendship is learned in interaction with concrete others, and in some ways it is learned anew every time we 'make' new friends, because no two friendships are alike. And it is here also that we may learn decency.

Decency as a normative standard for social relations at large cannot, and for good reasons ought not, mimic the decency of friendship as a personal and private relationship. But at the same time, there can be no full understanding of decency without having experienced it. No theoretical engagement or debate about what a decent society might look like can replace the practical knowledge of the generous give and take, the sometimes tense but mostly affectionate, being of oneself in the company of another. Here, in friendship, we may learn about decency by establishing its contents in interaction with a concrete, respected, and trusted other. Here we may also learn what it means to warm the cool and necessary hand of civility just enough to enable generative reconciliations of difference under conditions of complexity and contingency. To that extent alone friendship's freedom deserves to be protected, and its arbitrary as well as necessary limits to be more fully understood.

Notes

1 Modernity, Intimacy, and Friendship

1. For an alternative view that traces the formation of the individual back to the European Middle Ages, see Morris (1987).
2. The classic statement is Max Weber's *Zwischenbetrachtung* in his sociology of religion, where he elaborates on the tensions between the religious ethos of brotherly love and the modern logics of economy, politics, art, intimacy, and science (see Weber, 1977 for an English version).
3. Rössler (as does Honneth) draws on the German semantics of intimacy, which more narrowly than in English usage, has distinctly 'erotic or sexual connotations' (2005 p. 5).
4. In Rössler's conception privacy spans three analytically separate, but empirically overlapping, dimensions: 'I speak of *decisional* privacy when we claim the right to protection from unwanted access in the sense of unwanted interference or of heteronomy in our decisions and actions. I speak of *informational* privacy when people claim the right to protection against unwanted access in the sense of interference in personal data about themselves, in other words access to information about them that they have no desire to see in the wrong hands. And I speak of *local* privacy in a completely non-metaphorical sense when we claim the right to protection against the admission of other people to spaces or areas. Violations of a person's privacy can be defined, therefore, in these three ways: as illicit interference in one's actions, as illicit surveillance, as illicit, intrusions in rooms or dwelling' (2005, p. 9, original emphases).
5. A familiar misinterpretation is that of Ferdinand Tönnies (1887) conception of social change. Rather than describing a liner shift from premodern *Gemeinschaft* to modern *Gesellschaft* – so the common interpretation – Tönnies attempted to analyze their coexistence and constant tensions in modernity. Another example of fallacious common sense in sociology is the alleged social evolutionism of Herbert Spencer (see Francis, 2007).
6. In his *Nicomachean Ethics* (2012), Aristotle famously distinguishes between three types of friendship: friendships of utility, friendships of pleasure, and friendships of virtue. For an insightful discussion that includes the problem of justice in friendship, see Lorraine Smith Pangle's *Aristotle and the Philosophy of Friendship* (2003).
7. At the same time, Adam Ferguson was highly skeptical of new developments: 'Man is sometimes found a detached and a solitary being: he has found an object which sets him in competition with his fellow-creatures, and he deals with them as he does with his cattle and his soil for the sake of the profits they bring' (cited in Hill and McCarthy 1999: 46–47).
8. In 'Antinomies of "Culture"', Gyorgy Markus (2011, pp. 633–654), persuasively argues that the tensions between Enlightenment and Romanticism as attitudes, standpoints, and practices, continues to characterize modernity.

9. For Zaretsky, the second industrial revolution is marked by the psycho-analytic recasting of three Enlightenment 'promises': individual autonomy, women's emancipation, and democracy (2004, pp. 8–11.).

10. In his 1783 lectures on love and 'marital bliss' Von Drais states: 'But love only serves a function when friendship beats with it in the same breast' (cited in Luhmann, 1998a, p. 117).

11. The notion of recognition – as respect or validation – runs like a thread through the sociological literature. Apart from Goffman's distinction of cognitive and social recognition as briefly discussed in Chapter 2, Elias also raises the topic. In *The Court Society*, he has this to say: 'for a healthy person there can be no absolute zero-point in the relation between the image he has of his own value and of the values directing his efforts, and the confirmation or denial of his image through the behavior of other people. This interdependence of the valuations of many individuals in a society makes it difficult if not impossible for a single person to seek fulfillment of his efforts in a way that has no chance of bringing him present or future rewards in the form of respect, recognition, love, admiration – in short, the confirmation or heightening of his value in the eyes of others' (2006, p. 83). However, Elias refers to a fundamental fact of our sociality that is historically generalizable, while Honneth is specifically interested in *modern* forms of recognition that can no longer rely on fixed social statuses and the 'honour' they confer (1996, pp. 123–126).

12. On a greater level of abstraction, for Luhmann too, love is fundamentally about recognition: 'Here', he writes, 'the experience of an other is validated through my own actions' (2009a, p. 158, my translation).

2 Friends, Friendship, and Sociology

1. Uruguayan writer Eduardo Galeano (2001) coined the term 'Global North' to indicate the uneven distribution of wealth and poverty, whereby the rich of Montevideo, for example, have more in common with the rich in New York than with their poorer compatriots, which a geographical North/South divide captures only insufficiently.

2. Monoculture in whatever terms – linguistic, religious, ethnic – is rarely more than a wish-dream of those hoping for the rebirth of a simpler community. Cultural sensitivity among social researchers needs to be included into the register of what Zygmunt Bauman and Tim May (2001, p. 8) in their introduction to sociology call 'responsible speech'. My own observations pertain mainly to Anglophone, German, and (to some extent) Italian language and research contexts.

3. To the best of my knowledge, Gerhard Richter's article 'Siegfried Kracauer and the Folds of Friendship' (1997) remains the only scholarly analysis of Kracauer's thought on friendship in English.

4. I'm reminded here of a scene, typical of Prague until the annihilation of Jewish life, described by Friedrich Torberg in his wonderful autobiographical collection of anecdotes, *Die Tante Jolesch* (1977).

> Every Sunday, late morning at the Graben, the parade took place at whose occasion greeting and non-greeting were cultivated whereby first-practiced nuances were of the greatest significance. How low a greeting

person drew their hat and at which distance they initiated their greeting was as telling about the relationship between him and the person he greeted as it was about his social position. The person greeted, on the other hand, signaled through the promptness or friendliness of his reply to what degree he welcomed the greeting. Not infrequently, a rapprochement or cooling of relations was initiated in this way, not infrequently did it occur that business, personal relationships or even relationships between the sexes eventuated or fell apart at the Grabenparade – so that all in all the demise of this blessed institution, whose informal social yield in some respects even surpassed that of the café, is to be lamented. (1977, p. 92, my translation)

3   Love, Friendship, and Freedom

1. For a classic statement see Weber on 'legitimate authority' with his well-known distinction of the three ideal types, 'rational', 'traditional', and 'charismatic' authority (1978, pp. 212–301).
2. For a thought-provoking discussion of the history of love, sex, and eroticism, see Octavio Paz's essays in *The Double Flame* (2011).
3. The watershed moment in the demise of authoritarian parenting was the 1945 publication of Benjamin M. Spock's *Baby and Child Care* (2012). Spock was subsequently attacked by Norman Vincent Peale (who also happened to be author of *The Power of Positive Thinking*) who called him 'the father of permissiveness' – a critique taken up by Spiro Agnew and conservatives who thought the new style of parenting to be at the root of anti-Vietnam sentiment among the younger generation. For a more circumspect take on 'permissiveness', see Christopher Lasch's *The Culture of Narcissism: American Life in an Age of Diminishing Expectations* (1979).

4   Friendship, Intimacy, and the Self

1. Giddens' concept is similar to, but also sufficiently different from, the sense of home I am concerned with. In Giddens, ontological security refers to 'the practical mastery of how to "go on" in the context of social life' and thus presupposes a basic trust in the continuance of self and the social environment, essential aspects of which are acquired in early child development (1991a, p. 41).
2. For an attempt to marshal Mead's concept in empirical research see Margaret Archer, *Structure, Agency and the Internal Conversation* (2003).
3. As briefly sketched in Chapter 1, the practical playing out of the tensions between demands for the recognition of one's individual or collective uniqueness and extant criteria for recognition in plural, private, and public contexts constitutes Honneth's 'struggle for recognition' as driver of social change. In the first rendition of his theory of recognition Honneth (1996) draws liberally on Mead's conception.
4. I am not suggesting that the self is a monolithic, unchangeable essence. We are, of course, different 'selves' in different contexts (for interesting discussions on the topic see Burkitt, 1991; Craib, 1998; Jenkins, 2013).

5. Velleman explains: 'I suggest that it arrests our tendencies toward emotional self-protection from another person, tendencies to draw ourselves in and close ourselves off from being affected by him. Love disarms our emotional defenses; it makes us vulnerable to the other' (1999, p. 361).

6. For an introduction to the interplay between social and psychological dynamics in the creative process, see Mihaly Csikszentmihaly (1999).

7. In keeping with usage in some branches of philosophy, Cocking and Kennett choose the term 'companion friendship'.

8. Jamieson does not connect Giddens' conception of 'the pure relationship' to the long turn toward a therapeutic persuasion in all things intimate (Illouz, 2008; Swidler, 2001).

9. Others have attempted to fathom the 'communicative predicaments' of friendship, such as the tensions between affection and instrumentality, judgment and acceptance, and expressiveness and protectiveness (see Rawlins, 1992).

10. My use of the term 'communication' concurs with Luckmann's, and so is restricted 'to processes based on socially constructed sign systems; particularly, but not exclusively, language. The processes are social (inter)actions of a special kind. They are essential to the organization of human collective life; they are especially important in making possible the effective transmission of the traditions of a society, including that of its moral order. Communicative processes are either reciprocal or unilateral; they are either direct, face-to-face, or mediated in a number of ways. They occur between individuals as individuals or as incumbents of office, and as representatives of groups or socially defined categories. Correspondingly, individuals address themselves to individuals or to offices, groups and socially defined categories of individuals. Furthermore, communication may be between anonymous senders and equally anonymous receivers' (2000, p. 20).

11. Judith Shklar's (1998) essay on the friendship between John Adams and Thomas Jefferson is illuminating. Though their relationship was beset by fierce rivalry for much of their political careers, it's an exemplary instance of how the personal and the political, duty and love, can live in creative tension with each other. In fact, their friendship was both a political and – significantly – after both had retired from their offices, an intimate one.

12. The term 'function' is not intended here to connote the 'natural' givenness of social arrangements and institutions guaranteeing constant social equilibrium. At least according to the critique of functionalism, that version is unable to account for social change (for an early crititque of functionalism see, Dahrendorf, 1958; for an important reconceptualization see, Merton, 1968). I simply want to indicate that different social relationships, institutions, and organizations have contestable, contested, and changing purposes, aims, and roles; they offer orientation to individual and collective agents and may fulfill needs that other social arrangements cannot fulfill.

5 Gender and the Love–Friendship Paradox

1. Because I am dealing with gender in a mainstream context, and with pre-reflexive assumptions regarding the division male/female as read off from biological and representational signifiers, I am not including transgender

and indeterminate gender identities here. For a now 'classic' and powerful statement on the cultural elaboration of gender see especially that part of Gayle Rubin's 'The Traffic of Women' that critically analyzes Levi-Strauss' work on kinship systems, the incest taboo, obligatory heterosexuality, gender asymmetry, and the resultant curtailment of female sexuality (Rubin, 1975, pp. 170–183).

2. The term 'gender order' is not supposed to denote fixed social arrangements, but describes macrosocial patterns within which we identify as masculine or feminine, and within which there is leeway for context-specific 'gender regimes'. These gender regimes, states Connell, 'usually correspond to the overall gender order, but may depart from it' (2009, p. 73).

3. I use the term 'label' in the literal sense. Sex assignment surgery cases where newborns' genital development is deemed 'inadequate' is a case in point (Reiner, 1997). It is well to consider Judith Butler's suggestion that 'gender ought not to be conceived merely as the cultural inscription of meaning on a pre-given sex (a juridical conception); gender must also designate the very apparatus of production whereby the sexes themselves are established (1990, p. 10).

4. However, cultural change tends to lag behind changes in practices. In a different context I refer to the gap between collective practices and ideas as 'normative lag'. My example is the reconfiguration of 'adulthood' by young people who, largely due to the precariousness of labor markets and uncertainties about intimate life, tend to postpone the realization of the 'classic markers' of adulthood such as marriage and family formation, financial independence, and full-time careers. Their adaptive strategies to social change are often pejoratively commented up as 'prolonged adolescence', and have attracted labels such as 'kidults', 'adultescents', etc. The gap between social change and its negotiation by young people on the one hand, and entrenched notions about what it means to be a 'mature adult'– themselves artifacts of the postwar era when the notions where matched by social conditions conducive to their realization – can cause considerable uncertainties among young people with regard to their self-identification and so exacerbate the already considerable structural and cultural uncertainties that often mark their lives (Blatterer, 2009).

5. Jackson distinguishes four dimensions of 'the social' in which sexuality and gender are constituted and contested: a macrosocial structural dimension of 'patterned social relations'; a dimension of shared meanings; everyday, 'routine social practices through which gender and sexuality are constantly constituted and reconstituted within localized contexts and relationships'; and finally subjects 'who through their embodied activities construct, enact and make sense of everyday gendered and sexual interaction' (Jackson, 2006, p. 108).

6. Broad interest in the sport across the population is not reflected in teams' ethnic composition. The Anglo-Celtic bias in representations aligns with realities: the team fielded for the 2014 One Day International series against England was exclusively comprised of players from Anglo-Celtic backgrounds. On endemic, institutionalized racism in the sport, see Fraser (2004).

7. The term 'boys' is not to be read as denoting children or adolescents or as a diminutive form of 'men'. On the contrary: in the Australian context it is a collective label denoting Connell's ideal-typical 'hegemonic masculinities' (Connell, 2005), and is frequently invoked to express fraternal bonds (see also, Flood, 2008).
8. I take my cues here from Manuel Castells who maintains that 'identities organize the meaning while roles organize the functions' (Castells, 1997, p. 7)
9. In the Australian context, positive changes have been made on the level of state recognition of transgendered and intersex identified people: 'The Australian Human Rights Commission (*Addressing sexual orientation and sex and/or gender identity discrimination 2011*) defines the phrase 'sex and gender diverse' (SGD) as referring to the whole spectrum of sex and/or gender identity. For the purposes of issuing passports, this includes 'trans' and 'intersex' persons. 'Trans' is a general term for a person whose preferred gender is different from their sex at birth. The term 'intersex' refers to a person who has genetic, hormonal, or physical characteristics that are not exclusively male or female. A person who is intersex may identify as male, female, or as being of indeterminate sex' (Australian Government, Department of Trade and Foreign Affairs, 2011).

6 The Love–Friendship Paradox and Cross-sex Friendship

1. For an example set in the intellectual *milieu* of the early 20th century European *fin-de-siècle*, see Lou Andreas-Salomé's (1995) memoir, *Lou Andreas-Salome: The Intimate Story of her Friendships with Nietzsche, Rilke & Freud*.
2. Good cites an advice book from 1803 whose author exalts same-sex friendship as 'the noblest passion of the human breast ... a passion too refined, and of too platonic a nature to exist between those of different sexes'. Cross-sex friendship 'must repine into love, or degenerate into lasciviousness' (cited in Good, 2012, p. 20).
3. I wrote a friendly email to the association asking for their philosophy behind the banner's motto in February 2014, but did not receive a reply.
4. For an analysis of representations of bromance in Hollywood productions, see Diana Sargent's *American Masculinity and Homosocial Behavior in the romance Era* (2013).
5. Legal scholars have argued that these are social control mechanisms that have come into force as legal prescriptions concerning intimate relationships have increasingly moved into the background (Chen, 2011).
6. Reeder found differentiated kinds of attraction among her sample of 231 US college students: physical/sexual, romantic, and friendship attraction. The majority of her heterosexual respondents cited friendship attraction as most prevalent in their cross-sex friendships; those who professed to physical/sexual or romantic attraction tended to prioritize friendship attraction in order to protect and maintain the relationship.
7. For a more comprehensive review, see Blatterer (2013).
8. I owe much of the discussion in this section to conversations with Penelope Faulkner and to her thesis *Just Add Sex ... Then Stir: A Sociological Enquiry into 'Friends with Benefits'* (2011).

Conclusion: Friendship's Embedded Freedom

1. For Erikson (1994), generativity extends to the contribution of new generations to society.
2. Various engagements with Markus's argument are available in a special
   Festschrift issue of the journal *Thesis Eleven* (2010b, vol. 101, no. 1).
3. On a much smaller scale, Lewin and Lippitt's (1938) early study of dyads
   sought to analyze the influence of the social environment on friendship
   dyads. They found that dyads in 'autocratic' groups were marked by far
   greater hostility than those in 'democratic' groups'.

References

Abbey, A. (1982). 'Sex Differences in Attributions for Friendly Behavior: Do Males Misperceive Females' Friendliness?'. *Journal of Personality and Social Psychology*, *42*(5), 830.

Adams, R. G. (1985). 'People would Talk: Normative Barriers to Cross-sex Friendships for Elderly Women.' *The Gerontologist*, *25*(6), 605–611.

Adams, R. G., & Allan, G. (1998). *Placing Friendship in Context*. Cambridge: Cambridge University Press.

Adorno, T. W. (2005). *The Culture Industry: Selected Essays on Mass Culture*. London and New York: Routledge.

Adorno, T. W., & Kracauer, S. (2008). *Briefwechsel 1923–1966*. Frankfurt am Main: Suhrkamp.

Afifi, W. A., & Faulkner, S. L. (2000). 'On Being "Just Friends": The Frequency and Impact of Sexual Activity in Cross-Sex Friendships.' *Journal of Social and Personal Relationships*, *17*(2), 205–222.

Alberoni, F. (1984). *Movement and Institution*. New York: Columbia University Press.

Alberoni, F. (2009). *L'amicizia*. Milano: Biblioteca Universale Rizzoli.

Allan, G. (1989). *Friendship: Developing a Sociological Perspective*. Hertfordshire, England: Harvester Wheatsheaf.

Allan, G. (2008). 'Flexibility, Friendship, and Family.' *Personal Relationships*, *15*(1), 1–16.

Allan, G., & Adams, R. G. (2007). 'The Sociology of Friendship.' In *21st Century Sociology: A Reference Handbook* (pp. 123–31). London, Thousand Oaks: Sage Publications.

Allport, G. W. (1954). *The Nature of Prejudice*. Reading, MA: Addison-Wesley.

AMSA (Australian Men's Shed Organisation). (2014). 'Our Mission and Values',. http://www.nswmensshed.org/home/.aspx, accessed 16 February 2014.

Anderson, B. (2006). *Imagined Communities: Reflections on the Origin and Spread of Nationalism*. London and New York: Verso.

Anderson, D. C. (2001). *Losing Friends*. London: Social Affairs Unit.

Andreas-Salomé, L. (1995). *Looking Back: Memoirs*. New York: Marlowe & Company.

Archer, M. S. (2003). *Structure, Agency and the Internal Conversation*. Cambridge: Cambridge University Press.

Arendt, H. (1958). *The Human Condition*. Chicago: University of Chicago Press.

Argyle, M., & Henderson, M. (1984). 'The Rules of Friendship.' *Journal of Social and Personal Relationships*, *1*(2), 211–237.

Ariès and Béjin, A. (1985)., *Western Sexuality: Practices and Precepts in Past and Present Time*. New York: Barnes and Noble.

Aristoteles. (2012). *Aristotle's Nicomachean Ethics*. Chicago: University of Chicago Press.

Aron, R. (1967). *18 Lectures on Industrial Society*. (M. K. Bottomore, Trans.). London: Weidenfeld and Nicolson.

Australian Government, Department of Trade and Foreign Affairs. (2011). *'Sex.'* http://www.dfat.gov.au/publications/passports/Policy/Identity/Sex/index.htm

Bahr, H. (1968). *Zur Ueberwindung des Naturalismun: Theoretische Schriften, 1887–1904.* Stuttgart: W. Kohlhammer Verlag.

Banaji. (2001). 'Stereotypes, Social Psychology of.' In *International Encyclopedia of the Social and Behavioral Sciences* (pp. 15100–04). Oxford: Elsevier.

Banaji, M. R., & Hardin, C. D. (1996). 'Automatic Stereotyping.' *Psychological Science, 7*(3), 136–141.

Bank, B. J. (1995). 'Friendships in Australia and the United States: From Feminization to a More Heroic Image.' *Gender & Society, 9*(1), 79–98.

Barzun, J. (2003). *From Dawn of Decadence: 500 Years of Western Cultural Life: 1500 to the Present.* New York: Demco Media.

Bauman, Z. (1991). *Modernity and ambivalence.* Cambridge: Polity Press.

Bauman, Z. (1995). 'Searching for a Centre that Holds.' In *Global Modernities* (pp. 140–154). London: Sage.

Bauman, Z. (2001). *The Individualized Society.* Oxford: Blackwell.

Bauman, Z. (2003). *Liquid Love: On the Frailty of Human Bonds.* Cambridge: Polity Press.

Bauman, Z. (2013). *Liquid Modernity.* John Wiley & Sons.

Bauman, Z., & May, T. (2001). *Thinking Sociologically.* Oxford: Blackwell.

Bech, H. (1997). *When Men Meet: Homosexuality and Modernity.* Chicago: University of Chicago Press.

Beck, U. (1997). *Risk Society: Towards a New Modernity.* London: SAGE Publications.

Beck, U., & Beck-Gernsheim, E. (1995). *The Normal Chaos of Love.* Oxford: Wiley-Blackwell.

Beck, U., & Beck-Gernsheim, E. (1996). 'Individualization and 'Precarious Freedoms': Perspectives and Controversies of a Subject-Oriented Sociology.' In P. Heelas, S. Lash, & P. Morris (Eds), *Detraditionalization* (pp. 23–48). Cambridge and Oxford: Blackwell.

Beck, U., & Beck-Gernsheim, E. (2002). *Individualization: Institutionalized Individualism and its Social and Political consequences.* London: Sage.

Becker, H., & Useem, R. H. (1942). Sociological Analysis of the Dyad. *American Sociological Review, 7*(1), 13–26.

Beier, B. (Ed.). (1997). *Harenberg Lexikon Der Sprichwörter & Zitate: Mit 50000 Einträgen Das Umfassendste Werk in Deutscher Sprache.* Dortmund: Harenberg.

Bellah, R. N., Madsen, R., & Sullivan, W. M. (2007). *Habits of the Heart: Individualism and Commitment in American Life.* Berkeley: University of California Press.

Berger, P. L., Berger, B., & Kellner, H. (1974). *The Homeless Mind: Modernization and Consciousness.* London: Vintage Books.

Berger, P., & Luckmann, T. (1966). *The Social Construction of Reality; A Treatise in the Sociology of Knowledge.* New York: Anchor Books.

Bergmann, J. R. (1993). *Discreet Indiscretions: The Social Organization of Gossip.* New Jersey: Transaction Publishers.

Berlant, L., & Warner, M. (1998). 'Sex in Public.' *Critical Inquiry, 24*(2), 547–566.

Berlin, I. (1969). *Four Essays on Liberty.* Oxford: Oxford University Press.

Berlin, I. (2001). *The Roots of Romanticism.* Princeton: Princeton University Press.

Berman, M. (1983). *All That Is Solid Melts into Air: The Experience of Modernity.* London and New York: Verso.

Bevan, L. (2009). *Life Without Jealousy: A Practical Guide.* Ann Arbor: Loving Healing Press.

Bittman, M., Hoffmann, S., & Thompson, D. (2004). *Men's Uptake of Family-Friendly Employment Provision.* Canberra: Australian Government Department of Family and Community Services.

Blatterer, H. (2009). *Coming of Age in Times of Uncertainty.* New York and Oxford: Berghahn Books.

Blatterer, H. (2010). 'Social Networking, Privacy, and the Pursuit of Visibility.' In H. Blatterer, P. Johnson, & M. Markus (Eds), *Modern Privacy: Shifting Boundaries, New Forms* (pp. 73–87). New York and London: Palgrave Macmillan.

Blatterer, H. (2013). 'Review of A. Muraco, Odd Couples: Friendships at the Intersection of Gender and Sexual Orientation.' *Contemporary Sociology: A Journal of Reviews, 42*(4), 590–592.

Blatterer, H., Johnson, P., & Markus, M. R. (2010). *Modern Privacy: Shifting Boundaries, New Forms.* New York and London: Palgrave Macmillan.

Bleske-Rechek, A., Somers, E., Micke, C., Erickson, L., Matteson, L., Stocco, C., ... Ritchie, L. (2012). 'Benefit or Burden? Attraction in Cross-Sex Friendship.' *Journal of Social and Personal Relationships, 29*(5), 569–596.

Blumer, H. (1954). 'What is Wrong with Social Theory?' *American Sociological Review, 19*(1), 3–10.

Booth, A., & Hess, E. (1974). 'Cross-Sex Friendship.' *Journal of Marriage and Family, 36*(1), 38–47.

Bornstein, K. (2013). *Gender Outlaw: On Men, Women and the Rest of Us.* Routledge.

Bourdieu, P. (2001). *Masculine Domination.* Stanford: Stanford University Press.

Brain, R. (1976). *Friends and Lovers.* Glasgow: Hart-Davis MacGibbon.

Braudel, F. (1985). *Civilization and Capitalism: 15th–18th Century.* (S. Reynolds, Trans.) (Vol. 2). London: Fontana Press.

Bray, A. (2003). *The Friend.* Chicago: University of Chicago Press.

Broadie, A. (2003). 'Introduction.' In *The Cambridge Companion to the Scottish Enlightenment* (pp. 1–9). Cambridge: Cambridge University Press.

Budgeon, S. (2006). 'Friendship and Formations of Sociality in Late Modernity: the Challenge of "Post Traditional Intimacy"'. *Sociological Research Online, 11*(3).

Buhrke, R. A., & Fuqua, D. R. (1987). 'Sex Differences in Same- and Cross-Sex Supportive Relationships.' *Sex Roles, 17*(5), 339–352.

Burkart, G. (1998). 'Auf dem Weg zu einer Soziologie der Liebe.' In *Liebe am Ende des 20. Jahrhunderts: Studien zur Soziologie intimer Beziehungen* (Vol. 1, pp. 15–49). Opladen: Leske + Budrich.

Burkart, G., & Hahn, K. (1998). 'Einleitung: Liebe am Ende des 20. Jahrhunderts.' In *Liebe am Ende des 20. Jahrhunderts: Studien zur Soziologie intimer Beziehungen* (Vol. 1, pp. 7–13). Opladen: Leske + Budrich.

Burkeman, O. (2012). 'Facebook and Twitter: The Art of Unfriending or Unfollowing People.' *The Guardian.* http://www.guardian.co.uk/technology/2012/sep/14/unfollow-unfriend-on-facebook-twitter, accessed 4 February 2013.

Burkitt, I. (1991). *Social Selves: Theories of the Social Formation of Personality.* London: Sage.

Burleson, B. R. (1997). 'A Different Voice on Different Cultures: Illusion and Reality in the Study of Sex Differences in Personal Relationships.' *Personal Relationships, 4*(3), 229–241.

Butera, K. J. (2008). '"Neo-Mateship" in the 21st Century: Changes in the Performance of Australian Masculinity'. *Journal of Sociology, 44*(3), 265–281.

Butler, J. (1990). *Gender Trouble: Feminism and the Subversion of Identity*. New York: Psychology Press.

Caldwell, M., & Peplau, L. (1982). 'Sex Differences in Same-Sex Friendship.' *Sex Roles, 8*(7), 721–732.

Calhoun, C. (1992). 'The Infrastructure of Modernity: Indirect Relationships, Information Technology, and Social Integration.' In *Social Change and Modernity* (pp. 205–236). Berkeley: University of California Press.

Califia, P. (2003). *Sex Changes: The Politics of Transgenderism*. Cleis Press.

Cancian, F. M. (1986). 'The Feminization of Love.' *Signs*, 692–709.

Cancian, F. M. (1990). *Love in America: Gender and Self-Development*. Cambridge and New York: Cambridge University Press.

Carnegie, D. (2009). *How to Win Friends and Influence People*. New York: Simon & Schuster.

Carrier, J., G. (1999). 'People who can be Friends: Selves and Social Relationships.' In S. Bell & S. Coleman (Eds), *The Anthropology of Friendship* (pp. 21–38). Oxford and New York: Berg.

Castells, M. (1997). *The Power of Identity: The Information Age: Economy, Society, and Culture*. Malden: Blackwell.

Chen, E. J. (2011). 'Caught in a Bad Bromance.' *Texas Journal of Women and the Law, 21,* 241.

Cocking, D., & Kennett, J. (1998). 'Friendship and the Self.' *Ethics, 108*(3), 502–527.

Cohen, Y. A. (1961). 'Patterns of Friendship.' In Y. A. Cohen (Ed.), *Social Structure and Personality* (pp. 351–386). New York: Hot Rinehart Winston.

Cohen, Y. (1963). *Social Structure and Personality*. Holt, Rinehart, Winston: New York.

Connell, R. (2005). *Masculinities*. Cambridge: Polity Press.

Connell, R. (2009). *Gender*. Cambridge: Polity Press.

Connidis, I. A., & McMullin, J. A. (2002). 'Sociological Ambivalence and Family Ties: A Critical Perspective.' *Journal of Marriage and Family, 64*(3), 558–567.

Conrad, R. (2010). *Against Equality: Queer Critiques of Gay Marriage*. Oakland: A KPress Distribution.

Coontz, S. (2005). *Marriage, a History: From Obedience to Intimacy, or How Love Conquered Marriage*. New York: Viking.

Craib, I. (1998). *Experiencing Identity*. London: Sage Publications.

Cross, S. E., & Madson, L. (1997). 'Models of the Self: Self-Construals and Gender.' *Psychological Bulletin, 122*(1), 5.

Csikszentmihalyi, M. (1999). 'Creativity.' In *Handbook of Creativity* (pp. 313–35). Cambridge: Cambridge University Press.

Dahrendorf, R. (1958). 'Out of Utopia: Toward a Reorientation of Sociological Analysis.' *American Journal of Sociology*, 115–127.

Darroch, J. E., Landry, D. J., & Oslak, S. (1999). 'Age Differences Between Sexual Partners in the United States.' *Family Planning Perspectives, 31*(4), 160.

Davies, K. (2011). 'Friendship and Personal Life.' In V. May (Ed.), *The Sociology of Personal Life*. Basingstoke: Palgrave MacMillan.

Davies, N. (2010). *Europe: A History*. New York: Random House.

De Souza Briggs, X. (2007). "Some of My Best Friends Are ...": Interracial Friendships, Class, and Segregation in America.' *City & Community*, 6(4), 263–290.

Deaux, K., Winton, W., Crowley, M., & Lewis, L. L. (1985). 'Level of Categorization and Content of Gender Stereotypes.' *Social Cognition*, 3(2), 145–167.

Dovidio, J. F., Hewstone, M., Glick, P., & Esses, V. M. (Eds). (2010). *The SAGE Handbook of Prejudice, Stereotyping and Discrimination*. London: Sage Publications.

Durkheim, E. (1966). *The Rules of the Sociological Method*. New York: Free Press.

Düttmann, A. G. (2000). *Between Cultures: Tensions in the Struggle for Recognition*. London: Verso.

Eagly, A. H., & Steffen, V. J. (1984). 'Gender Stereotypes Stem from the Distribution of Women and Men into Social Roles.' *Journal of Personality and Social Psychology*, 46(4), 735.

Ehrenreich, B. (2009). *Brightsided: How the Relentless Promotion of Positive Thinking has Undermined America*. New York: Macmillan.

Eisenberg, M. E., Ackard, D. M., Resnick, M. D., & D. Neumark-Sztainer. (2009). 'Casual Sex and Psychological Health Among Young Adults: Is Having "Friends with Benefits" Emotionally Damaging?' *Perspectives on Sexual and Reproductive Health*, 41(4), 231–237.

Eisenstadt, S. N., & Roniger, L. (1984). *Patrons, Clients, and Friends: Interpersonal Relations and the Structure of Trust in Society*. Cambridge: Cambridge University Press.

Elias, N. (2006). *The Court Society*. In *Collected Works* (E. Jephcott, Trans., S. Mennell, Ed.) (Vol. 2). Dublin: University College Dublin Press.

Elias, N. (2011). *The Society of Individuals*. In *Collected Works* (M. Schroter & R. Van Krieken, Eds.) (Vol. 10). Dublin: University College Dublin Press.

Elias, N. (2012a). *On the Process of Civilisation: Sociogenetic and Psychogenetic Investigations*. In *Collected Works* (E. Jephcott, Trans., S. Mennell, E. Dunning, J. Goudsblom, & R. Kilminster, Eds) (Vol. 3). Dublin: University College Dublin Press.

Elias, N. (2012b). *What is Sociology?* In *Collected Works* (G. Morrissey, S. Mennell, & E. Jephcott, Trans.) (Vol. 5). Dublin: University College Dublin Press.

Engels, F. (2010). *The Origin of the Family, Private Property and the State*. London: Penguin UK.

Epstein, M., Calzo, J. P., Smiler, A., & Ward, M. L. (2009). 'Anything from Making out to Having Sex': Men's Negotiations of Hooking Up and Friends with Benefits Scripts'. *Journal of Sex Research*, 46(5), 414–24.

Erikson, E. H. (1994). *Identity: Youth and Crisis*. New York: W. W. Norton & Company.

Esser, H. (2000). *Soziologie. Spezielle Grundlagen 5: Institutionen*. Frankfurt: Campus Verlag.

Evans, M. (2003). *Love, an Unromantic Discussion*. Oxford: Wiley-Blackwell.

Evans-Pritchard, E. E. (1963). *Witchcraft, Oracles and Magic among the Azande*. London: Clarendon Press.

Eve, M. (2002). 'Is Friendship a Sociological Topic?' *European Journal of Sociology / Archives Européennes de Sociologie*, 43(03), 386–409.

Faulkner, P. (2011). *Just add sex ... then stir: A sociological enquiry into friends with benefits* (Unpublished Honours Thesis). North Ryde: Macquarie University.

Felmlee, D. H. (1999). 'Social Norms in Same-and Cross-Gender Friendships.' *Social Psychology Quarterly*, 53–67.

Felmlee, D. H., Sweet, E., & Sinclair, H. (2012). 'Gender Rules: Same- and Cross-Gender Friendships Norms.' *Sex Roles, 66*(7), 518–529.

Fischer, C. S. (1982). 'What Do We Mean by 'Friend'? An Inductive Study.' *Social Networks, 3*(4), 287–306.

Flood, M. (2008). 'Men, Sex, and Homosociality How Bonds between Men Shape Their Sexual Relations with Women.' *Men and Masculinities, 10*(3), 339–359.

Foucault, M. (1980a). *Power/Knowledge: Selected Interviews and Other Writings, 1972–1977*. Pantheon Books.

Foucault, M. (1980b). *The History of Sexuality* (Vol. 1). New York: Vintage Books.

Foucault, M. (2000). 'Friendship as a Way of Life.' In P. Rabinow (Ed.), (pp. 135–140). New York: Perseus Distribution Services.

Francis, M. (2007). *Herbert Spencer and the Invention of Modern Life*. Durham: Acumen.

Fraser, D. (2004). *Cricket and the Law: The Man in White is Always Right*. London: Routledge.

Fraser, N. (2000). 'Rethinking Recognition', *New Left Review* (3), May–June, 107–20.

Fraser, N., & Honneth, A. (2003). *Redistribution Or Recognition?: A Political-Philosophical Exchange*. Verso.

Frisby, D. (1986). *Fragments of Modernity: Theories of Modernity in the Work of Simmel, Kracauer, and Benjamin*. Cambridge, Mass: MIT Press.

Fromm, E. (2013). *The Art of Loving*. New York: Open Road Media.

Fuhrman, R. W., Flannagan, D., & Matamoros, M. (2009). 'Behavior Expectations in Cross-Sex Friendships, Same-Sex Friendships, and Romantic Relationships.' *Personal Relationships, 16*(4), 575–596.

Furedi, F. (2004). *Therapy Culture: Cultivating Vulnerability in an Uncertain Age*. London: Psychology Press.

Galeano, E. (2001). *Upside Down: A Primer for the Looking-Glass World*. London: St Martins Press.

Gans, H. J. (2012). 'Against Culture versus Structure.' *Identities, 19*(2), 1–10.

Garfinkel, H. (1967). *Studies in Ethnomethodology*. Oxford: Wiley-Blackwell.

Garfinkel, H., & Rawls, A. W. (2006). *Seeing Sociologically: The Routine Grounds of Social Action*. Boulder: Paradigm Publishers.

Gates. (2011). *How many People are Lesbian, Gay, Bisexual, and Transgender?* UCLA School of Law: The Williams Institute.

Gates, G. J., & Newport, F. (2013a). *LGBT percentage highest in D.C., lowest in North Dakota*. Gallup Politics, State of the States. http://www.gallup.com/poll/160517/lgbt-percentage-highest-lowest-north-dakota.aspx, 5 February 2014.

Gates, G. J., & Newport, F. (2013b). *3-4% of U.S. Adults Identify as LGBT*. http://www.gallup.com/poll/158066/special-report-adults-identify-lgbt.aspx, 5 February 2014.

Gay, P. (1999). *The Bourgeois Experience: Victoria to Freud: Education of the Senses* (Vol. 1). New York and London: Norton.

Gerson, K. (2010). *The Unfinished Revolution: How a New Generation is Reshaping Family, Work, and Gender in America*. Oxford and New York: Oxford University Press.

Giddens, A. (1984). *The Constitution of Society: Outline of the Theory of Structuration*. Cambridge: Polity Press.

Giddens, A. (1991a). *Modernity and Self-Identity: Self and Society in the Late Modern Age*. Stanford: Stanford University Press.

Giddens, A. (1991b). *The Consequences of Modernity*. Stanford: Stanford University Press.

Giddens, A. (1992). *The Transformation of Intimacy: Sexuality, Love and Eroticism in Modern Societies*. Stanford: Stanford University Press.

Glick, P., & Fiske, S. T. (2001). 'Ambivalent Sexism.' *Advances in Experimental Social Psychology*, *33*, 115–188.

Goffman, E. (1963a). *Behavior in Public Places: Notes on the Social Organization of Gatherings*. New York: Free Press.

Goffman, E. (1963b). *Stigma: Notes on the Management of Spoiled Identity*. New York: Simon and Schuster.

Goffman, E. (1977). 'The Arrangement between the Sexes.' *Theory and Society*, *4*(3), 301–331.

Goffman, E. (1990). *The Presentation of Self in Everyday Life*. London: Penguin.

Good, C. A. (2012). 'Friendly Relations: Situating Friendships Between Men and Women in the Early American Republic, 1780–1830.' *Gender & History*, *24*(1), 18–34.

Gouliquer, L. (2000). 'Pandora's Box: The Paradox of Flexibility in Today's Workplace'. *Current Sociology*, *48*(1), 29–38.

Granovetter, M. S. (1973). 'The Strength of Weak Ties.' *American Journal of Sociology*, 1360–1380.

Green, R. J., & Ashmore, R. D. (1998). Taking and Developing Pictures in the Head: Assessing the Physical Stereotypes of Eight Gender Types1. *Journal of Applied Social Psychology*, *28*(17), 1609–1636.

Green, R. J., Ashmore, R. D., & Manzi, R. (2005). 'The Structure of Gender Type Perception: Testing the Elaboration, Encapsulation, and Evaluation Framework.' *Social Cognition*, *23*(5), 429–464.

Greif, G. L. (2009). *Buddy System: Understanding Male Friendships*. Oxford; New York: Oxford University Press.

Gross, N. (2005). 'The Detraditionalization of Intimacy Reconsidered.' *Sociological Theory*, *23*(3), 286–311.

Grumley, J. (1988). Weber's Fragmentation Of Totality. *Thesis Eleven*, *21*(1), 20–39.

Guerrero, L. K., & Chavez, A. M. (2005). Relational Maintenance in Cross-Sex Friendships Characterized by Different Types of Romantic Intent: An Exploratory Study. *Western Journal of Communication*, *69*(4), 339–358. doi:10.1080/10570310500305471

Gulliver, P. H. (1971). *Neighbours and Networks: The Idiom of Kinship in Social Action among the Ndendeuli of Tanzania*. Berkeley: University of California Press.

Gurdin, J. (1996). *Amitie/Friendship: An Investigation into Cross-Cultural Styles in Canada and the United States*. San Francisco: Austin and Winfield.

Gurman, A. S., & Fraenkel, P. (2002). 'The History of Couple Therapy: A Millennial Review.' *Family Process*, *41*(2), 199–260.

Habermas, J. (1991). *The Structural Transformation of the Public Sphere: An Inquiry into a Category of Bourgeois Society*. Cambridge: MIT Press.

Haggerty, G. E. (2007). 'Male Love and Friendship in the Eighteenth Century.' In K. O'Donnell & M. O'Rourke (Eds), *Love, Sex, Intimacy and Friendship between Men, 1550–1800* (pp. 70–81). Basingstoke: Palgrave MacMillan.

Halatsis, P., & Christakis, N. (2009). 'The Challenge of Sexual Attraction within Heterosexuals' Cross-Sex Friendship'. *Journal of Social and Personal Relationships*, 26(6-7), 919–937.

Hartley, N. (2010). 'Friends With Benefits: 10 Relationship Rules.' http//: www. mademan.com/mm/friends-benefits-10-relationship-rules.html, accessed 12 June 2011.

Heaphy, B., Donovan, C., & Weeks, J. (2004). 'A Different Affair? Openness and Nonmonogamy in Same Sex Relationships.' In *The state of affairs: Explorations in Infidelity and Commitment* (pp. 167–186). New York: Lawrence Erlbaum.

Hegel, G. W. F. (1991). *Elements of the Philosophy of Right*. (A. W. Wood, Ed.). Cambridge: Cambridge University Press.

Heilbroner, R. L. (1999). *The Worldly Philosophers: The Lives, Times, and Ideas of the Great Economic Thinkers*. New York: Simon & Schuster.

Heinämaa, S., & Reuter, M. (2009). *Psychology and Philosophy: Inquiries into the Soul from Late Scholasticism to Contemporary Thought (Studies in the History of Philosophy of Mind)*. New York: Springer.

Heller, A. (1998). 'The Beauty of Friendship.' *South Atlantic Quarterly*, 97(1), 5–22.

Heller, Á., & Fehér, F. (1988). *The Postmodern Political Condition*. Cambridge: Polity Press.

Hill, L., & McCarthy, P. (1999). 'Hume, Smith and Ferguson: Friendship in Commercial Society.' *Critical Review of International Social and Political Philosophy*, 2, 33–49.

Hill, L., & McCarthy, P. (2004). 'On Friendship and Necessitudo in Adam Smith.' *History of the Human Sciences*, 17(4), 1 –16.

Hobsbawm, E. (2010). *Age of Revolution 1789–1848*. London: Hachette UK.

Hobsbawm, E., & Ranger, T. (2012). *The Invention of Tradition*. Cambridge: Cambridge University Press.

Hobson, B. (2002). *Making Men into Fathers: Men, Masculinities and the Social Politics of Fatherhood*. Cambridge: Cambridge University Press.

Hochschild, A. R. (1979). 'Emotion Work, Feeling Rules, and Social Structure.' *American Journal of Sociology*, 551–575.

Holmes, M. (2011). Emotional reflexivity in contemporary friendships: Understanding it using Elias and Facebook etiquette. *Sociological Research Online*, 16(1), 11.

Honneth, A. (2007b). 'Between Justice and Affection: The Family as a Field of Moral Disputes.' In *Disrespect: The Normative Foundations of Critical Theory* (pp. 144–162). Cambridge: Polity Press.

Honneth, A. (2007c). 'Love and Morality: On the Moral Content of Emotional Ties.' In *Disrespect* (pp. 163–180). Cambridge: Polity Press.

Honneth, A. (1996). *The Struggle for Recognition: The Moral Grammar of Social Conflicts*. MIT Press.

Honneth, A. (2011). *Das Recht der Freiheit: Grundriß einer demokratischen Sittlichkeit*. Frankfurt: Suhrkamp.

Hughes, J. A., & Sharrock, W. W. W. (1997). *The Philosophy of Social Research*. London and New York: Longman Publishing.

Illouz, E. (1997). *Consuming the Romantic Utopia: Love and the Cultural Contradictions of Capitalism*. Berkeley: University of California Press.

Illouz, E. (2007). *Cold Intimacies: The Making of Emotional Capitalism*. Cambridge: Polity Press.

Illouz, E. (2008). *Saving the Modern Soul: Therapy, Emotions, and the Culture of Self-Help*. Berkeley: University of California Press.

Illouz, E. (2012). *Why Love Hurts*. Cambridge: Polity Press.

Irmen, L. (2006). 'Automatic Activation and Use of Gender Subgroups.' *Sex Roles*, 55(7-8), 435–444.

Jackson, S. (2006). 'Gender, Sexuality and Heterosexuality: The Complexity (and Limits) of Heteronormativity.' *Feminist Theory*, 7(1), 105–121.

Jackson, S. and Scott, S. (2010). *Theorizing Sexuality*. Maidenhead: McGraw-Hill International.

Jagose, A. (2012). *Orgasmology*. Durham: Duke University Press.

Jamieson, L. (1998). *Intimacy: Personal Relationships in Modern Societies*. Cambridge: Polity Press.

Jamieson, L. (1999). 'Intimacy Transformed? A Critical Look at the Pure Relationship.' *Sociology*, 33(3), 477–494.

Jenkins, R. (2000). 'Categorization: Identity, Social Process and Epistemology''. *Current Sociology*, 48(3), 7–25.

Jenkins, R. (2013). *Social Identity*. London: Routledge.

Jerrome, D. (1992). *Good Company: An Anthropological Study of Old People in Groups*. Edinburgh: Edinburgh University Press. http://www.getcited.org/pub/103140574

Katz, J. (2007). *The Invention of Heterosexuality*. Chicago: University of Chicago Press.

Kaufmann, J.-C. (2009). *Gripes: The Little Quarrels of Couples*. Cambridge: Polity Press.

Kimmel, M. (2004). 'Masculinity as Homophobia: Fear, Shame, and Silence in the Construction of Gender Identity.' In P. S. Rothenberg (Ed.), *Race, Class, and Gender in the United States: An Integrated Study* (pp. 81–93). New York: Worth.

Kimmel, M. (2009). *Guyland: The Perilous World Where Boys Become Men*. New York: Harper Collins.

Klesse, C. (2014). 'Polyamory: Intimate Practice, Identity or Sexual Orientation?' *Sexualities*, 17(1-2), 81–99.

Kon, I., S. (1979). *Freundschaft: Geschichte und Sozialpsychology der Freundschaft als soziale Institution und individuelle Beziehung*. München: Rowohlt Taschenbuch Verlag.

Kracauer, S. (1990). *Über Die Freundschaft: Essays* (6. Aufl.). Frankfurt am Main: Suhrkamp Verlag.

Kracauer, S. (1998). *The Salaried Masses: Duty and Distraction in Weimar Germany*. London: Verso.

Krais, B. (2006). 'Gender, Sociological Theory and Bourdieu's Sociology of Practice'. *Theory, Culture & Society*, 23(6), 119–134.

Kristjánsson, K. (2006). 'Parents and Children as Friends.' *Journal of Social Philosophy*, 37(2), 250–265.

Kruglanski, A. W., & Sleeth-Keppler, D. (2007). 'The Principles of Social Judgment.' In A. W. Kruglanski & Hggins, Tory E. (Eds), *Social Psychology: Handbook of Basic Principles* (pp. 116–37). New York: Guilford Press.

Kundera, M. (1984). *The Unbearable Lightness of Being*. London: Faber and Father.

Kupfer, J. (1990). 'Can Parents and Children be Friends?' *American Philosophical Quarterly*, *27*(1), 15–26.

Kurth, S., B. (1970). 'Friendships and Friendly Relations.' In G. J. McCall, M. M. McCall, N. K. Denzin, G. D. Startles, & S. B. Kurth (Eds), *Social Relationships* (pp. 135–170). Chicago: Aldine.

Kwateng, D. (2010). 'Love and Marriage: 8 Rules for Being 'Friends with Benefits.'' http://madamenoire.com/5471/8-rules-for-being-friends-with-benefits/, accessed 12 June 2011.

Lambert, A. (2013). *Intimacy and Friendship on Facebook*. London: Palgrave Macmillan.

Langford, W. (2013). *Revolutions of the Heart: Gender, Power and the Delusions of Love*. London: Routledge.

Lasch, C. (1979). *The Culture of Narcissism; American Life in an Age of Diminishing Expectations*. New York: Norton.

Lasch, C. (1995). *Haven in a Heartless World: The Family Besieged*. New York: Norton.

Lazarsfeld, P., & Merton, R. (1964). 'Friendship as Social Process: A Substantive and Methodological Analysis.' In P. L. Kendall (Ed.), *Freedom and Control in Modern Society* (pp. 18–66). New York: Columbia University Press.

Lehmiller, J. J., VanderDrift, L. E., & Kelly, J. R. (2011). 'Sex Differences in Approaching Friends with Benefits Relationships.' *Journal of Sex Research*, *48*(2-3), 275–284.

Leib, E. J. (2011). *Friend v. Friend: The Transformation of Friendship--and What the Law Has to Do with It*. New York: Oxford University Press.

Lewin, K., & Lippitt, R. (1938). 'An Experimental Approach to the Study of Autocracy and Democracy: A Preliminary Note.' *Sociometry*, *1*(3/4), 292–300.

Lindholm, C. (1982). *Generosity and Jealousy: The Swat Pukhtun of Northern Pakistan*. Columbia University Press.

Lipman-Blumen, J. (1976). 'Toward a Homosocial Theory of Sex roles: An Explanation of the Sex Segregation of Social Institutions.' *Signs*, *1*(3), 15–31.

Lippmann, W. (1922). *Public Opinion*. New York: Harcourt Brace.

Livingstone, S. (2008). 'Taking Risky Opportunities in Use of Social Networking Sites for Intimacy, Privacy and Self-expression.' *New Media & Society*, *10*(3), 393–411.

Luckmann, T. (2002). 'Moral Communication in Modern Societies.' *Human Studies*, *25*, 19–32.

Luhmann, N. (1998b). *Die Gesellschaft der Gesellschaft* (7th ed.). Frankfurt am Main: Suhrkamp Verlag.

Luhmann, N. (2009a). *Einführung in die Theorie der Gesellschaft*. Heidelberg: Carl-Auer Verlag.

Luhmann, N. (1998a). *Love as Passion: The Codification of Intimacy*. Stanford: Stanford University Press.

Luhmann, N. (1994). *Trust: and Power*. New York: UMI.

Luhmann, N. (1995). *Social Systems*. Stanford: Stanford University Press.

Luhmann, N. (2010). *Love: A Sketch*. Cambridge: Polity Press.

Lukes, S. (1968). 'Methodological Individualism Reconsidered.' *The British Journal of Sociology*, *19*(2), 119–129.

Lyman, P. (1987). 'The Fraternal Bond as a Joking Relationship: A Case Study of Sexist Jokes in Male Group Bonding.' In M. S. Kimmel (Ed.), *Changing Men: New Directions in Research on Men and Masculinity* (pp. 166–71).

Magaraggia, S. (2013a). 'Tensions between Fatherhood and the Social Construction of Masculinity in Italy. *Current Sociology*, *61*(1), 76–92.

Magaraggia, S., & Cherubini, D. (2013b). *Uomini contro le donne? Le radici della violenza maschile*. Milano: UTET Università.

Mallory, P. (2012). 'Political friendship in the era of 'the social': Theorizing personal relations with Alexis de Tocqueville.' *Journal of Classical Sociology*, *12*(1), 22–42.

Margalit, A. (1996). *The Decent Society*. Harvard: Harvard University Press.

Markiewicz, D., Lawford, H., Doyle, A. B., & Haggart, N. (2006). 'Developmental Differences in Adolescents' and Young Adults' Use of Mothers, Fathers, Best Friends, and Romantic Partners to Fulfill Attachment Needs'. *Journal of Youth and Adolescence*, *35*(1), 121–134.

Markus, G. (2011). *Culture, Science, Society: The Constitution of Cultural Modernity*. BRILL.

Markus, M. R. (2001). 'Decent Society and/or Civil Society?' *Social Research*, *68*(4), 1011–1030.

Markus, M. R. (2002). 'Cultural Pluralism and the Subversion of the "Taken-for Granted' World." In P. Essed & D. T. Goldberg (Eds), *Race Critical Theories: Text and Context*. Oxford: Blackwell.

Markus, M. R. (2010a). 'Can Solitude be Recaptured for the Sake of Intimacy?' In H. Blatterer, P. Johnson, & Markus, Maria R. (Eds), *Modern Privacy: Shifting Boundaries, New Forms* (pp. 88–101). New York: Palgrave Macmillan.

Markus, M. R. (2010b). 'Lovers and Friends: "Radical Utopias" of Intimacy?'. *Thesis Eleven*, *101*(1), 6.

Martin, J. L. (2011). *Social Structures*. Princeton: Princeton University Press.

Matthews, S. H. (1986). *Friendships through the Life Course: Oral Biographies in Old Age*. Newbury Park: Sage Publications.

May, V., Bottero, W., & Davies, K. (2011). *Sociology of Personal Life*. London: Palgrave Macmillan.

McPherson, M., Smith-Lovin, L., & Brashears, M. E. (2006). 'Social Isolation in America: Changes in Core Discussion Networks over Two Decades.' *American Sociological Review*, *71*(3), 353–375.

Mead, G. H. (1964). *Selected Writings*. (A. J. Reck, Ed.). New York: Bobbs-Merrill.

Merton, R. K. (1968). 'Manifest and Latent Functions.' *Social Theory and Social Structure*, 19–84.

Messner, M. (1992). 'Like Family: Power, Intimacy, and Sexuality in Male Athletes' Friendships'. In *Men's Friendships* (pp. 215–38). Newbury Park: SAGE Publications.

Miller, S. (1992). *Men and Friendship*. Los Angeles: J.P. Tarcher.

Mills, C. W. (2000). *The Sociological Imagination*. Oxford: Oxford University Press.

Mirowsky, J., & Ross, C. E. (2003). *Social Causes of Psychological Distress*. New Jersey: Transaction Publishers.

Misztal, B. (1996). *Trust in Modern Societies: The Search for the Bases of Social Order*. Oxford: Wiley.

Monsour, M. (2002). *Women and Men as Friends: Relationships across the Life Span in the 21st Century*. New York: Lawrence Erlbaum.

Monsour, M., Harris, B., Kurzweil, N., & Beard, C. (1994). 'Challenges Confronting Cross-Sex Friendships: "Much ado about nothing?"'. *Sex Roles, 31*(1), 55–77.

Moody, J. (2001). 'Race, School Integration, and Friendship Segregation in Americ. *American Journal of Sociology, 107*(3), 679–716.

Moon, D. (1995). 'Insult and Inclusion: The Term Fag Hag and Gay Male "Community."' *Social Forces, 74*(2), 487–510.

Morgan, D. (2009). *Acquaintances: The Space Between Intimates and Strangers*. Maidenhead: McGraw-Hill.

Morris, C. (1987). *The Discovery of the Individual, 1050–1200*. Toronto: University of Toronto Press.

Muraco, A. (2012). *Odd Couples: Friendships at the Intersection of Gender and Sexual Orientation*. Durham: Duke University Press.

Nardi, P. M. (1999). *'Gay Men's Friendships: Invincible Communities'*. Chicago: University of Chicago Press.

Natanson, M. (1970). 'Phenomenology and Typification: A Study in the Philosophy of Alfred Schutz.' *Social Research, 37*(1), 1–22.

Nedelmann, B. (1991). 'Amicizia.' *Treccani, l'Enciclopedia italiana*. Retrieved August 1, 2012, from http://www.treccani.it/enciclopedia/ amicizia_(Enciclopedia_delle_Scienze_Sociali)/

Nisbet, R. A. (1973). *The Social Philosophers: Community and Conflict in Western Thought*. New York: Thomas Y. Crowell.

O'Meara, J. D. (1989). 'Cross-Sex Friendship: Four Basic Challenges of an Ignored Relationship.' *Sex Roles, 21*(7), 525–543.

OECD. (2012). Marriage and Divorce Rates. OECD 2012, 'Marriage and Divorce Rates', http://www.oecd.org/els/family/SF3.1%20Marriage%20and%20divorce %20rate%20-%20updated%20240212.pdf

OECD. (2013). Family Violence. http://www.oecd.org/els/soc/SF3_4_Family_ violence_Jan2013.pdf, 11 May 2013

Pahl, R. (2002). 'Towards a More Significant Sociology of Friendship. *European Journal of Sociology / Archives Européennes de Sociologie, 43*(03), 410–423.

Paine, R. (1969). In Search of Friendship: An Exploratory Analysis in 'Middle-Class' Culture. *Man, 4*(4), 505–524.

Paine, R. (1974). An Exploratory Analysis in 'Middle-Class' Culture. In *The Compact: Selected Dimensions of Friendship*. Toronto: Toronto University Press.

Parekh, B. (1994). 'An Indian View of Friendship.' In L. S. Rouner (Ed.), *The Changing Face of Friendship*. Notre Dame: Notre Dame University Press.

Paz, O. (2011). *The Double Flame: Essays on Love & Eroticism*. Random House.

Pinker, S. (2010). *The Language Instinct: How The Mind Creates Language*. HarperCollins.

Polanyi, K. (2001). *The Great Transformation: The Political and Economic Origins of Our Time*. Boston: Beacon Press.

Prentice, D. A., & Carranza, E. (2002). 'What Women and Men Should Be, Shouldn't Be, are Allowed to Be, and Don't Have to Be: The Contents of Prescriptive Gender Stereotypes'. *Psychology of Women Quarterly, 26*(4), 269–281.

Quigley, C. (2013). 'The Best Examples of Platonic Friendship between Men and Women in Popular Culture.' portable tv. http://portable.tv/culture/post/

the-best-examples-of-platonic-friendships-between-men-and-women-in-popu-lar-culture/, 19 February 2014.

Raley, S., Bianchi, S. M., & Wang, W. (2013). 'When Do Fathers Care? Mothers' Economic Contribution and Fathers' Involvement in Child Care'. *American Journal of Sociology*, *117*(5), 1422–1459.

Rapsch, A. (2004). *Soziologie der Freundschaft: Historische und Gesellschaftliche Bedeutung Von Homer Bis Heute*. Stuttgart: Ibidem-Verlag.

Rawlins, W. K. (1982). 'Cross-Sex Friendship and the Communicative Management of Sex-Role Expectations.' *Communication Quarterly*, *30*(4), 343–352.

Rawlins, W. K. (1992). *Friendship Matters: Communication, Dialectics, and the Life Course*. New Jersey: Transaction Publishers.

Rawls, J. (2009). *A Theory of Justice*. Harvard: Harvard University Press.

Reeder, H. M. (2000). I Like you... as a Friend': The Role of Attraction in Cross-Sex Friendship'. *Journal of Social and Personal Relationships*, *17*(3), 329–348.

Reiner, W. G. (1997). 'Sex Assignment in the Neonate with Intersex or Inadequate genitalia.' *Archives of Pediatrics & Adolescent Medicine*, *151*(10), 1044.

Ribbens McCarthy, J. (2012). 'The Powerful Relational Language of 'Family': Togetherness, Belonging and Personhood.' *The Sociological Review*, *60*(1), 68–90.

Rich, A. (1980). Compulsory heterosexuality and lesbian existence. *Signs*, *5*(4), 631–660.

Richardson, D. (2000). *Rethinking Sexuality*. SAGE Publications.

Richter, G. (1997). 'Siegfried Kracauer and the Folds of Friendship.' *The German Quarterly*, *70*(3), 233–246.

Rofes, E. (1997). 'Dancing Bears, Performing Husbands, and the Tyranny of the Family.' In R. E. Goss & A. S. Strongheart (Eds), *Our Families, Our Values* (pp. 151–162). Binghampton: The Harrington Park Press.

Rogers, E. M., & Bhowmik, D. K. (1970). 'Homophily-Heterophily: Relational Concepts for Communication Research.' *Public Opinion Quarterly*, *34*(4), 523–538.

Rose, S. M. (1985). 'Same- and Cross-sex Friendships and the Psychology of Homosociality.' *Sex Roles*, *12*(1), 63–74.

Roseneil, S., & Budgeon, S. (2004). 'Cultures of intimacy and care beyond "the family": personal life and social change in the early 21st century.' *Current Sociology*, *52*(2), 135.

Rössler, B. (2005). *The Value of Privacy*. (R. D. V. Glasgow, Trans.). London: Polity Press.

Rubin, G. (1975). 'The Traffic in Women: Notes on the "Political Economy" of Sex'. In Reiter, R. A. (Ed.), *Toward an Anthropology of Women*. New York: Monthly Review Press.

Rubin, L. B. (1985). *Just Friends*. New York: Harper and Row.

Rudman, L. A., & Fairchild, K. (2007). 'The F Word: Is Feminism Incompatible with Beauty and Romance?' *Psychology of Women Quarterly*, *31*(2), 125–136.

Rudman, L. A., & Glick, P. (2001). 'Prescriptive Gender Stereotypes and Backlash Toward Agentic Women.' *Journal of Social Issues*, *57*(4), 743–762.

Sargent, D. (2013). *American Masculinity and Homosocial Behavior in the Bromance Era*. Georgia State University, Atlanta.

Schmidt, J. F. K. (2000). 'Die Differenzierung persönlicher Beziehungen. Das Verhältnis von Liebe, Freundschaft und Partnerschaft.' In *Liebe: Grenzen und Grenzüberschreitungen. Studien zur Soziologie intimer Beziehungen* (Vol. 2, pp. 73–100). Opladen: Leske + Budrich.

Schnitzler, A. (1916). Der Weg ins Freie. In *Erzaehlende Schriften* (Vol. 3). Berlin: Fischer Verlag.

Schorske, C. E. (1981). *Fin-de-Siecle Vienna Politics and Culture* (First Printing edition.). New York: Vintage Books.

Schutz, A. (1962). 'The Problem of Social Reality.' In *Collected Papers* (Vol. I). The Hague: Martinus Nijhoff.

Schutz, A. (1973). 'On the Methodology of the Social Sciences.' In M. Natanson (Ed.), *Collected Papers: The Problem of Social Reality* (Vol. 1, pp. 1–98). The Hague: Martinus Nijhoff.

Sedgwick, E. K. (1985). *Between Men: English Literature and Male Homosocial Desire*. New York: Columbia University Press.

Seidman, S. (1997). *Difference Troubles: Queering Social Theory and Sexual Politics*. Cambridge: Cambridge University Press.

Selznick, P. (1994). *The Moral Commonwealth: Social Theory and the Promise of Community*. Berkeley: University of California Press.

Sennett, R. (1977). *The Fall of Public Man: The Forces Eroding Public Life and Burdening the Modern Psyche with Roles It Cannot Perform*. New York: Knopf.

Sennett, R. (2006). *The Culture of the New Capitalism*. New Haven: Yale University Press.

Sennett, R., & Cobb, J. (1972). *The Hidden Injuries of Class*. London: CUP Archive.

Settersten, R. A. (2003). 'Age Structuring and the Rhythm of the Life Course.' In J. T. Mortimer & M. J. Shanahan (Eds), *Handbook of the Life Course* (pp. 81–102). New York: Kluwer Academic.

Shils, E. (1981). *Tradition*. London: Faber.

Shklar, J. N. (1998). *Redeeming American Political Thought*. Chicago: University of Chicago Press.

Silver, A. (1989). 'Friendship and Trust as Moral Ideals: an Historical Approach.' *European Journal of Sociology*, *30*(02), 274–297.

Silver, A. (1990). 'Friendship in Commercial Society: Eighteenth-Century Social Theory and Modern Sociology.' *American Journal of Sociology*, *95*(6), 1474–1504.

Silver, A. (1996). ''Two Different Sorts of Commerce': Friendship and Strangership in Civil Society.' In *Public and Private in Thought and Practice: Perspectives on a Grand Dichotomy*. Chicago: University of Chicago Press.

Simmel, G. (1908b). 'Die Gesellschaft zu zweien.' *Der Tag*. Berlin.

Simmel, G. (1908a). *Soziologie: Untersuchungen über die Formen der Vergesellschaftung*. Frankfurt am Main: Suhrkamp.

Simmel, G. (1902a). 'The Number of Members as Determining the Sociological Form of the Group. I.' *American Journal of Sociology*, *8*(1), 1–46.

Simmel, G. (1902b). 'The Number of Members as Determining the Sociological form of the Group. II.' *American Journal of Sociology*, *8*(2), 158–196.

Simmel, G. (1906). 'The Sociology of Secrecy and of Secret Societies.' *The American Journal of Sociology*, *11*(4), 441–498.

Simmel, G. (1978). *The Philosophy of Money*. London: Routledge Keegan Paul.

Simmel, G. (1996). *Philosophische Kultur*. (R. Kramme & O. Rammstedt, Eds) (Vol. 14). Frankfurt am Main: Suhrkamp.

Singer, I. (1984). *The Nature of Love: The Modern World*. Cambridge: MIT Press.

Smart, C. (2007). *Personal Life: New Directions in Sociological Thinking.* Cambridge: Polity Press.

Smart, C., Davies, K., Heaphy, B., & Mason, J. (2012). 'Difficult Friendship and Ontological Security.' *The Sociological Review Online, 60*(1).

Smith, A. (1813). *The Theory of Moral Sentiments: Or, An Essay Towards an Analysis of the Principles by which Men Naturally Judge Concerning the Conduct and Character, First of Their Neighbors, and Afterwards of Themselves* (Vols. 1-2). Edinburgh: Hay.

Smith, E. R. (2001). 'Mental Representation of Persons, Psychology of.' In *International Encyclopedia of the Social and Behavioral Sciences* (pp. 9687–91). Oxford: Elsevier.

Smith Pangle, L. (2003). *Aristotle and the Philosophy of Friendship.* Cambridge: Cambridge University Press.

Solove, D. (2007). 'I've Got Nothing to Hide" and Other Misunderstandings of Privacy'. *San Diego Law Review, 44*(1), 445–472.

Spencer, L. (2006). *Rethinking Friendship: Hidden Solidarities Today.* Princeton, N.J: Princeton University Press.

Spencer, L., & Pahl, R. (2006). *Rethinking friendship: hidden solidarities today.* Princeton: Princeton University Press.

Spock, B. (2012). *Dr. Spock's Baby and Child Care: 9th Edition.* Simon and Schuster.

Stephens-Davidowitz, S. (2013). 'How Many American Men are Gay?' *The New York Times.* http://www.nytimes.com/2013/12/08/opinion/sunday/how-many-american-men-are-gay.html?pagewanted=all&_r=0, 4 February 2014.

Sternberg, R. (2008). *Cognitive Psychology.* Stamford: Cengage Learning.

Strauss, E. (1994). *Dictionary of European Proverbs.* London: Routledge.

Sumner, G. W. (1906). Folkways: *A Study of the Sociological Importance of Usages, Manners, Customs, Mores and Morals.* New York: Ginn.

Suttles, G., D. (1970). 'Friendship as a Social Institution.' In *Social Relationships* (pp. 95–135). Chicago: Aldine Pub. Co.

Swain, S. O. (1992). 'Men's Friendship with Women: Intimacy, Sexual Boundaries, and the Informant Role'. In *Men's Friendships* (pp. 153–172). Newbury Park: SAGE Publications.

Swidler, A. (2001). *Talk of Love: How Culture Matters.* Chicago: University of Chicago Press.

Tajfel, H. (1969). 'Cognitive Aspects of Prejudice1.' *Journal of Social Issues, 25*(4), 79–97.

Taormino, T. (2013). *Opening Up: A Guide To Creating and Sustaining Open Relationships.* Cleis Press.

Taylor, C. (1977). *Hegel.* Cambridge: Cambridge University Press.

Taylor, C. (1992). *The Ethics of Authenticity.* Harvard: Harvard University Press.

Tenbruck, F. H. (1989). 'Freundschaft. Ein Beitrag zu einer Soziologie der persönlichen Beziehungen.' In *Die Kulturellen Grundlagen Der Gesellschaft: Der Fall Der Moderne* (pp. 227–250). Opladen: Westdeutscher Verlag.

Todorov, T. (2002). *Imperfect Garden: The Legacy of Humanism.* Princeton and Oxford: Princeton University Press.

Tönnies, F. (1887) *Gemeinschaft und Gesellschaft.* Berlin: Fues.

Torberg, F. (1977). *Die Tante Jolesch, oder der Untergang des Abendlandes in Anekdoten.* Munchen: Deutscher Taschenbuch Verlag.

Turkle, S. (2011). *Alone Together: Why We Expect More from Technology and Less from Each Other*. New York: Basic Books.

Updike, J. (1995). *Rabbit Angstrom: A Tetralogy*. New York: Everyman's Library, Alfred A. Knopf.

Vanderdrift, L. E., Lehmiller, J. J., & Kelly, J. R. (2012). 'Commitment in Friends with Benefits Relationships: Implications for Relational and Safe-Sex Outcomes.' *Personal Relationships*, *19*(1), 1–13.

Velleman, J. D. (1999). 'Love as Moral Emotion.' *Ethics*, *109*(2), 338–374.

Vernon, M. (2006). *The Philosophy of Friendship*. London: Palgrave Macmillan.

Wade, L., & Heldman, C. (2012). 'Hooking Up and Opting Out.' In L. M. Carpenter & J. DeLamater (Eds), *Sex for Life: From Virginity to Viagra, How Sexuality Changes throughout our Lives* (pp. 128–145). New York and London: New York University Press.

Weber, M. (1977). From Max Weber: Essays in Sociology. In H. H. Gerth & C. W. Mills (Eds), (pp. 331–362). London: Routledge and Kegan Paul.

Weber, M. (1978). *Economy and Society: An Outline of Interpretive Sociology* (Vol. 1). Berkeley: University of California Press.

Weeks, J. (1996). 'The Idea of a Sexual Community.' *Soundings*, *2*, 71–83.

Weeks, J., Heaphy, B., & Donovan, C. (2001). *Same Sex Intimacies: Families of Choice and Other Life Experiments*. London and New York: Routledge.

Weintraub, J. (1997). The Theory and Politics of the Public/Private Distinction. In J. Weintraub & K. Kumar (Eds), *Public and Private in Thought and Practice: Perspectives on a Grand Dichotomy* (pp. 1–42). Chicago: University of Chicago Press.

Werking, K. (1997). *We're Just Good Friends: Women and Men in Nonromantic Relationships*. Guilford Publications.

Weston, K. (1997). *Families We Choose: Lesbians, Gays, Kinship*. New York: Columbia University Press.

Wierzbicka, A. (1997). *Understanding Cultures through their Key Words: English, Russian, Polish, German, and Japanese*. Oxford and New York: Oxford University Press US.

Willmott, P., & Policy Studies. (1987). *Friendship Networks and Social Support*. London: Policy Studies Institute.

Wittgenstein, L. (2010). *Philosophical Investigations*. John Wiley & Sons.

Wittig, M. (1992). *The Straight Mind and Other Essays*. New Jersey: Harvester Wheatsheaf.

Wohlrab-Sahr, M. (2011). 'Schwellenanalyse: Ein Plädoyer für eine Soziologie der Grenzziehungen.' In K. Hahn & C. Koppetsch (Eds) *Soziologie des Privaten* (pp. 33–52). Wiesbaden: VS Verlag fur Sozialwissenschaftern.

Wolf, E. R. (1966). 'Kinship, Friendship, and Patron-Client Relations in Complex Societies.' *The Social Anthropology of Complex Societies*, 1–22.

Wright, P. H. (1982). 'Men's Friendships, Women's Friendships and the Alleged Inferiority of the Latter'. *Sex Roles*, *8*(1), 1–20.

Zaretsky, E. (2004). *Secrets of the Soul: A Social and Cultural History of Psychoanalysis*. New York: Alfred A. Knopf.

Zeldin, T. (1994). *An Intimate History of Humanity*. New York: Harper Collins.

Index

Printed and bound in the United States of America